THE NATURE AND IMPACTS OF NONCOMPLIANCE

Over two billion people (61% of the world's employed population) work in the informal economy. Due to its pervasiveness, informality plays a major role in understanding a wide swath of ideas, such as development, work, employment, governance, and growth. Its scope, nonetheless, goes far beyond economic definitions and political agendas. As the book argues, at the root of informality lies another comprehensive, yet generally unnoticed – or at best improperly treated – phenomenon: that of noncompliance with the law. Whilst it is true that much attention has been paid to the economic aspect over the past five decades, the same cannot be said about the legal aspect, which is one of its constitutive features. This book takes the first steps in this direction.

The book provides an account of the phenomenon's legal nature through the lens of a case study on street vendors in Brazil, focusing on what can be conceived as noncompliance and by which forms noncompliant behaviour can be assessed. It goes on to set out the most striking impacts of noncompliance; specifically, what happens to the legal system when noncompliance becomes pervasive.

European Academy of Legal Theory Monograph Series: Volume 18

EUROPEAN ACADEMY OF LEGAL THEORY MONOGRAPH SERIES

General Editors

Professor Mark Van Hoecke

Professor François Ost

Titles in this Series

The Harmonisation of European Private Law
Edited by Mark Van Hoecke & Francois Ost

On Law and Legal Reasoning
Fernando Atria

Law as Communication
Mark Van Hoecke

Legisprudence
Edited by Luc Wintgens

Epistemology and Methodology of Comparative Law
Edited by Mark van Hoecke

Making the Law Explicit.
The Normativity of Legal Argumentation
Matthias Klatt

The Policy of Law
A Legal Theoretical Framework
Mauro Zamboni

Methodologies of Legal Research
Which Kind of Method for What Kind of Discipline?
Edited by Mark van Hoecke

Objectivity in Law and Legal Reasoning
Edited by Jaakko Husa and Mark van Hoecke

An Introduction to Comparative Law Theory and Method
Geoffrey Samuel

The Tapestry of Reason
An Inquiry into the Nature of Coherence and its Role in Legal Argument
Amalia Amaya

Democracy and Ontology
Agonism between Political Liberalism, Foucault and Psychoanalysis
Irena Rosenthal

Global Constitutionalism and Its Challenges to Westphalian Constitutional Law
Martin Belov

Legal Validity: The Fabric of Justice
Maris Köpcke Tinturé

Paradigms in Modern European Comparative Law: A History
Balázs Fekete

Agency, Morality and Law
Joshua Jowitt

The Nature and Impacts of Noncompliance
Edvaldo Moita

The Nature and Impacts of Noncompliance

Edvaldo Moita

•HART•
OXFORD • LONDON • NEW YORK • NEW DELHI • SYDNEY

HART PUBLISHING

Bloomsbury Publishing Plc

Kemp House, Chawley Park, Cumnor Hill, Oxford, OX2 9PH, UK

1385 Broadway, New York, NY 10018, USA

29 Earlsfort Terrace, Dublin 2, Ireland

HART PUBLISHING, the Hart/Stag logo, BLOOMSBURY and the Diana logo are trademarks of Bloomsbury Publishing Plc

First published in Great Britain 2023

This title was submitted in slightly modified form as a doctoral dissertation to the Faculty of Sociology at Bielefeld University and the Law School of the University of Brasília in February 2021. It won two awards: The European Award for Legal Theory 2022 from the European Academy of Legal Theory (EALT) and Prêmio Abrafi de Teses 2022 from the Brazilian Association for Philosophy of Law and Sociology of Law (Abrafi).

A catalogue record for this book is available from the British Library.

A catalogue record for this book is available from the Library of Congress.

Library of Congress Control Number: 2023932726

ISBN: HB: 978-1-50996-624-0
ePDF: 978-1-50996-626-4
ePub: 978-1-50996-625-7

Typeset by Compuscript Ltd, Shannon

'Die korrekte Bestimmung dieses Verhältnisses [zwischen Geltung und Wirksamkeit] ist eines der wichtigsten und zugleich schwierigsten Probleme einer positivistischen Rechtstheorie.'

Kelsen (1960: 215)

'Furthermore, far from being confined to economic approaches, informality needs to be addressed, surveyed and understood from the points of view of other social sciences [...]'

Charmes (2020: 1)

Preliminary Note

THIS RESEARCH WAS carried out from 2016 to 2020. I submitted it as a doctoral dissertation in February 2021. The defence took place in May 2021. Today, 19 August 2021, I woke up and read another not so surprising news report: a street vendor was shot and killed in a confrontation between the vendors from the midnight street market *Feira da Sé* and police officers.[1] This is what this book is about: the rule of law … or to put it better, the lack thereof.

[1] See: g1.globo.com/ce/ceara/noticia/2021/08/18/ambulante-morto-durante-confronto-na-rua-jose-avelino-e-velado-em-fortaleza.ghtml. Accessed on 19 August 2021.

A Note on Translations

THROUGHOUT THIS BOOK, quotations of foreign works and materials have been freely translated. When English translations were available, they were consulted and quoted, but not always adopted. Where an English translation of a book originally published in a different language is available, both references have been provided. The reference to the English translation is given first, followed by the reference to the original work enclosed in square brackets.

Contents

Abbreviations

CLT	*Consolidação das Leis do Trabalho* (Labour Law Code)
CNMP	*Conselho Nacional do Ministério Público* (National Council of Prosecution Services)
COPM	*Código de Obras e Posturas do Munípio de Fortaleza* – Law 5,530/1981 (Code of Construction and Use of the Public Space in the Municipality of Fortaleza)
CTPS	*Carteira de Trabalho e Previdência Social* (Labour and Social Security Card)
DANE	*Departamento Administrativo Nacional de Estadística* (Colombian's National Administrative Department for Statistics)
DIEESE	*Departamento Intersindical de Estatística e Estudos Socioeconômicos* (Inter-union Department of Statistics and Socioeconomic Studies)
ETCO	*Instituto Brasileiro de Ética Concorrencial* (Brazilian Institute for Ethics in Competition)
FGV	*Fundação Getúlio Vargas* (Getúlio Vargas Foundation)
GDP	Gross Domestic Product
IBGE	*Instituto Brasileiro de Geografia e Estatística* (Brazilian Institute of Geography and Statistics)
IBPT	*Instituto Brasileiro de Planejamento e Tributação* (Brazilian Institute of Planning and Taxation)
ICLS	International Conference of Labour Statisticians
ILO	International Labour Organization
INSS	*Instituto Nacional do Seguro Social* (National Institute for Social Security)
JFCE	*Justiça Federal no Ceará* (Federal Justice at the State of Ceará)
MPCE	*Ministério Público do Estado do Ceará* (State of Ceará's Agency for Law Enforcement and Prosecution of Crimes)
MPF	*Ministério Público Federal* (Federal Agency for Law Enforcement and Prosecution of Crimes)

OECD	Organization for Economic Co-operation and Development
SEFAZ	*Secretaria da Fazenda* (Department of Finance of the State)
SEWA	Self-Employed Women's Association
SEWU	Self-Employed Women's Union
SINFECE	*Sindicato dos Trabalhadores de Feiras Livres e Particulares e Vendedores Ambulantes do Estado do Ceará* (Union of Street Vendors and Workers of Street and Private Markets)
STF	*Supremo Tribunal Federal* (Supreme Federal Court)
STJ	*Superior Tribunal de Justiça* (Superior Court of Justice)
StreetNet	International Alliance of Street Vendors
TAC	*Termo de Compromisso de Ajustamento de Conduta* (Terms of Conduct Adjustment Commitment)
TJCE	*Tribunal de Justiça do Estado do Ceará* (Court of Appeals of the State of Ceará)
TRF5	*Tribunal Regional Federal da 5ª Região* (Federal Court of Appeals of the 5th Region)
UE	Unobserved Economy
WIEGO	Women in Informal Employment: Globalising and Organising
WTO	World Trade Organization

List of Figures

Table of Cases

Brazil

Supremo Tribunal Federal (STF; Supreme Federal Court)

Superior Tribunal de Justiça (STJ; Superior Court of Justice)

Tribunal de Justiça do Estado do Ceará (TJCE; Court of Appeals of the State of Ceará: https://esaj.tjce.jus.br)

Tribunal Regional Federal da 5ª Região (TRF5; Federal Court of Appeals of the 5th Region: www4.trf5.jus.br/InteiroTeor/)

Colombia

Constitutional Court (www.corteconstitucional.gov.co/relatoria)

India

Supreme Court of India (https://main.sci.gov.in/judgments; also available at the *All India Reporter* (AIR) at: www.aironline.in)

Table of Legislation

1. Treaty

2. Brazil

2.1. Federal Laws

2.2. Local Laws from Fortaleza

2.3. Other norms

3. Colombia

4. India

Introduction

NO ONE TODAY would dispute the fact that the law matters a great deal in various spheres of our lives. The ever-increasing number of statutes, codes, rules, regulations, treaties, ordinances, principles, doctrines, and additional kinds of legally binding directives that exist makes this very clear. Even though it might seem difficult to track all the effects of such an overburden of legal norms, some of them have long been quite conspicuous, whilst others become so only after scholarly scrutiny. For instance, in the United States in the mid-1970s there was a talk of 'legal pollution'. 'Thickening layers of legalism seem to surround our lives. We have far too many laws; we rely too heavily on law as an instrument of social change; we depend too much on courts, legislatures and administrative agencies to resolve our woes', wrote a law professor in a newspaper.[1] This complaint resonated with a concern that a year before had been tackled as an 'explosion of law', that is, 'the growing intrusion of law on every aspect of American society' (Barton 1975: 567).

Far from being solely an American phenomenon, the issue could also be found across the Atlantic. Under the concept of 'juridification' it gained even more elaborate contours. Habermas (1987a: 357 [1987b: 524]) used it to refer 'quite generally to the tendency toward an increase in formal (or positive, written) law that can be observed in modern society'. Seen under the viewpoint of the disentanglement – or rather uncoupling – between the system and the lifeworld, he identified a historical process of 'thrusts' that began with the bourgeois state and, with a flow of '*ambivalence of guaranteeing freedom and taking it away*' (1987a: 361 [1987b: 531]), finds its apex – at least up to that point – in the democratic welfare state; that is, the state able to tame not only politics but also the economic system and hence the affected domains of life. If one takes into account what this entails, namely, the transfer of the coordination of life-relations from 'consensual mechanisms' over to 'media such as power and money' (1987a: 364 [1987b: 534]), juridification could then perfectly be presented as clear 'evidence' of a much more dramatic diagnosis, that of the 'colonialization of the lifeworld' (1987a: 356 [1987b: 522]).

Indeed, it was not merely about a 'flood of norms', as Teubner (1987: 7 [1985: 295]) warned, for 'it still seems too narrow an approach to concentrate on the expansion of legal material, on the extension and intensification of law'. Instead of quantitative analyses, he suggested, 'juridification processes should

[1] See Thomas Ehrlich, 'Legal pollution', *The New York Times*, 8 February 1976, www.nytimes.com/1976/02/08/archives/legal-pollution-increasingly-often-there-ought-not-to-be-a-law.html. Accessed on 28 January 2021.

in fact be analysed in terms of the specific conditions of the modern social state, "the interventionist state"'. He was specifically concerned with the changes in law brought about by – or rather expressed in – the new kinds of intervention in various social fields put forward by the state using law as a means: 'change in the function of law, in its legitimation and in its norm structure' (Teubner 1987: 14 ff [1985: 306 ff]). His immediate finding was clear-cut: 'juridification does not merely mean proliferation of law; it signifies a process in which the interventionist social state produces a new type of law, regulatory law' (1987: 18 [1985: 312]). The new regulatory law, a mix of coupling between law, politics, and another social system, could then be characterised according to those changes demanded by the new historical arrangement of the state: 'In its function it is geared to the guidance requirements of the social state, in its legitimation the social results of its controlling and compensating regulations are predominant. In its structure it tends to be particularistic, purpose oriented and dependent on assistance from the social sciences' (Teubner 1987: 19 [1985: 313]).

One could certainly question the accuracy of these descriptions or, considering the backdrop against which they were made, doubt whether the characteristics of the state they depict hold until today.[2] In any case, it is hard to deny the growth of the state's tasks[3] – or, be that as it may, the performances ascribed to the state – vis-à-vis the emergence of a corresponding 'regulatory law', or simply 'regulation'.[4] The spread of administrative agencies, the multitude of field-level officials, the large pile of public policies, and the variety of legal standards targeting business, industry, employment, health, environment, education, social assistance, consumer relations, and so on, illustrate how pervasive law has become over the last decades. And it seems that the trend is continuing in such a way that it is highly unlikely to be reversed and, as could be expected, it is unfolding in several ways.

Among the wide range of effects from this boundary-expanding process of the state and the law, a very specific kind of discourse emerged with the motto 'compliance with the law'. Its driving source, roughly speaking, is a residual difficulty of that process: if it is already too strenuous for lawyers and enforcement agents to keep up with such an overburden of legal norms, imagine it from the standpoint of those whose activities are regulated. When caught up in the intricate web of varying regulations and the respective law enforcement

[2] Already speaking of a 'general state of crisis' of the welfare state in the late 1970s, Stanfield and McClintock (1999: 1247–48). Teubner (1997 [1996], 2012a [2012b]) himself in the following years seems to have downsized the role of the state in the global evolution of law.

[3] Among the rich literature, see the book organised by Grimm (1990). The preface sets the tone: 'One of the characteristics of the welfare state is that, unlike liberalism, it does not have any task limitation within itself, but is required to compensate for all conceivable deficits, disadvantages, and structural constraints, and in doing so, unlike absolutism, which in principle also has no limits, it encounters fewer and fewer natural boundaries to its activities' (1990: 7).

[4] For a summary of the state of the art until the 1990s regarding this field, including useful references, see Hutter (1997: 4–12), who also tackles the issue in the United Kingdom.

agencies, they all have to deal with a problem that, most visibly in the field of regulatory law, seems to be irremediable: identifying which behaviours or practices are in accordance with the law. This ends up entailing another set of challenges, ranging from the very definition of compliance to its assessment, achievement, and maintenance. However, the presentation of the issue tends to have contrasting directions.

On the one hand, the discourse takes the shape of a business. Multitudes of manuals, casebooks, and guidebooks offer routines, advice, guidelines, case studies, etc to help companies and enterprises to adhere to the laws and regulations in order to diminish the risk of violating them.[5] There is already a 'compliance industry' in need of professionals specifically trained to work in the field – the 'compliance officers'.[6] And considering how the needs of the market are captured, there are courses, degrees, and programmes which promise to equip one with the proper skills to break into it.[7] Companies are establishing 'compliance committees', organising 'compliance departments', and designating 'Chief Compliance Officers'.[8] If one looks at all the evidence and the pace at which the business is growing, then it makes sense to say that 'we now live in an era of compliance' (Griffith 2016: 2077).[9]

On the other hand, compliance with the law becomes an object of scholarly interest, especially that of a sociological nature. The emphasis is usually put on the field level, in which the phenomenon takes place, so that compliance is seen as a kind of dynamic occurring between those being regulated and the officials of regulation or law enforcement agencies. The point of departure tends to be the general idea that 'it is not always clear what the law means, and hence what compliance might look like and entail'. This is argued to be particularly

[5] A quick search on the internet provides an overview of the volume of material available. In the United States, for instance, publications range from books introducing the 'compliance field' to law students and lawyers (Miller 2020), to guides aiming at introducing the subject to 'professionals in information technology (TI), operations, finance, and supply chain' (Tarantino 2006).

[6] Advertising a Master of Legal Studies, a university blog presents the career of a 'compliance officer' and the opportunities in the 'compliance industry'; see Brian Eastwood, 'Working in the Compliance Industry: What You Need to Know', *Northeastern University*, 28 May 2019, www.northeastern.edu/graduate/blog/what-is-the-compliance-industry. In May 2019, the US Bureau of Labor Statistics reported 317,600 'compliance officers'; see: www.bls.gov/oes/current/oes131041.htm#(1). Accessed on 8 February 2021.

[7] Since 2014 the New York University School of Law has had a general compliance class as part of its curriculum: *Compliance and Risk Management for Attorneys*, its.law.nyu.edu/courses/description.cfm?id=26669. Accessed on 5 February 2021. For an assessment of the field in the United States, see Miller (2017). *cf* Baer (2009) and Griffith (2016). In Brazil, a similar trend is setting in, although it has been coping with the national reality. A university in Fortaleza, Ceará, provides, on a regular basis, training courses on compliance and anti-corruption law: *Formação e Gestão em Compliance*, www.escoladenegociosuni7.com.br/educacao-executiva/formacao-e-gestao-em-compliance. Accessed on 3 December 2022. The Getúlio Vargas Foundation (FGV) offers a degree for lawyers and related professionals on compliance: *Pós-Graduação em Compliance*, direitosp.fgv.br/cursos/pos-graduacao-lato-sensu/fgvlaw-compliance. Accessed on 3 December 2022.

[8] See Miller (2017: 438).

[9] Lin (2006), referring to the financial industry, also tries to show how compliance is on the rise.

problematic in the field of regulatory law, for it 'is often vague, involving broad legal standards and the exercise of discretion by officials' (Hutter 1997: 3).[10] Thus, law enforcement plays a central role in such kind of analyses. Some have even suggested that 'compliance in practical terms is what agencies involved define it to be' (Manning 1988: 561).[11] Others try to frame the issue more cautiously: 'compliance depends largely on the initiative and agenda of those persons within organizations who are charged with managing the compliance effort' (Edelman et al 1991: 73). In this sense, instead of being presented as a mere event whose existence can be assessed, compliance is regarded as 'a social and political process that evolves over time' (Edelman et al 1991: 74).[12] In the end, the result of such sociological enterprises is almost always a context-dependent definition, which is to be substantiated according to the concrete constellations of actors and resources involved with the process.

It would certainly be interesting to further examine the ongoing developments of the compliance business or expand sociological inquiries into compliance processes, but regardless of the direction taken one thing seems certain: the more the law grows, the more we have to deal with compliance issues. Nowadays, even public authorities and states themselves are subject to different compliance measurements and monitoring, in which case judicial rulings, international treaties, or even indexes gain prominence in determining the parameters according to which behaviours or state of affairs should be assessed as compliant.[13] And this invariably denotes the role that the concept has been playing in a society increasingly marked by quantitative and qualitative juridification thrusts. However, underlying these descriptions of the growth of law, the historical arrangement of the welfare state, and the increasing significance of the concept of compliance, there are some assumptions that, if not properly clarified, might obscure considerably important aspects of the role of law in society, in particular with regard to the law's function, performances, and ability to serve as a means for conveying political decisions in the form

[10] See also Hutter (1997: 67). In the same vein, see Hawkins (1984: xiii), DiMento (1986: 25–26), and Edelman et al (1991: 75).

[11] It is true that, following his review of Braithwaite, Manning (1988: 561) concedes that 'compliance is a process of extended and endless negotiation in which noted or potential violations are points in a field of forces'. Although this also does not say much about the concept, he was nonetheless capable of observing what was pressing at the time: '… the emergent meaning of compliance'.

[12] *cf* DiMento (1986: 26–28) and Hutter (1997: 13–17).

[13] The examples here are manifold. With some incursions into the state of the art regarding judicial rulings, see Kapiszewski and Taylor (2013). For a study focused on compliance with human rights tribunals, see Hillebrecht (2009). An example of international treaty is the 2010 Nagoya Protocol, which provides for the issuance of an 'internationally recognized certificate of compliance' (see Art 17, sections 2–4); for a short contextualisation in this regard, see Sands et al (2018: 404). In terms of indexes, the ones measuring the rule of law are noteworthy. See, for instance, the index produced by the World Justice Project, available at: worldjusticeproject.org/our-work/research-and-data/wjp-rule-law-index-2020. Accessed on 10 February 2021. See also the index produced by the World Bank within the World Governance Indicators, available at: info.worldbank.org/governance/wgi. Accessed on 10 February 2021. Elsewhere I have mentioned some problems in the measurement of abstract concepts such as rule of law (Moita 2018: 174–76).

of regulations. This is more easily seen when the issue is put into a regional perspective.

It must be said that one cannot take for granted that the expansion of the law and the state has been occurring in a homogeneous or symmetrical way worldwide, especially in terms of economic development and distribution of welfare. The discrepancies are so outrageous that one could ask 'whether the worldwide realization of the currently high level of welfare found in some industrial countries is at all possible' (Luhmann 2004: 490 [1993: 585]). In certain regions, such as Latin America, the problem has been so blatant and persistent that one may fairly call into question the degree of importance given to law in everyday life. This includes the application of the law by bureaucracies and law enforcement officials, and the ability of the state to properly intervene and cause changes by means of regulation. As Pinheiro (1999: 1–2) once reported, dispelling the hope brought by the democratic transitions in Latin America in the 1980s:

> Human rights abuses occur every day, and the majority of the perpetrators are not punished or otherwise held accountable for their heinous crimes. In certain areas, the state monopoly of legitimate violence has been relaxed, and survival may depend on an individual's ability to maintain his or her reputation by displaying a 'credible threat of violence,' a process which threatens the development of a democratic society. Growing criminality not only erodes democratic expectations (as many surveys in the continent have demonstrated) but also sanctions arbitrary violence, weakening the legitimacy of the political system. There are large portions of the territory, mainly in rural areas, where the local ruling classes continue to manipulate state institutions, including the judiciary and police. To complicate this situation, we face a paradox which undermines the efforts to fight crime: although the fundamental guarantees are well-defined by most of the democratic constitutions, the exercise of full citizenship is practically nonexistent for the majority of the population.

No wonder several authors have refrained from or at least hedged when using terms such as democracy or rule of law to describe many countries of the continent.[14] This is not to say that juridification and its consequences cannot be seen virtually everywhere. Nor that the law is absent in certain regions of the world, or that the state has not increased in its capacity to regulate the many spheres of life. The problem is much more nuanced. Paraphrasing Luhmann (2004: 489 [1993: 583]), it is not about whether the difference between legal and illegal exists and that there is legal programming (statutes, regulations, ordinances, etc) that regulate how the values of 'legal' or 'illegal' are attributed to facts, but rather to what extent this difference is important for people to orient their behaviour accordingly.

Any attempt to answer this question has to consider the increasing expansion of law. But, as this book will argue, when it comes to contexts where the legal system is marked by high grades of inefficacy, a proper response can only be achieved if the focus is geared toward the obverse of compliance, that is,

[14] See for all, Méndez et al (1999).

noncompliance. Whereas on the one hand the growth of law paves the way for compliance to emerge as a socially relevant theme, on the other it creates assessments of breaches of the law, which in certain regions have society-wide resonance. In this case, the phenomenon of noncompliance does not arise as a mere by-product of the analysis of compliant behaviour. It becomes pervasive to such an extent that it can structure actions and experiences within the space of the historical arrangements of the states that have not profited from the development of the high level of welfare seen in some parts of the world.

Against this background, this book is devoted to an in-depth examination of noncompliance – more specifically, noncompliance with the law. This work aims to explore the nature of noncompliance as a legal phenomenon and its impacts on the law, particularly its function, performances, temporal and spatial dimensions, and its ability to serve as a means for conveying political decisions by the state. In order to make this comprehensive endeavour empirically plausible, this book builds on a case of noncompliance. In this sense, it considers the regulation of economic activities whose violation falls under the so-called informality. In particular, it considers the activity of street vending with a special emphasis on the city of Fortaleza, Brazil. The book is structured as follows.

Part I is dedicated to a case of noncompliance. Chapter one provides an overview of the development of informality studies since the 1970s and shows how it is essentially a case of noncompliance. Chapter two reviews the literature studying street vending worldwide. Chapter three contains a qualitative analysis of street vending in Fortaleza, Ceará, drafted as a representative case study of street vending in Brazil.

Part II is a conceptual inquiry on the nature of noncompliance as a multi-leveled legal phenomenon. Chapter four delimits the conceptual presuppositions assumed, and chapter five presents the concept of noncompliance encompassing all of its degrees of occurrence.

Part III is a sociological investigation of the impacts of noncompliance. Chapter six assesses the impacts on the dimensions of time and space of legal norms. Chapter seven clarifies the concept of arenas of noncompliance, which is used throughout the book to narrow the scope of the conclusions drawn from the empirical evidence collected. Chapter eight sets out the findings regarding the impacts on the circulation of political power and bartering arrangements that are brought about by power deflation.

Part I

A Case of Noncompliance

1

On the Concept and Size of Informality

THIS PART OF the book aims to explore the concept of informality, especially in relation to working conditions and economic activities, and demonstrate how widespread the phenomenon is worldwide and in particular in Brazil (chapter one). It illustrates this further with the case of street vending (chapter two), which is the most striking example of informal work, and with an in-depth analysis of these activities in the city of Fortaleza, Brazil (chapter three), emphasising their legal aspects (eg, local regulations, inspections, and court decisions).

1.1. COMMON POLITICAL AGENDAS BUT DIFFERENT APPROACHES

In recent decades, many governmental agendas and public policies have been aimed at fighting informality. The year 2015 was a cornerstone in this process, when the United Nations, in the 2030 Agenda for Sustainable Development, included the transition to formality as a target for Sustainable Development (Goal 8 on decent work and economic growth, Global Target 8.3).[1] Indeed, the concept of informality seems to be usually used to describe a certain set of economic activities which do not comply with the law or some other standards of acceptable working conditions. The term, nonetheless, has a much longer history. It was used for the first time in the early 1970s, when the economic anthropologist Keith Hart, in his research on the economic activities in Ghana (K Hart 1973), coined the concept of the 'informal sector'.[2] The term was then

[1] See the Sustainable Development Goals: www.undp.org/content/undp/en/home/sustainable-development-goals.html. Accessed on 28 October 2019.

[2] Originally, he conceived of a distinction 'between formal and informal income opportunities' which was based on another difference, that of 'between wage-earning and self-employment', the key variable being 'the degree of rationalization of work – that is to say, whether or not labour is recruited on a permanent and regular basis for fixed rewards' (K Hart 1973: 68). In this sense, the informal sector would comprise both legitimate activities (such as farming, market gardening, shoemakers, tailors, street hawkers, musicians, borrowing, begging and so on) and illegitimate activities (mostly criminal, such as receiving stolen goods, usury, drug-pushing, prostitution, petty theft, larceny, peculation and embezzlement). Contesting the origin of the concept, Elwert et al (1983: 281 fn 1) named Hart its 'illegitimate father'.

used by and gained widespread acceptance when the International Labour Organization (ILO) (1972) carried out a mission to research economic activities in Kenya, revealing how some of these activities were unrecognised, unrecorded, unprotected, and unregulated.[3] The nomenclature was abandoned after some criticism, especially due to the fact that informal activities do not concentrate in one sector but rather cross many sectors simultaneously.[4]

From this point on, many debates took place attempting to define informality at an international level. In 2002, the ILO tried to reach a consensus on the definition. Through the resolution that followed the 90th Session of its General Conference, in opposition to the former concept of 'informal sector', they proposed among its conclusions the concept of 'informal economy',[5] which 'refers to all economic activities by workers and economic units that are – in law or in practice – not covered or insufficiently covered by formal arrangements' (ILO 2002b: conclusion 3). The idea was to shed light on worldwide economic activities that take place with a certain lack of compliance with the law, such as activities either located 'outside the formal reach of the law' or 'not covered in practice', as a consequence of no proper enforcement or application, or even because 'the law discourages compliance'.

Further attempts to make the concept more precise were also made, so that even formal workers could fall into informality by receiving undeclared remuneration or being subject to wages and working conditions typical of informal workers (ILO 2002b: conclusion 5). It is important to consider that, according to the resolution, this kind of work is marked by 'decent work deficits', since 'the negative aspects of work in informal economy far outweigh its positive aspects', meaning the impossibility for workers 'to enjoy, exercise or defend their fundamental rights' due to the lack of recognition, registration, regulation, or protection (ILO 2002b: conclusion 9). This conceptual enterprise towards achieving decent work patterns, arguably a commitment anchored in human rights declarations, made it possible to empirically measure the informality.

[3] As the report states, 'informal activities are the way of doing things, characterized by (a) ease of entry; (b) reliance on indigenous resources; (c) family ownership of enterprises; (d) small scale of operation; (e) labour-intensive and adapted technology; (f) skills acquired outside the formal school system; and (g) unregulated and competitive markets' (ILO 1972: 6).

[4] For a more detailed historical background about the concept and the respective school of thoughts concerning the informal sector, see Chen (2005). Other terms, nonetheless, are also used to designate the same phenomenon such as 'non-structured sector', 'non-organized sector', 'non-protected sector' (Jakobsen 2000: 5), and 'unorganized sector' (Bhowmik 2010a: 1). Some others point out close and sometimes overlapping phenomena such as the 'shadow economy' (Schneider, Buehn, and Montenegro 2010), 'underground economy' (Feige 1989, 1990), 'unobserved economies' (Feige 2016a), and 'non-observed economy' (OECD 2002). I will elaborate more on this in this section.

[5] Indeed, much of the discussion derived from the lack of common definitions at international levels and the difficult distinction between informal employment and employment in the informal sector. The term 'informal economy', however, would be more comprehensive since it included both. In this regard, see Charmes (2012). The technical definitions for statistical measurement purposes can be found in the ILO's statistical manual (ILO 2013b).

When the numbers of the informal economy are pointed out, one gains a broad picture of how pervasive and persistent the phenomenon is. At the international level, according to the Organization for Economic Co-operation and Development (OECD), in 2009, more than half of the global labour force, about 1.8 billion people, were working without formal labour contracts and social security.[6] In 2018 the ILO (2018: 13) published an even more striking report indicating that this number had grown to 2 billion people, which represented 61.2% of global employment. This increase could represent a long-standing effect of the 2008 Global Financial Crisis, however, when placed in a regional and historical perspective, the numbers are found to be persistent. In a study carried out by OECD, which is comprised of varying data from 1990 to 2007, 'informal employment accounts for more than 47 per cent of total non-agricultural employment in West Asia and in North Africa, and more than 70 per cent in sub-Saharan Africa, more than 50 per cent in Latin America, nearly 70 per cent in South and Southeast Asia and 24 per cent in transition economies' (Charmes 2009: 32). For instance, this means that in places like Latin America 84 out of each 100 new jobs created from 1990–95 were in the informal sector (ILO 1996: 8).

In Brazil, a representative case for Latin America, in 2001 54.7% of the employed workers were informal, while by 2012 the number had decreased, but nonetheless remained relatively consistent at about 47% of the employed workers, that is, about 44 million people.[7] This number includes employees without proper registration, own-account workers, non-wage workers, or underemployed people. For the first time in Brazilian history, in the last quarter of 2017 the number of workers without proper work registration and own-account workers (34.3 million) surpassed the number of workers with proper registration (33.3 million).[8] In 2019, the numbers continued to rise: the number

[6] For the numbers of informality around the world with a focus on developing countries, see the study of OECD (Jütting and Laiglesia 2009), especially the data gathered by Charmes (2009), following the concepts proposed by ILO on the informal economy and informal employment. See also: www.oecd.org/development/risinginformalemploymentwillincreasepoverty.htm. Accessed on 26 October 2018.

[7] These data were presented by the *Departamento Intersindical de Estatística e Estudos Socioeconômicos* (DIEESE; Inter-union Department of Statistics and Socioeconomic Studies); see DIEESE (2014: 5) with a general reference to the statistics provided by the *Instituto Brasileiro de Geografia e Estatística* (IBGE; Brazilian Institute of Geography and Statistics). For the specific details on the data, including the breakdown of informal workers according to gender, age, and the type of occupation in the years of 2001, 2006, and 2011, see IBGE (2012: 135–38 and 147–48). For the comprehensive data produced by IBGE, see the series synthesis of social indicators from 2001 to 2018 here: www.ibge.gov.br/estatisticas/sociais/trabalho/9221-sintese-de-indicadores-sociais.html ?edicao=17068&t=publicacoes. Accessed on 31 October 2019.

[8] The category 'own-account worker', in addition to informal workers, also includes autonomous professionals such as lawyers and dentists who might not be considered informal workers if they are duly registered as legal persons. For more accessible data, see the following article which includes a number of graphs: g1.globo.com/economia/noticia/trabalho-sem-carteira-assinada-e-por-conta-propria-supera-pela-1-vez-emprego-formal-em-2017-aponta-ibge.ghtml. Accessed on 6 August 2018.

of employees in the private sector without proper registration was 11.8 million, combined with the 24.3 million own-account workers giving a total of 36.1 million people (IBGE 2019b). In the same year, even though the unemployment rate decreased to 11.8%, the number of informal workers reached 41.4% of the employed population, that is, 38.6 million, which is the highest number since the IBGE came up with this indicator in 2016. In this case, the measurement considers informal workers to include employees in the private sector and domestic workers without proper registration, employers, own-account workers not registered as legal persons, and non-wage workers (contributing family workers).[9] Figures 1 and 2 illustrate this data on the approximate number of people in the labour force according to their position in Brazil and the relation between informal and formal workers.

Figure 1 Labour Force in Brazil, June–August 2019

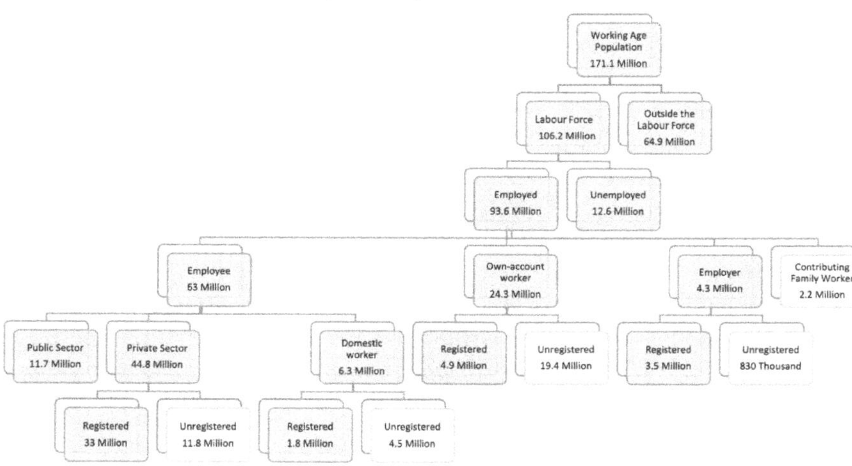

Source: own design with data from IBGE (2019a). Pesquisa Nacional por Amostra de Domicílio Contínua, Junho a Agosto de 2019, quadro sintético.

Notes: The groups constitute what IBGE considers informal workers.

Working Age Population: Persons aged 14 years or older at the reference date.

Employed: Persons who, during this period, worked at least one full hour in paid work by cash, products, goods, or benefits (housing, food, clothing, training, etc), or in work without direct remuneration in support of the economic activity of a member of the household or relative residing in another household, or those who had paid work from which they were temporarily away during that week. …

Unemployed: People who have taken some effective action to obtain work in the 30-day reference period and were available to take work in the reference week. Also considered as unemployed are those people without work in the reference week who did not take effective action to obtain work in the 30-day reference period because they had already found work that would begin in less than four months after the last day of the reference week.

Outside the Labour Force: People who were neither employed nor unemployed that week.

[9] That was the last figure produced by IBGE in the period of June, July, and August 2019, when this chapter was being written. See: agenciadenoticias.ibge.gov.br/agencia-noticias/2012-agencia-

Figure 2 Informal workers according to IBGE, June–August 2019

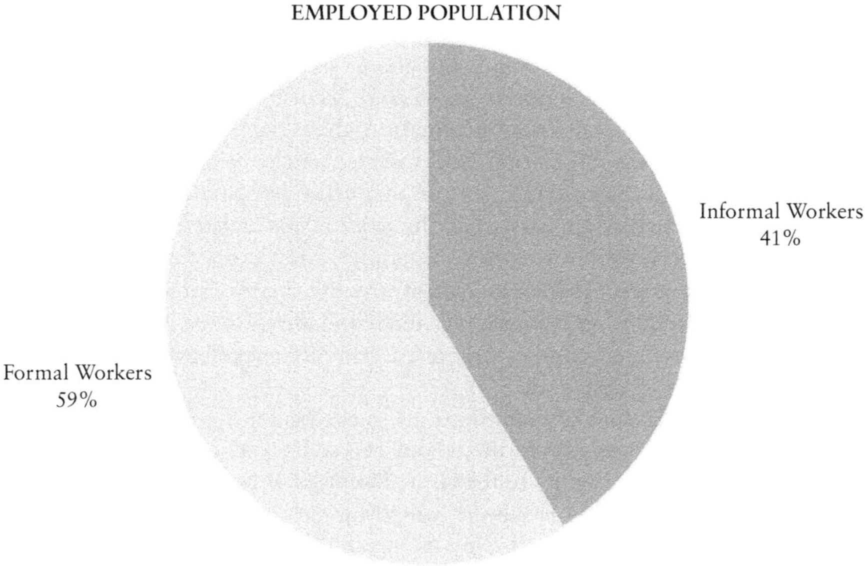

Source: own design with data from IBGE (2019a). Pesquisa Nacional por Amostra de Domicílio Contínua, Junho a Agosto de 2019, quadro sintético.
Note: The definition of informal and formal workers follows the definitions used by IBGE.

It is worth noting that, even though IBGE applies an internationally generalised framework on the methods and standards for work statistics developed by the 19th International Conference of Labour Statisticians (ICLS; ILO 2013a), the same cannot be said about all the categories that fall under informal work, as countries often have national peculiarities that are taken into consideration when labelling informal work.[10] Brazil, for instance, has a very specific system

de-noticias/noticias/25534-desemprego-cai-para-11-8-com-informalidade-atingindo-maior-nivel-da-serie-historica. Accessed on 28 October 2019. All these data on informality from IBGE are collected through the 'Continuous National Household Sample Survey' (Continuous PNAD), which began in 2012 and are available here: www.ibge.gov.br/en/statistics/social/labor/16833-monthly-dissemination-pnadc1.html?=&t=o-que-e. Accessed on 2 November 2019. The effects of the Covid-19 pandemic on informality were striking, since the overall standards of decent working conditions worsened. In some countries, informality was not even an option, for the pandemic forced people to leave the labour force. See, for instance, the United Nations (2022: 43) report regarding SDG 8.3. In Brazil, the numbers of informality remained somewhat consistent. From the first trimester of 2020 to the first trimester of 2022, Brazil gained 1.42 million informal workers; see: www1.folha.uol.com.br/mercado/2022/07/brasil-ganha-14-milhao-de-informais-em-apenas-2-anos.shtml. Accessed on 11 December 2022.

[10] For an updated and more comprehensive understanding of the international guidelines, see ILO (2018: 6–12). For the different definitions used in Latin America, Asia, and Africa, see the joint study carried out by the ILO and World Trade Organization (WTO) with sources collected up to 2008 (Bacchetta, Ernst, and Bustamante 2009: 163–69).

of work registration which was designed in 1932 and reformulated in 1943, when the *Consolidação das Leis do Trabalho* (CLT; Labour Law Code) was instituted by Presidential Decree 5,452/1943. According to its Article 13, every employee or own-account worker is obliged to have a *Carteira de Trabalho e Previdência Social* (CTPS; Labour and Social Security Card).[11] On this card, the employer must provide basic information about the labour contract, such as the date of admission, position, and salary (Article 29 of CLT), as well as details of vacations (Article 135, § 1) among other information. Therefore, a clear sign of informality appears when the work is not registered on the CTPS, or, if registered, crucial information is missing or incorrect data is registered, such as underpayments. This is the reason why the survey carried out by IBGE (see Figure 1) distinguishes between registered and unregistered work. However, in addition to these high numbers, there are still other segments of informality not captured by this framework.[12]

Despite the difficulties of definitions, the measurements are not restricted to size in terms of participation in the labour force. They also try to understand the contribution of informality to the Gross Domestic Product (GDP) of a country. Jacques Charmes, who has been compiling data over decades for OECD and ILO, is perhaps one of the leading figures in this regard. According to him, referring to the years 2000, 'the informal sector represents nearly two-third of total GDP in sub-Saharan Africa, more than 54 per cent in India[13] and nearly one-third in Latin America [29.2 per cent]', whilst in the Middle East North Africa (MENA) region the informal sector is estimated to contribute slightly more than one third (36.2%) and in transition countries it contributes 19.5% (Charmes 2012: 127–29). As the informal sector is only one sub-component of the informal economy, the numbers above do not account for informal employment outside the informal sector and, therefore, are not representative for the whole of the informal economy.

If the scope is broadened, other indicators of informality show a similar striking impact of what is produced outside the formal economy. In a

[11] The translation of '*Previdência Social*' as 'Social Security' can be somewhat misleading. Literally, 'Social Security' would be '*Seguridade Social*'. This difference is technically important because, in Brazil, the system of Social Security encompasses three different subsystems: (1) the health system, which is universal and free, ie, everybody regardless of economic condition or status has access with no cost to public hospitals, clinics, doctors, etc; (2) the *Previdência Social*, which accounts for work benefits, such as retirement, parental leave, sick leave, accidents during work, etc; and (3) social assistance, which gives social benefits to poor people in general. Whilst the health system functions autonomously, the *Previdência Social* and social assistance are under the *Instituto Nacional do Seguro Social* (INSS; National Institute for Social Security). Its main structure and sources of financing are given in the Brazilian Constitution in Arts 194 and 195.

[12] The growing forms of 'new informality' (Krein and Proni 2010: 27) and the informality in the public sector are striking examples.

[13] Due to the fact that estimates for Asia are partial and incomplete, he takes India as a representative case for the region (Charmes 2012: 120).

remarkable report supported by the World Bank (Schneider, Buehn, and Montenegro 2010: 457–59), informality was found to have reached 'a large size of a weighted (unweighted) average of 17.1% (33.0%) of official GDP over 162 countries over 1999 to 2007'. In terms of regions, the average in Sub-Saharan Africa was 37.6% of the GDP, in Europe and Central Asia (mostly transition countries) 36.4%, and in Latin America and the Caribbean 34.7%. Unlike the previous concept of informal sector employed by Charmes, informality here was measured in terms of the 'shadow economy', the literal translation of the term *Schattenwirtschaft* originally used.[14]

Brazil also matches the general situation of the many informality measurements in Latin America. In 2006, the contribution of its informal sector accounted for 21.6% of the GDP (Charmes 2012: 124). Its shadow economy, from 1999 to 2007, amounted to 39% (Schneider, Buehn, and Montenegro 2010: 454). In an exclusively national index produced by *Fundação Getúlio Vargas* (FGV) in collaboration with the *Instituto Brasileiro de Ética Concorrencial* (ETCO; Brazilian Institute for Ethics in Competition), the money collected from the entire production of what, based on Feige (1989), they call the 'underground economy' was estimated at 16.5% of the GDP in 2016, 16.8% in 2017, and 16.9% in 2018; this last number amounts to 1.17 trillion reals in the Brazilian currency, almost equivalent to the GDP of Colombia (1.2 trillion reals), Greece (1.1 trillion), and Chile (1 trillion).[15]

[14] For the indicators used to measure the shadow economy, see Schneider et al (2010: 444–47). It is worth noting that Charmes (2012: 119), referring to Schneider's works, does not accept the assimilation of the informal sector and the underground economy (the terms were used interchangeably by Schneider in previous works (Schneider, Buehn, and Montenegro 2010: 444 fn 2)), due to the fact that 'the comparison of the results with the current GDP is particularly misleading because the national accounts already include a part of the underground and illegal economy'. One of the major criticisms, however, comes from Feige (2016a), for whom Schneider's shadow economy 'estimates suffer from conceptual flaws, apparent manipulation of results and insufficient documentation for replication, questioning their place in the academic, policy and popular literature'. Indeed, some of the findings by Schneider et al (2010: 443 and 445) seem quite arbitrary, especially his claims that the main causes for the existence and increase of the shadow economy are increases in tax and social security contribution burdens and intensification of regulations, including labour market regulations. Brazil shows a counterexample of that: despite the big labour reform in 2017 (Law 13,467/2017), which among other things diminished tax social contribution burdens (for example by making the union contribution optional – formerly it was mandatory) and made labour relations more flexible, the rates of informality increased in the following years (see the reports mentioned in n 9 above). For proper criticisms regarding the fragility of the findings and methodology employed by Schneider et al, see Feige (2016a: 21–27), suggesting even that the relationship between tax rates and the shadow economy are either ambiguous or negative. For a response to Feige's criticisms, see Schneider (2016); and for the new rejoinder, confirming the previous criticisms, which include problems of documentation, normalisation, calibration, and replication, and asserting that Schneider's reply does not solve these issues, see Feige (2016b).

[15] The numbers pointed out were referred in the annual report of 2018 of the ETCO (2018: 32), which includes all the indexes since 2003. Nonetheless, the historical index in their website presents a slightly different figure for 2016: 16.3%. See: www.etco.org.br/economia-subterranea/?sub=indice_historico. Accessed on 18 November 2019.

1.2. THE COMMON FEATURE: NONCOMPLIANCE WITH THE LAW

Underlying almost every empirical measurement of informality is the necessity to settle distinctions between the illegal and the informal. The ILO itself, in the resolution mentioned earlier (ILO 2002b), tried to provide a strong boundary to make it clear that informal economic activities should 'be distinguished from criminal or illegal activities, such as production and smuggling of illegal drugs, as they are the subject of criminal law, and are not appropriate for regulation or protection under labour or commercial law' (ILO 2002b: conclusion 5). Moreover, in 2015, as a result of the 104th Session of its General Conference, the ILO launched Recommendation 204 concerning the transition from the informal to the formal economy (ILO 2015), which not only endorsed the previous 2002 concept of 'informal economy' (recommendation 2.a) but also clarified that it 'does not cover illicit activities, in particular the provision of services or the production, sale, possession or use of goods forbidden by law' such as 'the illicit production and trafficking of drugs, the illicit manufacturing of and trafficking in firearms, trafficking in persons, and money laundering, as defined in the relevant international treaties' (recommendation 2.b).

In a similar vein, the concept of 'shadow economy', as used by Schneider et al (2010: 444), or 'underground economy', as used by the World Bank and OECD (United Nations et al 1993: 153, para 6.34; OECD 2002: 37–38), comprises activities which, despite complying with certain standards and regulations, are

> … deliberately concealed from public authorities for the following kinds of reasons: to avoid the payment of income, value added or other taxes; to avoid the payment of social security contributions; to avoid having to meet certain legal standards such as minimum wages, maximum hours, safety of health standards, etc; to avoid complying with certain administrative procedures, such as completing statistical questionnaires or other administrative forms.

A similar rationale applies to the concept of 'underground economy' used by FVG/ETCO, framed in Feige's (1989) earlier work. Falling into a broader concept of informality that also encompasses illegal activities, it tries to measure the production of goods and services not reported to the government for one of the following reasons: evading taxes, evading social security contributions, avoiding compliance with labour laws and regulations, or avoiding costs arising from the legal rules applicable to each activity.[16]

The more one examines the literature, the more different kinds of economies there are to be found. In Feige's account (2016a: 5), the past half-century has seen an 'explosion' of the various descriptions: 'grey, black, subterranean, cash

[16] See their website: www.etco.org.br/economia-subterranea/?sub=resumo. Accessed on 18 November 2019.

in hand, off the books, moonlight, undeclared, hidden, unofficial, concealed, parallel, invisible, occult, irregular, shadow, underground, non-observed, unreported, unrecorded, illegal, and informal'. Furthermore, despite all the differences that those concepts might have, and the highly elaborated specific details in measurement procedures, Feige (2016a: 5–6) came up with what is perhaps the most overarching concept so far: that of 'unobserved economies (UE)' which 'comprise the activities of individuals, households and/or firms that evade, avoid, circumvent, elude, are excluded from, or not subject to the rules and conventions of established institutions'. What is interesting about his conceptual proposal is that it sheds light onto a constant commonality among all these definitions and measurements: 'They all involve economic agents engaged in non-compliant behaviours that they seek to hide.' In this sense, 'what distinguishes one UE from another is the particular rule being violated'. Therefore, 'different empirical methodologies are required to estimate the composition, magnitude and trend of these different unobserved economies' (Feige 2016b: 93).

Naturally, Feige is mostly concerned with the economic dimension of this phenomenon in order to empirically measure the magnitude of non-compliant behaviours and, hence, to assess its implications for governance, efficiency, equity, and growth. Indeed, this is no easy task. But out of the research done to date, two things seem clear: the phenomenon is big – or, in La Porta and Shleifer's (2014: 110–12) framing, it is 'huge'[17] – and, by its own nature, characterised by different grades of noncompliance with the law. As previously shown, there is plenty of specialised literature to account for the scope, but little attention is paid to the second aspect. All the concepts and definitions above seem to share a common basis, according to which noncompliance equals violation of a certain set of rules. Defining non-compliant behaviour, nonetheless, is no less difficult a task. There are many other different circumstances to consider, especially if one sees the law as a more of an encompassing social system and not only a given set of enacted laws, such as statutes, ordinances, and governmental decrees. The framing of the national and international legal orders is important, but their capacity to generalise normative expectations of behaviour, the way people perceive illegality, and, moreover, the way enacted laws are applied through organisations and public authorities are also circumstances that come into play when defining the standards from which compliant and non-compliant behaviour can be distinguished. This is especially significant when it comes to activities that are, despite legal regulations, pervasive and entrenched in society, which seems to dispute any clear notion of what is supposed to be legal or illegal

[17] They go even further to describe the phenomenon by adding other features: 'informal firms are small, unproductive, and stagnant', 'regulation is not what keeps informal firms down', 'informal firms rarely become formal', and 'as countries develop, informality becomes less important' (La Porta and Shleifer 2014: 112–19). Some of these theses seem difficult to take for granted; however, a proper criticism would go beyond the purposes of this book.

and, hence, compliant and non-compliant. In such cases, the borderline between these zones becomes much harder to identify.

Before taking a deeper look at the theoretical framework to describe those multilevel circumstances and providing a conceptual scheme to define compliant/non-compliant behaviour, which I will do in the second part of the book, it seems important now to further address the analysis of informality and account for more qualitative examples in order to see how the phenomenon occurs in practice. As already shown, the world of informality is huge, and there are many different cases that could be explored. For the sake of academic reasoning, I will focus on what is perhaps the most common visible informal activity, that of street vending. This choice was made for two reasons. First, street vendors are considered to be one of the largest occupational groups of people working in the informal economy,[18] which deems them as a representative case for the purpose of this work. Second, most of the literature focused on informality take street vendors as their main subject of study, as this provides a stable background from which to dive into an arena marked by high grades of noncompliance with the law and, hence, by many shades of invisibility. I aim to demonstrate how arenas of noncompliance are formed through groups of the population and within determined spaces inside the territorial boundaries of the state. In the following section, I will review major works on street vendors, with an emphasis on the legal aspects of the activity. Finally, in chapter three, I will present a case study of street vendors in one Brazilian City, Fortaleza, focusing on the way the activity is performed vis-à-vis the state regulations.

[18] In this sense, Skinner (2010: 185), quoting Charmes, says that 'after home-working, street trading is estimated to account for the largest share of these jobs'. Furthermore, Hummel (2017: 1526), referring to Bhowmik, de Soto, and Roever, asserts that 'street vendors constitute one of the largest occupational groups in the informal sector and are the main subjects in the literature on informal work'. Bhowmik (2010a: 15), in the same vein, says that they 'form a major part of the informal economy because of their large numbers' and they are 'the most visible section'. Roever (2010: 208) points out another aspect: 'Street commerce represents one of the most visible and dynamic segments of the informal economy in Latin America.' Nonetheless, none of the authors provide numbers or data that empirically support a generalised diagnosis. Indeed, national surveys do not usually distinguish the kind of informal work performed under the same category, which makes it difficult to measure the number of street vendors; see ch 2 n 9. Some of them, notwithstanding, point out sparse data from different places. In Donovan (2002: 89 fn 221), for instance, it is stated that, according to the *Departamento Administrativo Nacional de Estadística* (DANE; Colombian Census Bureau), there were 220,344 street vendors in Bogotá, Colombia; that is, 19.8% of Bogotá's informal labour force in 1995. Roever (2010: 212) goes further and, also collecting data from the DANE, estimated that the number has dramatically increased since then: '… the total number of people working in the streets or in stands or kiosks by 2003 was 521,606. The number continued to increase through 2005, when it totaled 557,934.' Kamunyori (2007: 10) estimated that, in Nairobi, whilst 50% of the working population was in the informal sector, 20–25% of these workers were street vendors. Other data on street vendors in some Latin American and African countries can be seen in ILO (2002c: 51–54) and in Charmes (2002: 25).

2

Getting Closer to the Phenomenon: An Overview of the World of Street Vending

2.1. ITS MANY LAYERS AND CONFIGURATIONS

STREET VENDORS ARE typical figures in the urban economies of most of the world. Even though one could argue that they had not for a long time attracted scholarly research (Bhowmik 2010b: xxi), nowadays there are an increasing number of academic events[1] and a considerable body of literature concerned with them,[2] ranging from long-lasting micro ethnography[3] to edited books that bring together studies across the globe.[4] Despite being a worldwide phenomenon, it is hard to deny that a cross-country comparison might conceal stark differences that the activity faces regionally. As Bhowmik (2010a: 16) points out:

> There does not seem to be any connection or comparison with a country like Brazil that claims first-world status with the battered, war-torn economy of Cambodia. What could there be in common between the poor street vendors of India who earns

[1] A quick search on the web points out the different kinds of events that thematise street vending. Worth mentioning is the conference 'Urbanization and Street Vendors' that happened in 2016 in Nairobi, Kenya, a city known for its street commerce; for the report of the conference, including general assessments of street vending in Africa and, particularly, in Kenya, with an emphasis in Kisumu and Nairobi, see Racaud and Schlegel (2016). For another appraisal of street vending in Africa with references to Nairobi, see Skinner (2010). In 2018, I took part in the workshop 'Street Vending and the Dynamics of Modern Urbanization' organised by Marius Meinhof and Ryanne Flock at the University of Frankfurt, Germany, which brought together scholars from different parts of the world to discuss street vendors. The call for papers, which summarises the topics brought to attention, can be seen here: www.hsozkult.de/event/id/termine-37783. Accessed on 29 November 2019.

[2] For example, departing from different perspectives but all related to describing the activity of street vending, in the US (Duneier 1999; Austin 1994), Chile (Llancar 2009; Contreras and Thomas 1993), Peru (Brizio, Bernales, and Zea 2013), Italy (Dawes 2018), India (Srivastava et al 2012), and South Africa (Motala 2002).

[3] The most striking example is, perhaps, the ethnographical study carried out by Duneier (1999) on magazines and books street vendors at a sidewalk on the Sixth Avenue, New York. The book, although considered by many a seminal work in the discipline, provoked strong criticism. See, for instance, Wacquant (2002) and Duneier's reply (2002).

[4] See, for instance, Bhowmik (2010c).

less than two U.S. dollars a day and who cart their wares on hand carts or other forms of cheap transport because they cannot afford anything else, and the street vendors of Peru or Korea who can drive down to their places of work in their cars and enjoy a fairly decent level of living?

But it is even harder to deny that there are, indeed, commonalities to be found worldwide, providing a handful of insights on the activity, and the social roles created in the world of street vending. The regional trends in this regard are quite conspicuous. Latin America, for instance, has experienced a substantial growth of street vendors in the 1990s and 2000s and the diffusion of policies aimed at cleaning up historic centres of capital cities, as well as the creation of thousands of associations of street traders (Roever 2010: 209–10).[5] In Africa, which presents different economic and demographic settings, increases in street vending after late urbanisation processes and international migration due to political crises and civil wars are two common features of a chaotic urban management that often involves violent evictions, such as large-scale operations to remove vendors in order to clean up the city (Skinner 2010: 184–86). Removal of street vendors is another constant trend, especially before major public and tourist events, as documented by Bromley (2000: 12) in his more than 25 years of research with street vendors across the world.[6]

Although there are different settings and considerable variations in working conditions, some core features of the activity can be highlighted to trace patterns. Street vendors are mainly characterised by the activity of commerce in streets or households of products (new or used) and services, which are often cheaper than those provided by the formal market. Due to the usually precarious conditions, low level of commercial design, and use of public spaces, the activity is almost par excellence embedded in different forms of noncompliance and, hence, imbued with highly entrenched informality.[7] As street vendors normally conduct their business where large numbers of people transit, the activity gains certain visibility, at least at its surface level, that is, the part of the activity in which the goods or the service are made available to the public for consumption. In this sense, one can talk about the many layers of the activity, from obtaining the goods or training to perform a service until the actual selling. This differentiation is important to understand adequately the multiple levels of illegality involved and the many ways to analyse the social role and

[5] This study carried out by Roever compared six major cities from different countries in Latin America, namely Bogotá (Colombia), Caracas (Venezuela), Lima (Peru), Mexico City (Mexico), Santiago (Chile), and São Paulo (Brazil).

[6] Examples are reported worldwide. For the eviction of vendors during Independence Day or Republic Day in New Delhi, especially in preparation for, at the time, US President Barack Obama's visit, see: www.indiatogether.org/futile-struggle-for-the-right-to-trade-laws. Accessed on 10 December 2019.

[7] Of course, it is possible to find vendors who do not live in extremely precarious conditions and have more complex commercial designs. But even in these cases the activity remains, to some extent, entangled with informal environments. See ch 3, text accompanying n 25, which shows examples of how the activity might gain other levels of complexity and formality.

the phenomena interlaced with it. There are many examples of different issues that might intersect with street vending, such as transnational networks of import and export that supply open-air markets; exploitation of child workers, migrants, and immigrants – sometimes even as slave labour – to produce goods for selling; the spatial dynamics of street vending; and the urban management of public space.[8]

Of course, a thorough examination of all these layers would entail a far more comprehensive work than the one I propose here and, thus, is beyond the scope of this text. Consequently, the surface level of the activity will be enough to demonstrate the pervasive variety of noncompliance with the law, at least regarding the specific relation between street vendors and the state. The surface level is naturally the most visible level of the activity, that is, the selling, which per se entails two different relations with legal regulations. The first concerns the constitutive legal relationship between individuals in transferring property or performing services and presupposes therefore legal regimes of trade, contract, and business. The second – perhaps the most problematic one – entails a core feature that distinguishes street vendors from other kinds of informal workers: their place of work.[9] And this is what triggers almost every research on street vending: a specific use of space or, to put it more precisely, urban public space. If one understands it as 'all physical spaces and social relations that use that space within the non-private realm of the city' (Bhowmik 2010a: 8), then it becomes easy to imagine where those activities take place. Squares, parks, sidewalks, streets, pavements, entrances of shopping malls, public buildings and events, common areas of seaports, and beaches are some examples. Wherever potential consumers may appear, street vendors are likely to come out to offer food, goods, clothing, and services, creating what Bhowmik (2010a: 13–14) called 'natural markets'. But, when certain places during specific times become so popular that the space itself is transformed into a commercial area that resembles a marketplace, often in open-air, one can observe the rise of some sort of 'street markets',[10] where street vendors gather together and, instead

[8] A good example of how these issues might come together can be seen in the *Feira da Madrugada* (Midnight Market) in São Paulo. For a newspaper report on such problems, see: www.theguardian.com/cities/2017/nov/28/sao-paulo-night-market-bras-feirinha-da-madrugada. Accessed on 26 November 2019. Figure 3 shows one single point in this market. For a map of the clandestine routes through which merchandise illegally enters Brazilian territory and is supplied to São Paulo street markets, see Itikawa (2006: 166, 2010: 261).

[9] This is what makes it somewhat difficult to know precisely the number of street vendors among informal workers in international and national statistics. Normally they fall under the category of 'self-employed worker' or 'own-account worker'. Due to the huge differences in the kinds of work that fall under these categories, overarching public policies and political agendas that try to formalise informal work are hardly successful. For the initial discussions about the pertinence of 'place of work' to better capture the phenomenon, see ILO (2002a). Nowadays, the category is widely accepted by ILO (2018: 8–9), which uses it as one of the criteria to characterise employment in the informal sector.

[10] For a short account with some references on this type of market, see Bromley (2000: 4).

of walking throughout the city to sell, they form fairs, which are sometimes specialised. These are normally known to the townsfolk and attract consumers to the space and its vicinity. Figure 3 shows an example of this kind of open-air market in São Paulo which operates after midnight. Specialising in clothing, it is the largest open-air market in Latin America.[11]

Figure 3 'Feirinha da Madrugada' (Midnight Market) in São Paulo at 5:30am in September 2018. Photo: personal archive

This notion of natural markets and street markets gives a first glance at the different ways through which street vendors use public space. Basically, the use varies with respect to time and mobility. As Bromley (2000: 2) summarises,

> Street vending may be practiced full-time, part-time, seasonally or occasionally. It can be fixed, occasionally mobile, or almost continuously mobile, and it can go on at any or all times of the day and night. The firms involved can range from one-person micro-enterprises, through numerous forms of partnership and family business, up to franchisees, pieceworkers and wageworkers of larger off-street businesses. Some street vendors are branch operations of off-street stores, sometimes right outside the store, at other times some distance away. Other street vendors create their own branch operations, dividing their merchandise and sending some of it with a relative, partner or employee to sell at another location.

[11] See n 8 above.

This implies two different perceptions of the urban public space: whilst for some it is a space for leisure or transit, for others it is the place to work and to earn a living. In the latter sense, occupying public space with profit purpose calls for legal regimes of space governance and public management in which the state is called to play the pivotal role.

2.2. SPACE: A MATTER OF PRIVATE AND PUBLIC CONTROL (OR COMPETITION?)

As the use of public spaces by street vendors normally lacks compliance with the law, the activity is commonly portrayed as unorganised, chaotic, non-modern, backward, or illegal, triggering discourses of organisation, civility, modernisation, planification, and development that pits local government and the public sphere against vendors.[12] This is mostly due to the different externalities produced by the occupation of spaces in which the transit of people is intense: large agglomerations of street vendors block pavements, disrupt traffic, hinder pedestrian mobility, erode historical sites, and litter communal areas. State response comes either through daily harassment by the police, evictions, confiscation, arrests, displacement, municipal raids, or large-scale operations to recover the public space.[13] Such responses make uncertainty and risk some of the core features in the occupation of space by vendors, and conflict with state authorities becomes a general pattern of these arenas. Depending on the constellation of interests involved and the intensity of enforcement, the conflict might also even be described in terms of 'war'.[14]

[12] Many examples in this regard could be given since street vending is often reported as a 'problem' in newspapers worldwide. For a comprehensive account of 102 newspapers reports, collected from 1998 to 2006, in São Paulo, Brazil, see Itikawa (2006: 413–520). There are also studies worth mentioning that focus on these types of discourses. For the tension between 'desired modernization of the city' and the '"un-modern" activity of street vending' in Nairobi – which is also replicated in other African cities – and how a 'growing space for dialogue' is being created among local government, formal businesses, and street vendors to change these discourses, see Kamunyori (2007). For a more embracing approach taken by state-initiated projects along with real estate developers in terms of modernisation and economic development or urban centres against the 'sense of lateness' and 'backwardness' of street markets and historical sites, see Zhang (2006), building on the case of Kunming, China.

[13] For examples of such operations, see the study by Donovan (2002) in Bogotá, Colombia, where space recovery became a long-standing political campaign by the elected mayors from 1988 onwards. Skinner (2010: 190–91) reports what was perhaps 'the largest and most violent eviction of street traders' in Africa: the operation Murambatsvina, which took place in Zimbabwe in May 2005 and, according to estimates, affected about 700,000 people, including arrests of 20,000 vendors country-wide. Campaigns to 'clean up the streets' in many Chinese cities invoking the notion of 'civility' to support state regulation of public space are also mentioned by Zhang (2006: 473 fn 31).

[14] For instance, Duneier (1999: 231) used the expression 'space wars' to describe how business associations could manage their political influence to pass laws to regulate space against street vendors in New York. Donovan (2002: 112–18) used the same expression, but to describe the situation in Bogotá, also making some references to cases in La Paz, Seoul, and New York. Zhang (2006: 472) talks en passant about 'guerrilla wars' in Kunming, China.

Regardless of how successful governmental operations might be, including the ones which aim at relocating and relodging vendors, full control over the space can hardly be taken as granted.[15] Since attempts for control always imply the possibility of physical conflicts, those who are located at the fore of the enforcement, namely street vendors and government officials, are often open to pursuing alternatives in order to avoid a clash. Sometimes, a game of cat-and-mouse is played,[16] and certain abilities, such as 'rule-challenging' and 'alliance-making' with vendors and public authorities, turn street clandestinity into what Itikawa (2010: 257) called, referring to the situation in São Paulo, Brazil, the 'supreme art of escaping, evading and skirting'. At other times, bribes become the means to overcome the problem.[17] In this confusing, chaotic, and fuzzy state of affairs, both vendors and public authorities profit, with profit not being restricted to economic terms. Frequently, the uncertainty of the activity is used by politicians to explore the public space as coin to buy votes near elections or manoeuvre vendors to their advantage.[18] In the same context, street vendors' associations and leaders might become useful intermediaries to facilitate this relationship, which can eventually develop into forms

[15] Relodging operations are a good example of how even operations that are successful at first glance fail in the long run, for different reasons, to control the space. Donovan (2002: 24–28) exemplifies this with the case of San Victorino, a neighbourhood in Bogotá, where the mayor in 1960 wanted to take the vendors out of the streets and organise them into a market. The problem was, 'rather than control street vending, relocating street vendors to San Victorino transformed the area into a vending magnet. Unauthorized vendors established their stands on the periphery of San Victorino and quickly outnumbered the authorized, relocated merchants.' The market is still in full force today. A newspaper reported in 2017 that more than 200,000 people visited there daily, meaning around 10,000 per hour, for Christmas promotions. See: www.eltiempo.com/bogota/unas-200-000-personas-van-al-madrugon-de-san-victorino-en-diciembre-163450. Accessed on 05 December 2019. In 2019, also in the period before Christmas, due to the protests and manifestations against the government of Iván Duque in Colombia massive losses were reported, because people feared to go out on the streets. See: www.dinero.com/pais/articulo/en-san-victorino-estan-preocupados-por-el-paro/279658. Accessed on 05 December 2019.

[16] Kamunyori (2007: 29) reports a very interesting system of 'look-out' in Nairobi's Central Business District, in which information about the approach of city inspectors is transmitted through whistles. The escape plan can also 'include waiting taxis that whisks away the street vendors' stock as soon as the look-out signals'.

[17] In order to see how bribes play a role in street vending, see the study by Hummel (2017, 2018) in La Paz, Bolivia; Peña (1999: 386) in Mexico City, Mexico; and Itikawa (2006: 188–90) in São Paulo, summarising the widely known case 'Máfia da Propina' (Bribe Mafia) and its relation with street vending in the city.

[18] Donovan (2002: 30–31) brings some examples of this 'vote buying' practice in Colombia, especially through the position of city councillors. In Mexico City, in the 1990s, as described by Peña (1999: 368), vendors not only had to pay fees to street vendors' organisations, which used the fees to pay bribes or gifts to 'government officials in exchange for tolerance', but also had to 'attend political rallies to support candidates from the Revolutionary Institutionalized Party (PRI)'. Brazil does not lag behind. Itikawa (2006: 185) verified that, in the elections of 2000 and 2004 in São Paulo, 'street vendors' associations were invariably called by the candidates to collect votes from the members in exchange for promises of benefits to the category', which had still not been fulfilled in 2006 when she wrote her doctoral dissertation.

of clientelism or patronage depending on the characteristics it acquires.[19] Naturally, that does not prevent the rise of leadership among vendors to absorb the latent political capital.[20]

All in all, controlling the public space is problematic not only at the fore of enforcement. The lack of regulations or clear guidelines which specifically target street vending is another major issue. Even in cases where regulations do exist and are clear, and the occupation of the space can be done through proper licences, this often does not guarantee a safe and stable environment, for harassment may occur despite the regulations.[21] Further to this are the many ways in which legality is commodified and becomes itself a currency for another type of informal business, such as the trade of the licences themselves.[22] In the cases where regulations exist but are not clear, a new set of problems is generated. Ambiguity and vagueness in legal texts or overlapping competences give rise to collisions at many levels: among public authorities, state institutions, and government bodies,[23] as well as different branches of Power. In regard to the latter, cases in which the judiciary goes against administrative resolutions,

[19] In a survey conducted by Peña (1999: 367–70) on the functions of street vendors' organisations in Mexico City in 1997, 'the majority of vendors (51%) believe they benefit from being members because the organization negotiates on their behalf with the local government authorities regarding issues that directly affect their work. Almost a third (29%) of the vendors also believe that they benefit from the organization because it is a mechanism to address the problems of distribution of work spaces in the market.' Despite the problems of generalisation of a such specific sample (Peña 1999: 365), the accuracy of the answers sheds a light on the roles associations play in these arenas. For an assessment of the benefits and costs of organisation for street vendors and the respective state incentives to facilitate collective action, see Hummel (2017), who illustrates this with an ethnographic study in La Paz, Bolivia.

[20] During my field research in Fortaleza, I also observed how leadership could be converted into electoral aspirations. Some street vendors who earn trust from the others and enough confidence to face a campaign might also engage in politics. At the time, September 2018, I visited a street market where two different candidates were competing for votes from the vendors. See ch 3, Figure 15.

[21] Kamunyori (2007: 28–30) exemplifies this with the 'second round' fees in Nairobi: 'Even though vendors are mandated to pay the 70cts (KES 25) daily licensing fee, this license does not protect them from the *askaris* [Nairobi City Council Inspectorate]. A common occurrence is when one set of city *askaris* come round after an earlier set has already been by providing daily licenses at US$ 0.75 per vendor. When this second round comes by, they demand the "going rate" of US$ 7.10. When the vendors tell them that they have already paid their daily fee, the inspectors response is "have you seen me here collecting your KES25?"' The '"changing of the guard" at the executive branch of the City Council' is another example in which 'the person in charge wants everyone to know that he is in charge; so he voids all licenses making the license becomes invalid even though the expiry date has not reached'.

[22] Itikawa (2010: 258) reports this practice in the street markets of São Paulo Downtown: '… some permit-holder street vendors rent a trading spot to a third party, and in some cases increase the official permit's value 10 times.'

[23] Bhowmik (2010a: 10–11) points out that this is a general problem in street vending, and many examples can be found worldwide. He mentions the case of Mumbai, India, where the Municipal Corporation competes with other authorities, such as the Mumbai Metropolitan Region Development Authority, the Port Trust of India, and the police. Another example is given by Roever (2010: 220–21) on the conflict between the metropolitan and municipal mayors' offices in Caracas, Venezuela. In Brazil, inspections may also violate the legal framework of competences; in the next chapter, I will provide some examples from Fortaleza.

police actions or governmental practices are somewhat common. This happens especially when the Constitution provides for rights that can be invoked to justify the use of public space[24] or to protect it against private use.[25] As one might imagine, in the same way political agendas and governmental programmes to recover public space are frequently doomed to fail to control space, court decisions are destined to encounter noncompliance, regardless of whether they are aimed at issuing orders to public authorities or to street vendors.

In summary, due to this multitude of noncompliance, controlling the public space, instead of being strictly under legal rules, is constantly under dispute. The dispute assumes the form of competition, which happens not only at the level of the occupation of the public space, but also spreads throughout other layers of the activity: street vendors compete for the best spots; associations compete for members; leaders compete for influence; politicians compete for votes; officials compete for bribes; institutions compete for competences; Powers compete to rule. In such conditions, as space is by definition a limited resource, a varying pool of strategies come into play in order to rationalise its use and outcomes. Sometimes, they pave the way for integration with the formally constituted democratic institutions, such as coalitions of organisations,[26]

[24] One striking example is the case *Sodan Singh etc etc v New Delhi Municipal Committee & ANR etc* (1989 AIR 1988), in which the Constitutional Court of India recognised that, under certain circumstances, harassment of street vendors by public authorities violates the constitutional right to trade as part of their livelihood. This right was an expression of the constitutional right to freedom according to the Art 19(1)(g) of the Indian Constitution: '1. All citizens shall have the right – … (g) to practice any profession, or to carry on any occupation, trade or business.' The court ruled that 'the right to carry on trade or business mentioned in Article 19(1)(g) of the Constitution, on street pavements, if properly regulated cannot be denied on the ground that the streets are meant exclusively for passing or re-passing and for no other use' (p 11). Even though it could be considered a landmark case in India, local journals report that little has changed since then in Delhi as well in the rest of India. See: www.indiatogether.org/futile-struggle-for-the-right-to-trade-laws. Accessed on 10 December 2019.

[25] That was the case of the Colombian Constitution of 1991, which, in comparison with the earlier Constitution of 1886, brought in its Art 82(1) an interesting novelty: 'It is the duty of the State to watch over the protection of the integrity of public space and for its assignment to common use, which has priority over the individual interest.' This article was consistently invoked by many administrations in Bogotá in order to evict street vendors; see Donovan (2002: 56–58). Many of these evictions led to a huge number of lawsuits – more specifically *acciones de tutela* – brought by street vendors during the 1990s against the local administrations of Bogotá. In 1999, the Constitutional Court of Colombia (case SU-360/99) had to judge the constitutionality of the evictions. The case, which covered 1,016 street vendors from different sites of Bogotá, was ruled in favour of the ones who could prove that they had their right to work violated by the city administration. Among other reasons, the decision enforced the need for an 'integrated reading' of the Arts 334(2), 25, and 54 of the Constitution, which provide for, respectively, the duty of the State to provide full employment, the right to work, and the right to a job.

[26] Perhaps the most striking example is the International Alliance of Street Vendors (StreetNet), which was established in 2002 in Durban, South Africa, and brings together unions, co-operatives, and associations of street vendors from all over the world. Other important organisations played a central role in the constitution of StreetNet, such as the Self-Employed Women's Association (SEWA) in Ahmedabad, India; the Self-Employed Women's Union (SEWU) in Durban, South Africa; Women's World Banking in New York; the International Coalition of Women and Credit in New York; Women in Informal Employment: Globalising and Organising (WIEGO). See: streetnet.org.za. Accessed on 11 December 2019.

self-regulatory agreements between vendors and authorities,[27] and benevolent and accommodating public policies.[28] At other times, they aim to supersede or decouple the democratic institutions, as happens with networks of corruption and criminality.[29,30]

Either way, this state of affairs profoundly impacts the performances that legal texts, whether enacted law or common law, are expected to have within certain arenas inside the state. Ultimately, one could even cast some doubt onto the existence of a rule of law in such contexts, where the extent of noncompliance is so high that having rights or obligations does not affect immediately expectations of behaviour. Or, at least, it may be recognised that the legal rationality is submitted to factual constraints which change the performances of the law in these arenas. I shall explore this discussion in the coming chapters. However, first I will expand on the analysis for the sake of academic precision. For, even though the literature on street vending always makes references to the illegality of the activity, especially when it comes to the interplay between vendors and government, most of the time they consist of very general and superficial references.[31] There is little comprehensive analysis of the legal

[27] See ch 3 regarding the case of *Feira da Sé*. I will elaborate more on this point in section 8.2.2.

[28] The National Urban Street Vendors Policy launched in 2004 in India is an example of that. For a policy brief which reports its process of development, content, and implementation, see Sinha and Roever (2011). For a more detailed study of the emergence of this policy using the Advocacy Coalition Framework, see Lintelo (2010).

[29] In 2017, an operation of the Civil Police of the state of Ceará, Brazil, with the cooperation of the *Secretaria da Fazenda* (SEFAZ; Department of Finance of the State) and the *Ministério Público do Estado do Ceará* (MPCE; Government Agency for Law Enforcement and Prosecution of Crimes of the State of Ceará), uncovered a criminal organisation which involved businessmen and public officers of SEFAZ. They created ghost companies to buy products, especially textiles and clothing, from other states without paying the taxes due. These products were destined to supply street vendors' open-air markets in Fortaleza. See: g1.globo.com/ceara/noticia/treze-sao-presos-em-esquema-de-sonegacao-que-causou-prejuizo-de-mais-de-r-300-milhoes-ao-ceara.ghtml. Accessed on 12 December 2019. See also: www.opovo.com.br/noticias/fortaleza/2018/03/justica-aceita-denuncia-contra-19-acusados-de-fraude-no-setor-textil.html. Accessed on 12 December 2019.

[30] I borrowed here, with some adaptations, the conceptual framework of Mascareño et al (2016) on the relationship between informal networks and democratic institutions.

[31] This is clearly seen, for instance, in the work of Itikawa. Despite being an impressive study of street vendors and what she calls their 'clandestinity' in São Paulo, the analysis of the legislation is considerably weak. When she mentions, for instance, the crime of 'corruption' (2006: 186–88), there is a fuzzy mix of different categories of crimes against the public administration and unjustified assertions on the causes of corruption. Let alone the fact that the Brazilian Penal Code is quoted by *apud*, this amalgam of different categories of corruption – the ones stated by the Penal Code and a more general understanding of corruption as '… the transfer of income that takes place outside the rules of the economic game *stricto sensu* (SILVA, 2000)' [the paraphrase of Silva is hers, the translation into English is mine] – leads her to poorly grounded conclusions, such as that 'the regulation of the activity [of street vending] far from the reality of the streets has facilitated the expansion of the corruption scheme and the growth of bribes' (2006: 189). The meaning of being 'far' or 'close' to the reality is not clear, and the details of the regulations and their changes are not properly described.

framework, which includes not only the enacted laws, but also the interpretations conveyed by public authorities and courts.[32] In order to fill this gap and shed light on the many forms of noncompliance entrenched in street vending, the next chapter will be dedicated to exploring the legal framework which regulates the activity and observing the many ways it is breached. This will be done with a case study of the city of Fortaleza, capital of the state of Ceará, Brazil.

[32] So far, I have not come across any work that could accomplish such a task. It is true that some studies go into this direction, eg, the one carried out by Rincon (2010) in Caracas, Venezuela. She rightly casts light on the 'two distinct "layers"' of legal framework: the constitutional and national level, on the one hand, and the municipal level, on the other. However, many of her assertions do not come with proper references and cannot, therefore, be relied upon. For instance, she says that 'over the years, vendors had made appeals to the courts over the alleged unconstitutional nature of the ordinances and decrees, yet they were never successful' (2010: 244). But which ordinances and decrees were exactly contested, how many lawsuits were filled or even what were the rulings, are unanswered questions. To make this a strong criticism would be nonetheless a bit unfair, since it demands a trained legal scholar to do so – and, to my knowledge, none has been concerned with these questions. Regardless, given that a great part of the studies on street vending rely on the concept of illegality, a precise account of the legal framework cannot be simply dismissed.

3

Stepping into the Field: The Example of Fortaleza, Ceará, Brazil

3.1. STREET VENDING

IT IS IMPORTANT to begin by noting that in countries such as Brazil, making sense of the enacted laws is an incredibly difficult task even for the most trained eyes. An extensively analytic Constitution, which has 250 main articles plus 114 from the transitory dispositions, and an intricate, complex system of federal, state, and municipal laws[1] provide for different, often overlapping, regimes of regulation which cover every single layer of street vending. Any attempt to capture the legal framework of this activity, therefore, is doomed to face at least two basic challenges: finding the applicable norms and observing how institutions and authorities are applying them. In the previous chapter I focused my analysis on one aspect of the most visible layer of the activity, that is, the occupation of the public space for the purpose of profit. For the sake of consistency, I will continue with this focus to address these challenges.

The occupation of public space is in general deeply connected to municipal regulations in Brazil. From the forms of occupation to the types of merchandise, goods, and services allowed, there are many legal regulations a street vendor must fulfil in order to comply with the law. Although these vary from city to city, two general patterns can be observed: occupation is allowed through somewhat simplified administrative licences, normally in the form of a vending permit; and no matter how detailed or precise they may be, administrative regulations are rarely enforced to the full extent. This can be seen at different levels, and Fortaleza, in this sense, seems a representative case to illustrate the phenomenon.

The main administrative regulations of the municipality are the *Código de Obras e Posturas do Munípio de Fortaleza* – Law 5,530/1981 (Code of Construction and Use of the Public Space in the Municipality – hereafter

[1] A study conducted by the *Instituto Brasileiro de Planejamento e Tributação* (IBPT; Brazilian Institute of Planning and Taxation) found that more than 6 million pieces of legislation (from Constitutional amendments to statutes, decrees, city ordinances, etc) had been issued in Brazil since the Federal Constitution of October 1988 – an average of 776 pieces of legislation per working day; see Amaral et al (2019).

referred to as COPM),[2] the mayor's decree which implements the COPM, namely *Decreto 9.300/1994* (regulates the exercise of itinerant commerce activity), Law 8,222/1998 (application of penalties for violations of health legislation), and Law 9,477/2009 (regulates the commerce of alcoholic beverages). Some other sparse pieces of legislation which take care of secondary matters[3] or give special treatment to similar activities[4] can also be found. These regulations cover almost all of the types and forms of street vending found in Fortaleza, including detailed regulations on how to obtain permits, comply with certain standards for selling, and the penalties to be applied in the case of violations.

Perhaps the most direct regulation is Decree 9,300, issued by the mayor in 1994 to regulate the activity of street vending (*comércio ambulante*). Following the general rules contained in the COPM,[5] it provides the core concept for that activity:

> Article 1 – It is considered as itinerant commerce any commercial or service activity, of a permanent or occasional character, exercised in a stationary or itinerant way, in public roads or public places, by persons who do not have any type of employment or functional link, with public or private person.

[2] The Code is highly complex and overarching. It comprises 770 main articles, many of which have paragraphs and subsections. Regarding the activity of street vending, the most important are Chapter XLVII, Section II – *Da Licença do Comércio Ambulante e Feiras Livres* (Licence for Itinerant Commerce and Open Markets), which comprises Arts 708 to 717; Chapter XLVIII – *Do Comércio de Gêneros Alimentícios* (Trade of Foodstuffs), Arts 718 to 724; and Chapter XLIX – *Das Infrações e Penalidades* (Offenses and Penalties), more specifically its Section II – *Das Multas* (Fines) and Section VI – *Da Apreensão e Perda de Bens e Mercadorias* (Seizure and Loss of Goods and Merchandise). *Postscriptum*: The COPM was revoked in August 2019 by the 'Municipality Legal Code' (*Lei Complementar 270/2019*), after the case study carried out in this chapter was already complete. As the changes are not relevant for my analysis, only the COPM will be mentioned here.

[3] Such as Law 9,232/2007, which presents three short articles to authorise the mayor to offer or afford space for street vendors from the city centre for storage or to park their equipment; and Law 10,870/2019, which authorises the mayor to issue permits to street vendors who were already working in the markets on Avenue Beira Mar, the city shore most popular with tourists.

[4] This is the case of Law 10,474/2016, which regulates the activities of 'food truck', 'food bike', and 'food cart' [no translation made here]. For their own nature, as the law itself recognises, they are a kind of 'food trade activity' carried out in 'public streets and areas' (Art 2, I, II, and III). Interestingly, Art 3 states this regulation shall not be applied to street vendors. This exclusion, however, is difficult to understand, since they are, within their own category, the same kind of activity. In addition to that, the law, which is written in Portuguese, uses terms in English to describe the three categories mentioned above. This might suggest – even though the bill justification says otherwise (*Projeto de Lei Ordinária 253/2015*, proposed by the Representative Cláudia Gomes) – that the law was brought in to give special treatment not to those activities themselves, given that they are categorically the same as street vendors in general, but rather to a very specific middle class of street workers who tend to sell gourmet products, often more expensive than the ones sold by common street vendors. Naturally, this kind of food commerce usually takes place in richer neighbourhoods and are part of the so-called 'gourmetisation' of street food. For a more general study on the different strategies of products and prices differentiation in the Brazilian food industry, including the gourmetisation trend in recent decades, and their impact on social inequalities, see Palmieri Júnior (2017).

[5] Chapter XLVII, Section II of the COPM, which includes Arts 708 to 717, grants the mayor competence to regulate the activity of itinerant commerce and street markets, but, at the same time, provides a set of rules that constrain the activity, such as a maximum validity of 180 days for the administrative permits (Art 708, § 1), the conservation and preservation of the landscape in public areas (Art 709 (II)), common obligations for vendors at street markets (Art 717), and so on.

The concept is then followed by a list of goods and services that can be provided by street vendors (Article 2):

I – cigarettes and candy;
II – general clothing;
III – jewelry, things of small value, toys, household utilities, and varieties;
IV – used discs and cassette tapes;
V – hardware and scrap of domestic appliances;
VI – fast snacks;
VII – newspapers and magazines;
VIII – used books and school supplies;
IX – ice cream, popsicles, popcorn, and juices;
X – shoes, bags, belts, and similar;
XI – regional or seasonal products;
XII – medicinal herbs and dry spice;
XIII – fruit and vegetables and grocery products;
XIV – telephone cards;
XV – raffle tickets;
XVI – lotteries;
XVII – tickets;
XVIII – polishing and repair of footwear;
XIX – clock repairs and the like;
XX – making of keys.

Additionally, the municipal decree expressly excludes the 'sale of popsicle, popcorn, and lottery ticket, when they are exercised in an itinerant manner' (Article 2, sole paragraph). This exclusion, however, is difficult to understand, since the same goods are simultaneously admitted to street vending (Article 2, IX and XVI). In a first look, it could be understood as a prohibition, but, as one public inspector tried to explain, 'the idea was to exempt them from licensing/authorization because they are common activities of low economic value'.[6] These three activities would, according to him, be permitted, being exempt from inspection and control, although, as the same inspector admits, 'the right thing, from the perspective of the sanitary surveillance, would be to pass through at least an inspection to prove the certification for food manipulation, the origin

[6] The interviews mentioned in this chapter were carried out by me during field research in Brazil in August and September 2018. They lasted from one hour to one hour and a half and were done separately in different opportunities and in an unstructured manner, with the purpose of acquiring more information about the legal issues involved in the activity. One interviewee was a former street vendor specialised in the selling of clothes who has worked in all areas of an open-air market (the street, the tent, and the store). Another interviewee was Heron Moreira (see Figure 15), one of the most important leaders of the *feirantes* in Fortaleza. The last interviewee was a public inspector who, for many years, had been in charge of inspecting the area where the biggest open-air market in Fortaleza is located.

of the inputs'. Even though the explanation regarding the sales of popcorn and popsicle seems plausible, it becomes problematic when one realises that the majority of other goods and services stated in Article 1 of the decree are also of low economic value. In addition to that, the selling of popcorn is usually done along with candies, which would place the vendor in a grey zone, and the selling of popsicles is often done through a small number of companies that monopolise the market, sometimes employing the vendors. Figure 4 shows how popcorn is normally offered in the city. Figure 5 shows a vendor selling popsicles for the leading company in the region, which is, not out of coincidence, owned by a former street vendor.[7] Furthermore, it remains unclear as to whether street vendors whose products are similar to these exempted goods but were not expressly mentioned in the decree, such as the selling of boiled and roasted corn, should be exempted or not. Since there is no express regulation to deal with these, the public inspectors, in practice, as stated by one who was interviewed, 'usually ask them to leave the site, freeing up the public space under the penalty of apprehension of their equipment'. Figure 6 shows a seller of boiled and roasted corn.

Figure 4 Popcorn seller with candies in the middle of a sidewalk in Fortaleza. Photo: Deisa Garcês

[7] For a brief history of the company, which produces daily more than 40,000 popsicles and 8,000 litres of ice cream, and how the owner began as a street vendor, see: blogs.opovo.com.br/radardocomercio/2020/09/11/sabor-de-conquista-conheca-a-historia-de-sucesso-da-pardal. Accessed on 13 December 2022.

Figure 5 Popsicle seller on a weekend at the beach in Fortaleza. Photo: Fernanda Araujo

The case of the lottery, however, is more complicated since games of chance in general are prohibited under federal law. Lotteries and gambling in Brazil are considered penal contraventions, that is, a sort of misdemeanour which is punished primarily with fines and simple incarceration and, secondarily, with suspension of political rights and of state-given licences or authorisations for

Figure 6 Seller of boiled and roasted corn in Fortaleza. Photo: Deisa Garcês

the exercise of a professional activity.[8] The lottery can exclusively be offered by the federal union and, in specific cases, by the states; in other words, as a general rule, it cannot be explored by persons or private companies.[9] For this reason, when municipal Decree 9,300/1994 mentions lottery, it only permits the street vending of legally authorised lottery tickets. Nonetheless, in Brazil, informality also embraces this activity, which includes possibly the largest illegal lottery game in the world: the *jogo do bicho* (animal game), which is more than 125 years old and, in many ways, a clandestine lottery.[10] It is difficult to measure exactly how

[8] The prohibition is stated in Arts 50 to 58 of the *Lei das Contravencões Penais (Decreto-Lei 3.688/1941*; Law of Penal Contraventions). Simple incarceration, for the purpose of this law, means that, in general, the convicted is not submitted to rigorous confinement discipline, does not stay with common prisoners, and cannot be incarcerated for more than five years; see Arts 6 and 10. The secondary punishments are stated in Art 12.

[9] The legal regime of lotteries in Brazil is, to a certain extent, chaotic, especially due to the fact that unauthorised lotteries, as well as games of chance and gambling, have always been widely practised. In 1944, the service was regulated and permitted to be used only by the Union and states themselves or through public concessions to private persons limited to one concession per state and to the Union (Arts 1, 2, and 4 of *Decreto-Lei 6.259/1944*). In 1967, another regulation came into force during the military dictatorship. This is the regulation still in force, with minor changes made in the 1960s, 1970s and 2018. It limits the operation of lotteries exclusively to the Union, forbidding the creation of new state lotteries and public concession to third parties, keeping only those existing under the previous regulation as legal (Arts 1, 2, 32, and 33 of the *Decreto-Lei 204/1967*).

[10] In an investigation into the markets in Brazil, even Lévi-Strauss (1957: 148 [1955: 164]), during the 1930s, noted how this lottery was offered on the middle of the streets. Freyre (1986: 147 [2003: 206]), in his masterpiece from 1933, suggested that the great popularity of the game was due to the 'animistic and totemistic residuum of Amerindian culture, later reinforced by the African'. A comprehensive and detailed history of the game, including an account of the process of its criminalisation, can be found in Chazkel (2007, 2011) with evidence of its creation in the 1890s.

pervasive and entrenched this lottery is in Brazil.[11] The activity is so widespread throughout the country that, in order to avoid any ambiguity regarding its illegality, both the Law of Penal Contraventions, from 1941, and the 1944 lottery regulation had specific provisions to expressly state the prohibition.[12] However, in the same way as Chazkel (2011: 63) once referred to the animal game in the early twentieth century in Rio de Janeiro, one could mutatis mutandis say that its 'characteristically paradoxical status as a ubiquitous cultural phenomenon and criminal infraction' still remains today. The game, which since its beginning has been connected to the famous Brazilian Carnival in Rio de Janeiro, is also often associated with other types of crime, such as bribery of police, judges, and journalists, as well as money laundering.[13] The street vendors occupied only with the selling of tickets for the animal game and the ones who manage the activity are even given a special name: *bicheiros* (animal game sellers).[14] If the animal game alone has been a litmus test for the proper enforcement of legislation, the situation has become much more problematic in the last years, as other informal lotteries have emerged, sometimes with more sophisticated mechanisms, to reinforce this market, adopting not only the theme of animals, but also other themes such as dreams and soccer teams.[15] In many cases, street vendors sell more than one kind of lottery ticket, including both legal and illegal ones. In Fortaleza, it is common to see lottery vendors on sidewalks and street corners. Figure 7 shows a vendor on a sidewalk.

[11] For an account of its economic impact and cultural significance, see DaMatta and Soárez (1999) and, with an emphasis on rational choice theory, Freire (2019).

[12] See Art 58 of both laws. The Law of Penal Contraventions, for instance, states that 'exploring or performing the lottery called animal game, or practicing any act related to its performance or operation' may lead to punishment of 'simple incarceration, from four months to one year, and fine, from two to twenty *contos de réis* [the currency at the time of enactment]' (Art 58 of the *Decreto-Lei 3.688/1941*).

[13] For an international newspaper report on the animal game, its connection with Carnival in Rio de Janeiro, and some of the police operations attempting to take it down, see: www.bbc.com/news/world-latin-america-16634941. Accessed on 17 December 2019.

[14] In the glossary of Portuguese terms, Chazkel (2011: 313) describes only the seller of tickets as *bicheiro*. But nowadays, as many other informal lotteries besides the animal game are on the market for street vendors to sell, the name is instead used in some regions to designate the managers or bosses of the lottery, as can be seen in newspaper reports (see n 13).

[15] In Rio de Janeiro, a newspaper reports how animal game sellers started to diversify their business with sports bets; see: www1.folha.uol.com.br/esporte/2017/08/1910912-ilegais-apostas-esportivas-sao-oferecidas-por-bicheiros-no-rio.shtml. Accessed on 27 December 2019. Sometimes, however, the new lotteries compete against the animal game. For example, a new illegal sports lottery was born in the North and Northeast regions and has spread throughout the country. A newspaper article reports its coming to São Paulo and provides more information about its novelties, such as the new betting system in which bets can be taken not only through street vendors, but also via WhatsApp and online websites; see: www1.folha.uol.com.br/esporte/2017/11/1934937-loteria-esportiva-clandestina-toma-conta-das-ruas-de-sao-paulo.shtml. Accessed on 27 December 2019.

Figure 7 Lottery seller on a sidewalk in Downtown Fortaleza. In his stand, it is stated 'here we have the dreams lottery'. Photo: personal archive

Noncompliance with the municipal aforementioned decree, however, goes far beyond lotteries, popcorns, and popsicles. Among the requirements for the exercise of the activity, it prohibits the 'sale of meat, fish, shellfish, alcoholic beverages, weapons and ammunition of any kind, explosives or products of easy combustion' (Article 13, II, of Decree 9,300/1994). Despite this, most of those activities can also easily be seen throughout the city. The itinerant selling of fish and shellfish, for instance, is one of the key features of the beaches in

Fortaleza, which is famous for its local production of seafood.[16] It is hard to find a day or time in which there is no vendor within reach. Particularly on the weekends, when there is high traffic of people, the number of vendors – not only of food, but also handicraft, imported goods, candies, sunglasses, swimsuits, coconut water, and alcoholic beverages – increases considerably, which encourages turmoil when public authorities try to control them[17] and creates a sense of competition between the vendors and the restaurants located at the seashore.[18] Managers, waiters, and private security guards are often instructed by the restaurant owners not to allow vendors within the area of the beach they cover, often leading to conflicts between them,[19] even though the occupation of the seashore by restaurants is likewise legally controversial under federal law[20] and has also been a matter of judicial litigation in which legislation and rulings

[16] The state of Ceará is also known for its coastal fishing communities whose main activities are traditional artisanal fisheries. For a general account of these communities in Brazil with a special emphasis on their legal regulation, see Araujo (2021) and Araujo and Moita (2018).

[17] For newspaper reports on the irregular occupation, public inspections and turmoil at *Praia do Futuro*, one of the busiest beaches of Fortaleza, see: https://diariodonordeste.verdesmares.com.br/editorias/metro/presenca-de-ambulantes-na-praia-do-futuro-gera-polemica-1.1785845. Accessed on 04 January 2020; see also https://g1.globo.com/ce/ceara/noticia/2019/07/03/fiscalizacao-recolhe-produtos-de-ambulantes-e-gera-tumulto-na-praia-do-futuro.ghtml. Accessed on 03 January 2020.

[18] In January 2020, a newspaper reported that one restaurant was charging extra from clients who were buying from vendors. The manager, however, denied this practice, saying that the money was charged not from the vendors, but from the waiters instead; see: g1.globo.com/ce/ceara/noticia/2020/01/14/barraca-da-praia-do-futuro-cobra-r-60-de-clientes-que-consumirem-produtos-de-ambulantes.ghtml. Afterwards, the restaurant was notified by the local department of defence and protection of consumer rights that the practice was illegal; see: g1.globo.com/ce/ceara/noticia/2020/01/20/procon-notifica-barraca-de-praia-por-cobrar-r-60-de-clientes-que-consumissem-produtos-de-ambulantes-em-fortaleza.ghtml. Accessed on 23 January 2020.

[19] In 2014, the *Ministério Público Federal* (MPF; Federal Agency for Law Enforcement and Prosecution of Crimes) filed an *Ação Civil Pública* (Public Civil Action) against a very famous seaside restaurant involved in many conflicts, including verbal and physical assault on vendors. The Federal Justice held in 2018 that the restaurant could not impede the free transit of vendors and selling activities within its perimeter, because such competence was exclusively of the State; as the activity of itinerant vendors could be illegal, it should be reported to authorities instead (case 0010153-75.2014.4.05.8100, 2 *Justiça Federal no Estado do Ceará* (JFCE)). In 2015, a similar practice by another restaurant was reported in a newspaper; see: g1.globo.com/ceara/noticia/2015/11/barraca-de-praia-e-autuada-no-ceara-por-expulsar-cliente-que-comprou-de-ambulante.html. Accessed on 05 January 2020. In 2019, a third restaurant was required to compensate a customer for prohibiting her from inviting a vendor to sit at her table (case 0149322-93.2016.8.06.0001, *Tribunal de Justiça do Ceará* (TJCE)). The case happened in 2016 and went viral on social media, exposing the conflicts between vendors and restaurants at the seashore. See: politica.estadao.com.br/blogs/fausto-macedo/justica-ordena-que-barraca-de-praia-de-fortaleza-indenize-cliente-expulsa-por-convidar-ambulante-a-mesa. Accessed on 03 January 2020. The lawsuit, however, included the vendor as a witness only and not as the plaintiff.

[20] In Brazil, the portion of the seashore that consists of 33m from the mean high water in the year 1831 towards the continent is under dominion of the Union as its real estate and can only be used for private purposes in very specific cases (see Arts 1, 2, and 64 of *Decreto-Lei 9.760/1946*). On the other hand, beaches, which include the areas of the backshore, are assets of common use and their occupation cannot hinder the public's access, except for national security reasons or in the case of protected areas (Art 10 of Law 7,661/1988). Therefore, municipalities do not have competence to authorise use within these areas, except for interventions on the seashore as defined in Presidential Decree 5,300/2004, which regulates Law 7,661/1988. This legal framework – as it

are scarcely enforced.[21] Nonetheless, Fortaleza is nationally known for the appeal to tourists of such commercial encroachment of the beaches, with some of the restaurants being more than 50 years old.

Regarding alcoholic beverages, the prohibition was further extended and specified in 2009, when Law 9,477/2009 came in place to regulate sale of alcohol in bars, pubs, stores, clubs, near stadiums, and even during school hours and other school activities. Article 3 expressly stated:

> It is prohibited to sell alcoholic beverages in public spaces, such as public places, squares, flowerbeds, and sidewalks.

The only exception to using public spaces for this purpose was in the case of celebrations and popular events, such as carnival and new year's parties, given that the proper licence had been previously issued (Article 3, sole paragraph, of Law 9,477/2009). Nevertheless, street vending of alcoholic beverages was and is common in almost every surrounding of all kinds of public events, especially outside nightclubs and stadiums, as well as in places where people gather for leisure, such as beaches and squares. Figure 8 shows street vendors in one of the most important cultural public spaces of the city. In September 2017 this Article 3 was revoked by the Law 10,608/2017, because, as argued by the bill's author, it was clear that the volume of sales, instead of diminishing, had increased even more.[22]

And the examples of permitted and prohibited goods and services provided by the decree in discussion do not fully cover the whole range of activities that constitute street vending in Fortaleza as a pervasive and entrenched practice. Due to the ease with which vendors can distribute small goods throughout the city, one can even observe how certain consumption patterns have developed to such an extent that they might even distort the lay understanding of the illegality of some of these goods.[23] Even when it comes to those goods which are legally permitted, it is rather hard to find a vendor with proper administrative licence to sell, especially when vendors are spread throughout the city in isolated spots, which makes any kind of control virtually impracticable. Figure 9 and Figure 10 show some examples of such isolated street vendors.

seems – would technically make all the restaurants on the *Praia do Futuro* illegal for their own design and the way they demarcate their service area. For a proper discussion and detailed legal reasonings, see the case mentioned in n 21 below.

[21] For the ongoing case, which was filled in 2005 and whose aim is to remove the 154 restaurants located at the seashore, see the case 0017654-95.2005.4.05.8100, *Tribunal Regional Federal da 5ª Região* (TRF5). The structural incapacity of the judiciary to enforce its decisions in Brazil has been used as a motive underlying the advent of a bartering rationality over law enforcement (see section 8.2.1).

[22] One of the justifications pointed out by the Representative who proposed the revocation was the fact that, because many public squares were reformed in the previous years, 'many people began to use this public space as an alternative form of work, selling snacks, food and drinks, guaranteeing the sustenance of their families, generating income, reducing idleness and reducing the rate of violence' (*Projeto de Lei Ordinária 239/2017*, proposed by the Representative Adail Júnior).

[23] One of the most illustrative cases in this regard is perhaps the selling of pirate and counterfeited goods, which can be found in many commercial areas of the city. These can range from CDs and DVDs of music, films, computer software, and videogames, to fake shoes, clothes, and purses

Figure 8 Street vendors of alcoholic beverages near the Centro Dragão do Mar de Arte e Cultura, one of the most important cultural squares of Fortaleza. Photo: WhatsApp/Jornal O Povo

Figure 9 Street vendor on a sidewalk of a residential neighbourhood in Fortaleza where traffic is low, offering hammocks, tapestry, and upholstered chairs. Photo: personal archive

Figure 10 Street vending at traffic lights. When the light turns red, vendors show up to offer goods to the drivers stuck in the traffic jam. The vendor on the left sells imported gadgets (some of them clearly fake), and the other behind him, bottled water.
Photo: personal archive

3.2. STREET MARKETS

Notwithstanding the number of street vendors wandering throughout the city, who are also known as *ambulantes* (street vendors who are not fixed at one point but keep walking and offering their products or services to those passing by), the activity becomes more acute when vendors join together in a large contingent in the streets – sometimes setting up stalls, sometimes displaying the goods on the ground – to form what are known as *feiras*,[24] a name commonly used in Portuguese to describe street markets that take place in very specific places during certain days and times of the week. From this name, comes another designation for one kind of street vendor: the *feirante*, whose main place of work is the street market. They can be either *feirantes de rua*, that is, sellers who sell their goods

of famous brands. A newspaper reported a survey from 2016 in which 75% of the people from Fortaleza admitted to having bought some pirated goods; see: www20.opovo.com.br/app/opovo/cotidiano/2016/10/27/noticiasjornalcotidiano,3666148/tres-em-cada-quatro-fortalezenses-admitem-comprar-itens-piratas.shtml. Accessed on 18 May 2021.

[24] The Portuguese term *feira* is, nonetheless, polysemic. It may refer to a 'meeting of sellers and buyers in a certain place and time for the purpose of trade', a 'competitive exhibition, or for display of new products', the 'commercialization of various articles, for charitable purposes or for the sell-off of old supply'; it can also be used to refer to 'what one buys in *feiras*' (see the entry '*feira*' in the Portuguese Dictionary licensed by Oxford University Press).

literally in the streets, sometimes using stalls, carts, or even trunks of vehicles to display the products; or, if the open-air market gets big enough to support a more structured commerce, they may rent a private or public space specifically designed for that purpose, normally fronting the market. In the latter case, they may have a *banca*, which is a small, fixed place, mostly located inside a big storage shed shared with many other sellers in the surroundings of the street market; or they may become a *lojista* – a vendor who can afford to rent a store.[25] Figure 11, Figure 12, and Figure 13 illustrate the three kinds of vendors one can find in some markets. As one former street vendor who specialised in the clothing trade said, 'it is like the *feira* has three stages of evolution: the first one begins at streets; in the second one, the seller goes to a *banca*; and, in the third, he or she acquires a store'. As they become more successful, they may advance in their investments, being able to carry more products and hire other people to work for them. It also seems that the grade of informality decreases somewhat from one stage to another, although remaining at very high levels most of the time.

Figure 11 Street vendors offer T-shirts in the middle of the street at Rua Sobral, 70 metres away from the City Hall and on the left side of the Metropolitan Cathedral in the city's downtown. Photo: personal archive

[25] It seems that the difference, however, between a *banca* and a *loja* is more related to their size: while the first is a small place, similar to a box, of 1.5m long by 1m wide and 1.30m high, the second can vary between a floor area of $5m^2$ to $50m^2$. Even though the store looks like a normal shop or outlet in comparison to other stores, it definitely belongs to the open-air market system, that is to say, the products they sell, the clients they dispute, the suppliers they buy from, and the networks of relationships they are part of are basically the same. It is even common to see a *lojista* to describe themself as a *feirante*.

Figure 12 'Bancas' and 'Lojas' in the 'Mercado Central' (Downtown Market), a multi-level covered market built by the municipality, near 'Feira da Sé'. Photo: personal archive

Figure 13 Vendors in a private shed on José Avelino Street. Photo: Sousa (2016: 128)

According to Eronildo Moreira, President of the União dos Feirantes do Ceará (since 2017, Sindicato dos Trabalhadores de Feiras Livres e Particulares e Vendedores Ambulantes do Estado do Ceará (SINFECE)), an association that seeks to include all the feirantes in the State of Ceará, there are 68 street markets just in Fortaleza alone. They vary according to the products sold: some are focused on food, some on clothing and textiles in general, and others on used or illegal goods, such as stolen items, firearms, and exotic birds and wild animals that cannot be commercialised.[26] Figure 14 and Figure 15 show one of these street markets and a glimpse of its extension. The precise number of existing markets, however, is difficult to confirm because most of them do not have a stable and fixed location and do not occur on fixed schedules, except for those traditionally known in the city, some of which have existed for over a century.[27]

According to the legal framework applicable to these street markets, roughly all major street markets in Fortaleza are, to some extent, illegal, as they take place in public spaces that are forbidden to be occupied for commercial activities in such manner. The Constitution of the Municipality (*Lei Orgânica 1/2006*), for instance, makes it clear in Article 107, § 1:

> The following are prohibited: the donation, exchange, sale, lease or concession of use of any fraction of areas of public parks, squares, gardens or lakes, admitting only the permission to use small spaces for the sale of newspapers, magazines, handicrafts or snacks, in conditions to be established by an act of the Mayor.

Furthermore, Article 672, VII of the COPM prohibits 'embarrassing or impeding by any means the free transit of pedestrians or vehicles in public places'. Even if one considers that street markets could be, legally speaking, authorised by the municipality (Article 708 of the COPM), the market in any case shall not 'impair the transit, traffic, circulation and safety of pedestrians' (Article 709 of the COPM). Compliance with those legal commands would demand, in practical terms, almost every traditional street market in Fortaleza to cease its activities, because they occur mainly in streets, avenues, and sidewalks in such a way that vehicles are unable to pass through, and pedestrians must walk as if they were crossing a labyrinth. *Feira da Sé* – or if one wants to emphasise its

[26] Commonly, local newspapers try to cover this kind of commerce. A known street market in Fortaleza specialising, among used products, in illegal goods is the *Feira da Parangaba*. For reports on the apprehension of rare birds offered for sale in 2010, see: http://diariodonordeste.verdesmares.com.br/editorias/metro/passaros-raros-apreendidos-em-feira-1.472237. Accessed on 08 January 2020. Another report shows a video of the selling of a pistol, which is per se a crime (Arts 14, 16, and 17 of Law 10,826/2003), during daylight in this same market in 2017; see: g1.globo.com/ceara/noticia/homem-e-flagrado-oferecendo-arma-de-fogo-na-feira-da-parangaba-em-fortaleza-veja-video.ghtml. Accessed on 8 November 2018.

[27] This is the case, for instance, of the previously mentioned *Feira da Parangaba* (see n 26 above), whose origins date back to the nineteenth century and may have started as an alternative market for cattle for breeders who wanted to sell their animals in Fortaleza but did not want to pay the money for the necessary public licences (Lopes 2006: 63). At the time, Parangaba was not integrated into the city of Fortaleza, but was just a small town in its surroundings. Nowadays, it is one of Fortaleza's neighbourhoods.

Figure 14 Street market in the neighbourhood 'Granja Portugal' in Fortaleza, where most of the products are fruits and vegetables. The stalls start at the beginning of the street and go beyond the visible horizon. Photo: personal archive

Figure 15 Inside the market of 'Granja Portugal', Eronildo Moreira is active in his electoral campaign to be a federal deputy for the State of Ceará. The 'feirante' in the left side offers mangos, avocados, and apples. Photo: personal archive

continuity, *Feira da José Avelino* – the biggest street market in Fortaleza, is a good example of noncompliance with this set of rules. Located at the city centre and having its core at the crossroad of José Avelino Street and Alberto Nepomuceno Avenue, the market is famous in the whole region for its clothing trade. With a many-sided shape, it is made up of a dynamic interplay of formal and informal commerce that includes a mix of vendors located in large storage sheds, whose interior is populated by *bancas* and *lojas*, as well as in the streets, sidewalks, and public squares on the perimeter. The street market is particularly dense at *Praça da Sé*, one of the first public spaces in the city and where the Metropolitan Cathedral is situated, and in José Avelino Street. It is precisely from the square, *Praça da Sé*, and the street, José Avelino, that the market draws its name. During the days in which the market takes place, a crowd is formed, populating its core areas and moving across streets.[28] Curiously, just behind the Cathedral lies the City Hall, a configuration that casts a doubt on whether its informality could be characterised, in fact, as clandestine. Figure 11, Figure 16, and Figure 17 show some vendors constituting part of *Feira da Sé* and its surroundings. Figure 18 presents a map of the market elaborated by Sousa (2016: 127).

Figure 16 Street vending of clothing (on the left) and sugar-cane juice, water, and soda (on the right) near the Metropolitan Cathedral in Fortaleza. In the background, behind the Cathedral, lies the City Hall. Photo: personal archive

[28] A similar observation can be found in Sousa (2016: 129): 'Regarding the dynamics of the market on José Avelino Street it was observed that on the days of the activity the road has its use as passage to vehicles and passers-by replaced almost exclusively by commerce.' For more historical information about the different commercial occupations of the square and its continuity through José de Avelino Street, useful maps, and some pictures of this and other markets, see her master thesis (Sousa 2015).

Figure 17 Around the Cathedral, vendors set up tables on sidewalks, streets, and squares, forming the 'Feira da Sé'. Photo: Diário do Nordeste

Figure 18 Map of the 'José Avelino' market. The highlighted lighter grey space demarcates the 'Centro' neighbourhood (downtown), and the darker grey within, the market itself according to the City Hall

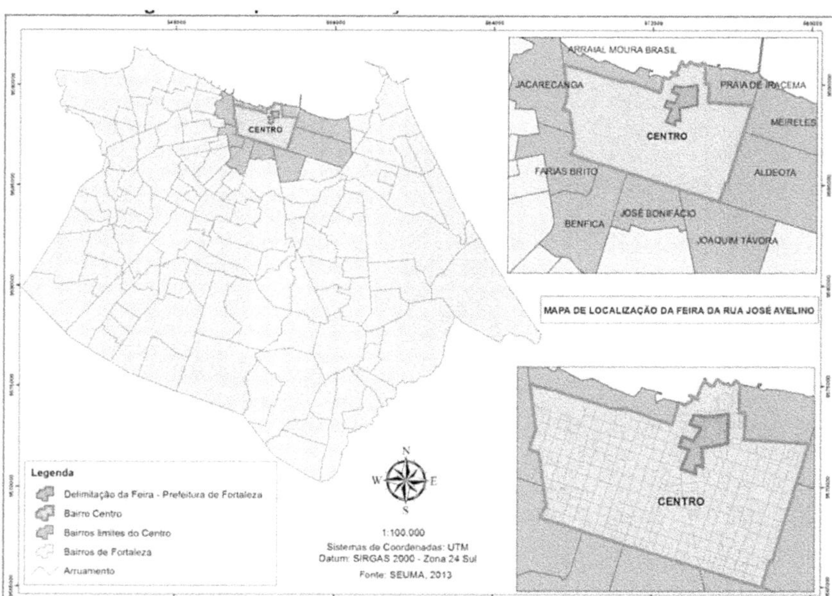

Source: Sousa (2016: 127)

Like every street market that emerges spontaneously, it is hard to define exactly how old *Feira da Sé* is.[29] Street vending in what today is the city's downtown is, it seems, as old as the city's urbanisation process.[30] On the other hand, it is true, as argues Dantas (2014: 150–51), that the activity underwent quantitative and qualitative changes throughout the history of the city, 'with the increase in the number of people involved in this activity and in the area occupied by it in downtown Fortaleza' and with some sort of state-driven force toward its fixation, which gave it an ambiguous mobility, 'by being able to fix itself, though mobile, and, though fixed, to move around downtown'.[31] This might explain how street vendors were able to move around in order to escape authorities and still occupy the same area for a long time. In this sense, there is a sort of reciprocal caution between the parts involved. On the vendors' side, they try to organise themselves in order to avoid inspections and major chaos taking place during the market. For this reason the most intense movement starts around midnight during certain days of the week and on the weekend, which generally has lower vehicle traffic – since this schedule is public knowledge, those who do not want to go to the market will avoid passing nearby.[32] On the public authorities' side, in order to avoid riots and uprisings, strong-armed attempts at enforcing the law are carried

[29] Sousa (2016: 127) suggests that the José Avelino market begun in the early 1990s, but no further evidence for that is provided. She contradicts herself later on, by stating that, at the end of the 1990s, vendors started to gather on the street (Sousa 2016: 132–33). Furthermore, it is not possible to understand the dynamic of the street market in this region properly without paying careful attention to the series of court decisions that started in 2007 against the municipality to remove the vendors from *Praça da Sé*. As I will explain (see section 3.3), attempts at removal by the public authorities played a major role in the growing occupation of José Avelino.

[30] One can find various references to the activity in different sources, such as in the chronicles of Nogueira from 1848 (*apud* Dantas (2014: 149)) and the famous novel *A Normalista* written by Adolfo Caminha, only published in 1893 [see, especially, Caminha (1893: 71)]. The history of the *Praça da Sé* and its almost intrinsic commerce are, time and again, the subject of newspaper reports; see, for instance: https://diariodonordeste.verdesmares.com.br/editorias/metro/por-que-a-feira-da-rua-jose-avelino-resiste-ao-passar-dos-anos-1.2175600. Accessed on 13 December 2022.

[31] For a more detailed study on these changes and the respective roles of the local administration in controlling the public space and street commerce, especially from 1975 to 1995, see Dantas (2014). For an account of local newspaper reports from the 1930s, 1940s, and 1950s on the impacts of the activity in the city's life, see Aragão (2012: 63–76).

[32] An account of the history of the open-air street markets in Fortaleza would give us a more precise idea about their timing dynamic and the causes of its adjustments. In regard to *Feira da Sé* there are some sources available that indicate its schedule. In a court hearing in 2007, an alleged organiser stated that the market used to take place from 4am to 8am, but since May 2007, due to its growth over the previous five years, they decided to start at midnight (see p 45 of case 0063506.61-2007.8.06.0001). In 2008, it was agreed that the market, as a form of transition before the removal of the vendors, would take place from midnight to 7am (see pp 117–122 of the same case; I will discuss later the details that led to this agreement; see section 3.3, more specifically after n 39). In 2015, an official letter sent by the municipal authority responsible for the street vending in the city's downtown confirmed that, since 2013, the market in José Avelino was allowed to happen on Wednesday 7pm until Thursday 7 am and on Saturday 7pm until Sunday 11am (see p 19 of case 0022413-06.2016.8.06.0001). The removal, nonetheless, was never fully accomplished, and the midnight market is still happening; see, eg, a newspaper report on the intensity of vendors on the Black Friday in November 2019: https://g1.globo.com/ce/ceara/noticia/2019/11/29/vendedor-ambulante-madruga-no-centro-de-fortaleza-vender-roupa-durante-a-black-friday.ghtml. Accessed on 15 January 2020.

out only in extreme cases, for instance, when sellers are warned many times to leave but still ignore the requests. One cannot deny that law enforcement, due to the extension of street markets, the number of street vendors involved, and the mobility that characterises their activity, is heavily compromised in many dimensions. In daily operations, state control is most of the time reduced to a friendly oral admonition, for the officers always have to ponder the possibility of a physical conflict. The oral admonition itself seems to be more of an informal attempt by inspectors to inform vendors that they should avoid violating the norms. It has no legal grounds since the sanctions expressly provided by the COPM are fines, embargos, seizures and loss of goods and merchandise, interdiction, suspension, licence cassation, and dismantling, demolition, or removal (Article 737). Depending on the lenience of the mayor towards the vendors, however, the approach of the inspectors may vary.[33] Figure 19 shows one of the most important newspapers of the state questioning candidates for mayor about their plans regarding the informal commerce in downtown.[34]

Figure 19 The thoughts of the main mayoral candidates and their voters about the removal of street vendors in downtown

Eleições e o comércio informal

O que propõem os candidatos e o que querem seus eleitores a respeito do comércio informal no Centro de Fortaleza

Roberto Cláudio PDT

Pretende estimular a formação de pequenos empreendedores por meio da consolidação e ampliação do programa Empreendedorismo Sustentável

A opinião dos eleitores dele sobre desocupação do comércio informal

A favor 49% | Contra 43%

Capitão Wagner PR

Propõe requalificação cultural, urbanística e econômica do Centro por meio de políticas de mobilidade urbana, segurança, limpeza e regulamentação das atividades comerciais. Ainda, quer reorganizar a feira da Sé/José Avelino para que as atividades dos comerciantes não prejudiquem comércios próximos e a circulação de veículos

A opinião dos eleitores dele sobre desocupação do comércio informal

A favor 37% | Contra 58%

Luizianne Lins PT

Afirma que vai remodelar o Centro da Cidade. Estuda redefinir o trânsito de pedestres e veículos, regular estacionamentos, criar banheiros públicos, padronizar calçadas e cadastrar, fiscalizar e disciplinar o trabalho dos ambulantes

A opinião dos eleitores dela sobre desocupação do comércio informal

A favor 52% | Contra 42%

Heitor Férrer PSB

Sugere que a Prefeitura adquira ou construa um espaço para abrigar o comércio ambulante, que deve ser retirado das calçadas para que os pedestres possam transitar livremente

A opinião dos eleitores dele sobre desocupação do comércio informal

A favor 49% | Contra 40%

Observação: neste item, a pesquisa leva em consideração somente os candidatos com mais intenções de voto em Fortaleza

Source: O Povo, 10 September 2016, p 2

[33] In 2016, for example, it was publicly said that a more 'educative approach' was preferred rather than seizure and loss. See the newspaper report from 2016 in n 36.

[34] All the results of the survey and the respective report can be accessed online at www20.opovo.com.br/app/opovo/cotidiano/2016/09/16/noticiasjornalcotidiano,3659131/retirada-de-vendedores-ambulantes-e-controversa.shtml. Accessed on 11 September 2020.

The tension is always present and, when the vendors feel there is a risk they will lose their goods, they try to pack everything up and leave, and authorities, most of the time, avoid chasing every vendor. Sometimes, however, special task forces of public inspectors and policemen, equipped with trucks and vans, are organised to do so. In a daily language, they are called '*o rapa*' by the vendors, a colloquial expression used to refer to the task force which does not come to warn or to offer friendly instruction about illegality, but rather to seize goods and merchandise. Even in these state-driven operations, noncompliance with the law is a common feature, for the seized goods are, with some frequency, not properly accounted, itemised, and categorised, which makes it practically impossible to recover them after the payment of the due fine. Not out of coincidence, this was, according to Eronildo Moreira, one of the biggest problems faced by vendors besides the lack of structure of the markets and the uncertainty of the activity. Figure 20 presents a formal answer from the municipality, denying that the goods were even seized. Cases of harassment, intimidation, abuse of authority, corruption, and embezzlement of the seized goods are also reported with some frequency by vendors.[35]

Figure 20 An answer given by the municipality to an administrative request to recover seized goods. Besides the lack of the signature and identification of the competent authority, the request was denied in one line: 'Denied! There was no such seizure.'

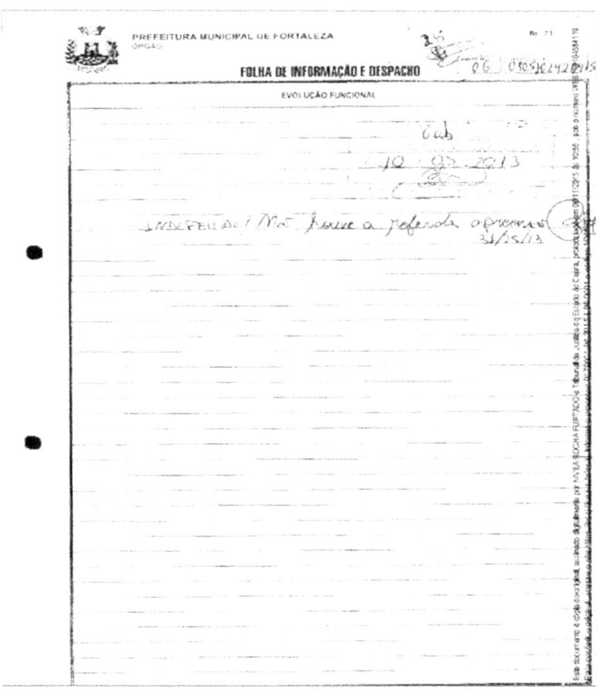
PREFEITURA MUNICIPAL DE FORTALEZA

FOLHA DE INFORMAÇÃO E DESPACHO

EVOLUÇÃO FUNCIONAL

Source: case 0179601-96.2015.8.06.0001 (p 71); see n 35

[35] See Arts 34 to 36 of Decree 9,300/1994 and Arts 753 to 758 of the COPM for the proper procedure of seizure and recovery of goods. On 6 December 2019, the municipality of Fortaleza was

3.3. THE CASE STUDY: *FEIRA DA SÉ*

The resilience of the market has set the stage for different conflicts between vendors and public authorities[36] as well as judicial disputes over the roles played by all those involved in using and regulating the public space. One can even observe the emergence of a lawfare initiated by the *Ministério Público do Estado do Ceará* (MPCE), in order to force the municipality to remove street vendors from public squares. In this sense, instead of a unity, the state presents itself as a highly fragmented constellation of different political interests and competing agendas of legality. Perhaps the most illustrative case in this regard is the Public Civil Action filed in 2007 by the MPCE against the municipality of Fortaleza (case 0063506.61-2007.8.06.0001), from which many others are derived.[37] The plea was to force the mayor to remove the unlicensed street vendors from Pedro II Square, where part of *Feira da Sé* takes place. On 1 April 2008, a first-instance judge ordered, in a preliminary ruling (see pp 92–97 of the case), that the municipality remove the unlicensed vendors under the

sentenced to pay moral and property damages to a street vendor who had her stall and goods seized in a midnight operation in *Praça Castro Carreira*, commonly known as *Praça da Estação*, another public square in the city's downtown, less than 1km away from *Praça da Sé*, even though she had the proper permit; see case 0179601-96.2015.8.06.0001. Figure 20 shows the administrative denial of the seizure, which took place on 26 April 2013 during the midnight removal operation. The seizure was widely publicised at the time, and many vendors witnessed it. See, for instance, a newspaper report about the incident: g1.globo.com/ceara/noticia/2013/04/prefeitura-retira-ambulantes-da-praca-da-estacao-em-fortaleza.html. Accessed on 16 January 2020. A major lawsuit was filed in 2017, aiming at recovering all the goods and merchandise seized from vendors since 2007, when the case *Feira da Sé* started (case 0183455-30.2017.8.06.0001; see also n 37). The case brings a lot of evidence of precarious seizure notices and harassment. For video footage of one of these operations in 2016, which includes harassment practised by the municipal authorities, see the following newspaper report: g1.globo.com/ceara/noticia/2016/07/secretaria-abre-inquerito-de-caso-de-apreensao-de-mercadorias-no-centro.html. Accessed on 16 January 2020. In the same context, SINFECE along with some state representatives requested the MPCE to start a criminal investigation against the public officers who participated in those removal operations for abuse of power, unnecessary damages, and even bribes (see case 0022413-06.2016.8.06.0001). The police chief in charge of the investigation, however, concluded in a very brief report without any account of the accusations that the only problem was that 'there is too much delay in the return' (p 129 of the case), referring to the goods seized. The MPCE decided, then, to dismiss the request due to the lack of 'apparent solution' and the existence of doubts (p 1). The decision was followed without further consideration by the judge (p 133).

[36] See, for instance, the media coverage of such conflicts over the last years: 2013, diariodonordeste.verdesmares.com.br/editorias/metro/ambulantes-nao-obedecem-fiscais-e-ficam-no-centro-1.125682; 2014, www.opovo.com.br/noticias/fortaleza/2014/08/feirantes-da-se-e-guarda-municipal-entram-em-conflito-neste-domingo.html; 2015, https://diariodonordeste.verdesmares.com.br/editorias/metro/online/feira-jose-avelino-tem-novo-confronto-entre-vendedores-e-policiais-1.1255226 and g1.globo.com/ceara/noticia/2015/02/feira-da-jose-avelino-ocorre-sem-transtornos-nesta-quinta-em-fortaleza.html; 2016, https://diariodonordeste.verdesmares.com.br/editorias/metro/ocupacao-irregular-gera-confronto-em-feira-no-centro-1.1678521; 2017, www.opovo.com.br/noticias/fortaleza/2017/05/feirantes-e-guardas-municipais-entram-em-confronto-na-jose-avelino.html; 2018, g1.globo.com/ce/ceara/noticia/2018/11/25/feirantes-e-fiscais-da-prefeitura-de-fortaleza-entram-em-conflito-na-rua-jose-avelino.ghtml. Accessed on 10 April 2019.

[37] In 2017, two other associations filed writs before the Tribunal de Justiça do Estado do Ceará (TJCE; Court of Appeals of the State of Ceará) in order to suspend the removal operation announced by the mayor to be carried out on 14 May 2017, Mother's Day (case 0000546-23.2017.8.06.0000, *SINFECE v Fortaleza*, and 0000537-61.2017.8.06.0000, *AFAECE v Fortaleza*). Also in 2017, as

penalty of R$ 5,000.00 for each day of noncompliance.[38] Among other justifications, the judge stated that the market impaired the transit of pedestrians and cars and that the municipality was in clear situation of noncompliance with the Constitution of the Municipality and the COPM (see p 95 of the case). However, due to the number of people involved, compliance to this standard would demand, in practical terms, a substantial detour of the government programme for which the mayor was voted. According to one piece of evidence used by MPCE to support the lawsuit, a report from 2007 carried out by the *Secretaria Executiva Regional II*, which is the municipal office responsible for issuing the permits in the area of the city's downtown, there were approximately 2,000 vendors without permission just in the *Praça Pedro II*, whilst merely five had the proper permit to work there (see pp 48 and 49 of the case). As this number was just an approximation, due to the fluidity of the activity, and as the market was not restricted to that square but was rather a flow of commercial activities spread through the surrounding streets, sidewalks, and other squares, it is hard to assess the economic and political costs involved in such an endeavour, let alone the human resources needed to equip a proper task force. On 23 June 2008, for instance, the judge, by the request of the MPCE, asked the Military Police of the State of Ceará to provide additional policemen to assist the public inspectors with the removal (see p 111 of the case), since the last contingent provided, made up of four men, was not enough to enforce it. It is in this context that the removal operations were never, in fact, completely successful. Some of them, it could even be said, were just for the record.[39]

The steady failures to enforce the decision resulted in different strategies and compromises. On 2 July 2008, the MPCE, the municipality along with some of its concerned authorities, and a committee representing the vendors came to a *Termo de Compromisso de Ajustamento de Conduta* (TAC; Terms of Conduct Adjustment Commitment),[40] which is a type of legal agreement in

mentioned earlier (see n 35), SINFECE filed a major lawsuit to recover all the goods seized and damages caused by the municipality since 2007, obtaining a partial provisional decision; the case, however, is under trial by the TJCE (case 0183455-30.2017.8.06.0001). Another Public Civil Action was filed by the MPCE in 2009 against the municipality to remove the vendors from *Praça Capistrano de Abreu*, or as it is commonly known, *Praça da Lagoinha* (case 0025421-35.2009.8.06.0001); and also another in 2012, aiming at the removal of vendors from *Praça da Estação*, which resulted in midnight operations to seize the stalls and goods of vendors working on the square, regardless of whether they had the proper permit (see case 0144481-94.2012.8.06.0001 and n 35).

[38] On 13 May 2008, an association of about 820 street vendors who worked mainly after midnight tried to extend the deadline of the provisional ruling that ordered the municipality to remove the vendors (case 0139959-63.2008.8.06.0001), but the plea was never heard. The procedural movements have gaps of years between them, and the case has not yet been closed.

[39] There are many requests from the MPCE to the judge, requesting that the judge ask the military police to help the municipality. See pp 108–109, 135–137, 155–157, and 349–350 of the case. This is somewhat curious, since these requests could be made by the mayor himself, and the assistance could be provided *ex officio* by the military police, if they were willing to put forward the removal operations. In the lawsuit, it is only in 2012 that the municipality asks for such assistance (pp 343–345).

[40] This form of legal agreement was created by Art 113 of Law 8,078/1990 (which creates the Consumer Defence Code and provides for other issues), which included Art 5, § 6 in Law 7,347/1985 (Public Civil Action Act): 'The competent public bodies may commit the interested parties to adjust

which the parties recognise that they have committed illegalities but will henceforth covenant to legalise the situation, *in casu*, to facilitate the vacancy of the public squares and their surroundings. Among the terms agreed was that the market should take place only from midnight to 7am during the transition period, and the municipality would provide another space with proper structure for the vendors (see pp 117–122 of the case). Despite the plans of action developed (pp 124–133 and 171), the agreement, somehow, served as a token for all parties to claim the legality of their role in using and controlling the public space in *Feira da Sé*, which started to grow exponentially towards José Avelino Street. As could then be expected, the deadline, 2 November 2008, was not met. The municipality reported that, on the last day of the transition time, there were more than 1,000 vendors gathered to resist any attempt of removal, which hampered the task force to enforce the judge's order to remove every vendor from *Feira da Sé* (p 148). It was not long until the MPCE, on 29 December 2008, asked the judge to resume the first provisional ruling, arguing that the vendors were recalcitrant, the municipality delivered poor planning, and not enough police officers had been provided to help with the compliance (p 156). On 12 January 2009, the plea was accepted, and a new order of removal was issued (pp 178–179).[41] However, shortly afterwards, on 3 February 2009, an addendum to the above-mentioned agreement was made between the MPCE and the municipality, without the street vendors. This time, instead of removing the vendors from *Praça da Sé* to José Avelino Street, the new plan was to remove the vendors to a new neighbourhood, *Conjunto Prefeito José Walter*, where a public market would be constructed and fully equipped for the vendors, and a new deadline for that was agreed, 120 days after the signature (pp 182–185).

The new plan was promising. The displacement of vendors to new areas did take place. Some even went voluntarily to the neighbouring city of Maracanaú. Others rented a space inside the private sheds built on the José Avelino Street. By the end of the deadline, the municipality, arguing that its duty was fulfilled, asked the judge to close the case (see p 199 of the case). However, in the following months, as someone acquainted with the dynamics of informality and especially street vending might suspect, new vendors appeared to occupy the *Praça da Sé*

their conduct to the legal requirements, by means of sanctions, which shall be effective as an extrajudicial enforcement instrument'. Even though its use is quite common in Brazil, it seems to me, as I will show later (see section 8.2), to be an odd feature, since it allows the will of committing parties to prevail, under certain circumstances, over hierarchically higher norms, such as statutes, laws, decrees, and, to a certain extent, the Constitution itself.

[41] Curiously, the order was issued by another judge who was, at the time, responsible for the court (*7a Vara da Fazenda Pública*). This normally happens when the main judge is on leave. The decision's reasoning brought without previous or further discussion a new argument to the case: 'the attitude of the Municipality of Fortaleza stimulates the continuity of environmental damage caused by improper occupation of public space'. (p 179) The decision did not clarify, however, what the environmental damage is and the evidence used to support the conclusion that there is ongoing environmental damage. The issue was the violation of municipal and not environmental legislation.

and many others returned, enlarging the market even more, which was already growing towards the nearby street, José Avelino. To increase the complexity of the situation, another player came into the game: the House of Representatives of the City passed a law (Law 9,559/2009) by the end of the year, authorising the creation of a business area for individual entrepreneurs in the city's downtown, covering, among other surrounding streets, the perimeter where *Feira da Sé* was located. The idea was to facilitate the use of buildings and storage sheds to gather vendors inside, granting, for instance, collective operating licences and dismissing the need for individual licences (Article 4, § 2). It is true that the law did not contemplate street vending – actually, it forbid commercial activities outside the proper buildings (Article 4) – but, in the context, which was 'to support the street vendors removed due to a judicial decision from Pedro II Square and surroundings' (*Projeto de Lei Ordinária 414/2009*, proposed by the Representative José do Carmo, bill justification), it served as a new stimulus for vendors, since it boosted the economic attractiveness of the area for the commerce of clothing (Article 3, I) – assets for which *Feira da Sé* was already widely known.

From 2009 to 2011, the case remained dormant; however, the market grew steadily over the years. It expanded not only towards José Avelino, but also throughout the whole extent of Alberto Nepomuceno Avenue and the surrounding streets, such as Conde D'Eu, Governador Sampaio, and Travessa Icó. This led the MPCE, on 27 June 2011, to request the enforcement of the previously agreed TAC, accusing the municipality of being idle in preventing the situation (see pp 202–205 of the case). A photographic study of the occupation and the new configuration of *Feira da Sé*, which by now was already being known as *Feira da José Avelino* too, supported the request (pp 221–244). On 15 September 2011, the request was reinforced because the occupation, according to the MPCE, had worsened (pp 266–288).[42] Even the Metropolitan Cathedral, located at *Praça da Sé*, announced at the time that it would stop its activities due to the uncontrolled occupation of the square and its surroundings by street vendors.[43] Recognising that 'this problem was becoming chronic due to the lack of ability of the Municipality of Fortaleza in fulfilling its legal duties', the judge issued, without hearing the municipality, a new provisional ruling on 9 November 2011, demanding once more the removal of the vendors from *Feira da Sé*, but this time within

[42] By August 2011, the market was already reported as the biggest open-air market in the state and one of the biggest of the Northeast Region. The peak was after midnight from Sunday to Monday and from Wednesday to Thursday. The competition for space was so high that some vendors arrived on Saturday night to keep their place until Sunday midnight. See: diariodonordeste.verdesmares.com.br/editorias/negocios/madrugada-na-jose-avelino-tem-maior-comercio-ao-ar-livre-1.696937. Accessed on 23 January 2020. Some newspapers even reported the market as 'urban chaos'; see: diariodonordeste.verdesmares.com.br/editorias/metro/estudo-avalia-ambulantes-da-jose-avelino-1.719234. Accessed on 23 January 2020.

[43] See: blogs.opovo.com.br/ancoradouro/2011/11/06/catedral-de-fortaleza-fechara-as-portas. Accessed on 21 January 2020. There were even complaints about the undergarments for sale being exposed in the parking grid of the cathedral.

only five days and increasing the fine to R$ 10,000.00 per day of noncompliance (pp 289–290). Notified to enforce the order, the municipality, however, argued that, due to the very nature of the problem, permanent efforts were necessary to remove the vendors and, if a definitive solution was to be given, the military police should help with the task, which otherwise could not be fully completed (pp 297–301). On 20 June 2012, the judge, due to the persisting noncompliance, instead of enforcing the previous decision, decided to follow a suggestion of the MPCE to have a court hearing with the municipality along with its concerned administrative authorities, the representatives of the association of vendors of the *Mercado Central* (Downtown Market; see Figure 12), and the military police in order to discuss the problem once again and develop a new plan to remove the vendors (p 328). The hearing took place on 27 June 2012, and it was agreed that all the parties present would develop a common plan to be enforced by 8 July 2012 (pp 339–340). Near the deadline, on 5 July 2012, the municipality informed the judge (pp 343–345) that the operation would not be carried out, because the military police had sent an official letter, stating that a study of the case should first be made due to its yet unknown impacts on that part of society and afterwards submitted to the Governor of the State (p 348). It seems that, from this point on, the municipality could somehow share its noncompliant behaviour with the military police – an institution, legally speaking, under the state's government and not the municipality – in order to share responsibilities for controlling the public space in the area. It is also difficult to assess whether the recalcitrance of the military police was indeed due to the complexity of the operation or just an attempt to postpone it indefinitely, since in terms of priority removing vendors from public areas would lie far behind preventing other more harmful crimes.[44] In any case, on 13 July 2012, the MPCE requested that the judge ask the military police to speed up the study (pp 349–350). This was done by the judge on 2 August 2012 (p 358), and the study was finally delivered by the military police on 7 August 2012 (see the study at pp 369–372). The operation lasted a couple of weeks and once it had been carried out, the intensive control over the area was loosened. The supposedly definitive solution to be carried out with the assistance of the military police turned out to be a token to show that the municipality was employing efforts to solve the problem. If it is already hard for skilled researchers to understand the causes of informality and street vending, it is even harder to imagine how security forces and administrative personnel would propose an end to such a complex state of affairs. Already by the end of

[44] Fortaleza, for the past decade, has been one of the most violent cities in the whole world. According to the World Atlas, in 2019 Fortaleza had the seventh highest homicide rate per 100,000 habitants (Dillinger 2019). From 2013 to 2017, the city had been in the top 12 in the ranking of the 50 most violent cities produced by the ONG *Seguridad, Justicia y Paz*, except 2016, when it was in the 35th position. But naturally these processes of increasing violence date back years. For a newspaper report on how Fortaleza became the most violent metropolitan region in Brazil, including interviews with some experts, see: g1.globo.com/ce/ceara/noticia/2019/03/07/como-fortaleza-se-tornou-a-regiao-metropolitana-mais-violenta-do-brasil.ghtml. Accessed on 22 January 2020.

that year, one could see street vendors everywhere.[45] On 20 November 2012, the MPCE required again that the order of removal should be enforced by the municipality (pp 378–379). And this was the last meaningful movement of the lawsuit,[46] which remained frozen until 5 January 2015, when the MPCE informed the court that it had developed, along with the municipality, a new plan of action to remove the vendors (pp 385–393). It then stalled again until 7 April 2017, when the SINFECE, represented by its President, Eronildo Moreira (see Figure 15), made a request to participate in the lawsuit (pp 394–408). On 7 March 2018, the MPCE, once more, required that the lawsuit move forward in the hope of triggering new operations, but one could say that the last important procedural movement, technically speaking, was the above-mentioned request by MPCE on 20 November 2012, which was never heard. On 4 May 2020, the judge decided to dismiss the case because the plaintiff did not bring 'any information regarding the plan of action prepared jointly with the municipality' and did not report that there had been 'noncompliance with the Terms of Conduct Adjustment Commitment' (p 720). Since this information was already in the case file and evidence of noncompliance was notorious – the street market was still as vibrant as ever – it seems that the reasoning was just a pretext, as if the judge himself had 'given up' on the case.

In summary, the situation, despite successive court orders to remove the vendors and consecutive removal attempts, has not yet come to a solution. On the contrary, it caused different forms of backlashes, such as the intensification of conflicts, creation of vendors' associations, and organisation of mass protests.[47] In contact with one public inspector in April 2019, I was informed that, in the city centre, where *Feira da Sé* and others take place, there were just 157 street vendors formally registered and about 4,000 unregistered.[48] This shows how not

[45] See, for instance, the newspaper reports: diariodonordeste.verdesmares.com.br/editorias/metro/ambulantes-voltam-a-lotar-ruas-e-calcadas-1.688960. Accessed on 21 January 2020.

[46] In 2014, the MPCE also attempted to force the municipality to pay a fine of R$ 3,510,000.00 for not complying with the terms of their common agreement (case 0902324-05.2014.8.06.0001 and 0142354-81.2015.8.06.0001), but so far the judge has not provided a ruling on this issue.

[47] The intensification of conflicts and the protests are vivid memories for Eronildo Moreira, who came to the fore as a political leader among the vendors at the time. According to him, physical conflicts and contends between vendors and inspectors/policemen started to happen on a daily basis in this period. As President of the SINFECE, an association of street vendors created in 2009 (renamed in 2017), he took part in many negotiations between the street vendors, the municipality, and the MPCE and knows by heart the timeline of the events triggered since the main case started. But even before 2009, more specifically in 2007, another association was created to organise the vendors that were in particular working after midnight: the *Associação das Alianças dos Multi-Empreendedores* (Association of Aliances of Multientrepreneurs, formerly named *Associação dos Empreendedores da Sé* (Association of Entrepreneurs of Sé)), which originally had about 820 members. For the cases in which those associations were actively representing the affected vendors, see n 37. For the conflicts, see the newspaper reports on n 36.

[48] The number of registered vendors, however, does not correspond to the number of licensed vendors. The vendor must first register in order to acquire the licence (see Art 715 of the COPM). As the number of licences available per area is far less than the number of registrations, a waiting list is normally created. For the intensification of the density of vendors in 2019 during Black Friday, see n 32.

only regulations[49] and law enforcement operations[50] but even court decisions, in fact, are prone to noncompliance, regardless of whether they are aimed at private persons or state authorities. If one bears in mind that the situation of noncompliance is acute in the most conspicuous case, that is, the city's downtown, then it is easy to imagine how pervasive it becomes in less known areas where there is less state control.[51]

Even though legal norms are constantly violated, the number of cases brought to justice is paradoxically scarce. Despite the fact that there is no systematised data on this, a rough picture can be gained by searching the database of the TJCE, the court of appeals of the state.[52] When the words *ambulante* or *feirante* or *camelô* or *vendedor(a) de rua* are searched (these are various Portuguese terms for street vendor), the results are: at the first instance of jurisdiction, 754 decisions; at the second instance, 139 collegiate decisions and 14 monocratic decisions.[53] But, as the vast majority of the cases are related to penal law, the condition of being a street vendor is mainly secondary and is not related directly to the activity itself. In the second instance, for which the jurisdiction belongs to the state court of appeals, only eight cases are directly concerned with the activity of street vending, such as the discussion about the lack of permits or the collective occupation of public spaces.

Such diagnosis of a general noncompliance with the law, of course, does not exclude the many different strategies that governmental entities take to control the activity, at least within the range of resources available to do so. Sometimes, administrative agencies attempt to mount large-scale operations for inspection and control. At other times, the legislation itself is changed in order to have some social resonance. But, in the majority of cases, noncompliance is

[49] If one goes further into other concerned ordinances, more breaches can be found. This is the case, for instance, of Decree 13,035/2012, which classified the pavement of the José Avelino Street as historical heritage due to its 'ineluctable reference to the identity and history of the Fortaleza society'.

[50] I had access to one internal document of the municipal agency responsible for inspecting the street markets in the city's downtown. The document consisted in a plan for a strategic inspection of the street vending and commercial facilities near the Metropolitan Cathedral and the José de Avelino Street. At many points the authors refer to the failures of different attempts in the last decades to control the expansion and the compliance with legal rules within the area of the market, to oral admonitions that are not respected, to risks and dangers that public officers face when they attempt to enforce the administrative regulations, to actual conflicts that had taken place, and even to the local and national media coverage given when such conflicts happen.

[51] In the interview with Eronildo Moreira (see Figure 15), he told me that in *Feira do Genibaú*, for instance, there were more than 3,000 vendors, but only 96 were registered. As this market takes place in a neighbourhood distant from the city's downtown, conflicts and media coverage are much rarer.

[52] In Brazil, the common justice, which embraces every branch of law except those ones for which the Federal Constitution prescribes a special justice (namely, labour law, electoral law, and military law), is divided into federal justice and state-level justice. As we are dealing here with non-federal matters, the state-level justice is, in the majority of cases, the one with the respective jurisdiction (for an exception, see n 21). A database of court decisions at this level can be accessed here: http://esaj.tjce.jus.br.

[53] Data collected on 16 January 2020.

so pervasive that such initiatives are hardly capable of overcoming it. On the contrary, they often trigger conflicts and stimulate new forms of noncompliance, which may become instead socially dynamised due to organisations and associations created as a backlash against state-driven enforcement attempts. This diagnosis may easily lead one to ask whether there is law at all in this context or – to pose the doubt in other terms – whether the rule of law has any meaning in guiding expectations and steering the behaviours of those concerned. The question becomes even trickier when one observes how legal norms, despite high grades of noncompliance, are used by judges and public authorities in decisions and administrative acts as well as by vendors to claim rights to certain behaviours and activities. Indeed, this sets up a complex scenario in which legal texts, instead of directly regulating and steering behaviour, are frequently used as tokens for purposes other than compliance with the law.

All in all, what remains clear is that noncompliance, far from being an intuitive concept used by scholars to characterise informality as mere violation of a set of rules, such as standards of working conditions, is rather a complex phenomenon in itself, which takes place at different levels and involves a variety of actors, interactions, and organisations. Furthermore, it drastically impacts the performances that a legal system is expected to have in arenas characterised by such high grades of noncompliant behaviours. In order to go deeper into this phenomenon, the following chapters will carefully examine all the levels of noncompliance with the law.

Part II

The Nature of Noncompliance

INFORMALITY HAS TWO clear characteristics: it is large in scale and marked by high grades of noncompliance with the law. Some definitions try to delimitate a boundary between what is informal and what is illegal, but rarely achieve this in a convincing manner. Others equate both, which brings essentially different activities together under a general umbrella. Scholars and international agendas, in order to assess its magnitude and economic impacts, seem to be satisfied with an intuitive concept of noncompliance as violation of a rule or set of rules, despite the variety of different conceptual approaches and measurement methodologies. As I argued in part I of this book, there are many other circumstances to consider in determining the standards from which noncompliance can be assessed. For rules are not restricted – as a layman intuitively may assume – to simple interpretations of enacted laws; they entail a far more complex web of organisations, networks, interactions, and social roles that come into play when defining what are the valid rules as well as framing the conditions to enforce them. With the framework of street vending, I tried to demonstrate with various examples how this web plays a role in the creation of multiple levels of noncompliance; that is to say, the phenomenon is not restricted to street vendors, but also encompasses public authorities, judges, inspectors, policemen, politicians, government agencies, associations, and customary practices. This creates what I roughly called an 'arena of noncompliance': a certain context in which it becomes, in many cases, somewhat difficult to draw clear lines between what is supposed to be legal or illegal and where the state itself is fragmented through a constellation of different political interests and sometimes competing agendas of legality. In this chapter, I will return to the concepts of noncompliance and arena, in order to explore them from the specific point of view of the legal scholarship. Equipped with this conceptual framework, instead of focusing on the economic dimension or urban configurations as most of the literature on informality does, I will be able to assess the impacts of noncompliance – anchored in our case study – on the legal system, which is an unexplored topic within the legal scholarship so far.

A natural point of departure is the common understanding of noncompliance as a violation of a rule or a set of rules which might trigger the application of another rule or set of rules, such as sanctions, as result of the violation. However, this describes just some of the operations of a multileveled phenomenon. When violations become so common and systematic that they become entrenched and pervasive in society, noncompliance might reach structural levels, bringing about far more complex scenarios. At extreme levels, this might even cast some doubt regarding whether the rules violated can still be taken as valid rules in the sense that they must be followed and, if not, whether the respective consequences will indeed be applied. At high and intermediate levels of noncompliance, in which the rules remain valid but without the ability to promote the legally desired state of affairs, the performances of the legal system seem to change in various ways. Whilst the challenge in the first scenario is to understand whether a rule or a set of rules can still be taken as valid, in the second the challenge is to observe the actual performances delivered by the legal system instead of promoting the state of affairs provided for in the rules. First, I will examine the operational levels of the phenomenon and then, in part III of this book, I will look at each of these scenarios in detail, for they will, respectively, give us insights into the very nature of noncompliance and its impacts on the legal system.

4

Conceptual Presuppositions

4.1. THE NORM AND ITS EFFICACY DIMENSION

THE CONCEPT OF noncompliance demands an initial understanding of two specific notions: first, that a norm exists as such and, therefore, a behaviour ought to be performed or a state of affairs ought to be achieved; and, second, that this behaviour is not performed or the state of affairs is not achieved, despite the existing norm. Whereas the former leads to discussions about the existence of a given norm, the latter focuses on its actual concretisation. Despite the polysemy of the term[1] and all the wide-ranging discussions and literature on the concept of (social or legal) norms,[2] it seems that there is a common ground in distinguishing the fact that a rule ought to be followed from the fact that it is or is not followed. This distinction, although at first glance might appear basic, is theoretically loaded, for it derives from an older, philosophically deep debate on the distinction between 'is' and 'ought'.[3]

[1] For a rich systematisation in English of different meanings of the term norm and its manifold logical differences, see von Wright (1963: 1–16). In his terminology, norm is being used here more in the sense of 'prescriptions or regulations' (1963: 7), although in arenas of noncompliance it becomes difficult to distinguish 'prescriptions or regulations' from 'rules'. For a list of different meanings of norm and their respective uses in sociology, along with illustrative bibliographical references, see Lautmann (1971: 54–68). With reference to the descriptions given in Lautmann's summary, I am using 'norm as rule' ('Norm als Richtschnur') and not 'norm as average' ('Norm als Durchschnitt'); whereas the former points out a regulative prescription, that is, what one ought to do, the latter relates to statistical facts, that is, what is numerically most frequent.

[2] Although I have been using the terms norm, rule, and regulation interchangeably up to this point, I do not ignore the specific discussions that permeate the concept of legal norm in legal theory or sociology of law. Two are worth mentioning. One deals with the elements of the concept of legal norm itself (and the most important to us is the element of validity). In this regard, there are countless examples in the literature that may be quoted with drastic variations of methodology and approaches, such as norm as 'directive' (Ross 1959: 7), 'social rule' (HLA Hart 1994: 55), and 'counterfactually stabilized behavioural expectations' (Luhmann 2014: 33 [1987: 43]). The other deals with the difference between norms as rules and norms as principles; in this regard, see esp Dworkin (1977b: 24–28) and, in terms of norms of fundamental rights, Alexy (1986: 71–104). I will come to these discussions when needed, for they will have important consequences in understanding the different forms of noncompliance.

[3] It can be traced back to Hume's (1960 [1739]: 469–70) famous claim on the impossibility of deriving propositions of 'ought' or 'ought not' from propositions of 'is' or 'is not'. It is hard to account for all the scholarship that followed either developing or criticising this claim. Kant (2004: 7 and 10, [1920: 4 and 7]) himself, for instance, considered this Humean line of thought, along with the impossibility of an a priori relation between cause and effect, to have interrupted his 'dogmatic slumber'. Later on, the deduction of an 'ought' from an 'is' became, after the work of Moore

The most traditional appropriation in terms of legal scholarship can be found in the work of Kelsen (1967: 5 [1960: 5]), to whom this distinction 'is directly given to our consciousness'.[4] Based on this assumption, he develops some lines of reasoning, out of which two are strictly important here. One refers to the distinction between the subjective and objective meanings of the act of will from which an 'ought' emerges. As he puts it,

> 'Ought' is the subjective meaning of every act of will directed at the behavior of another. But not every such act has also objectively this meaning; and only if the act of will has also the objective meaning of an 'ought,' is this 'ought' called a 'norm'. (Kelsen 1967: 7 [1960: 7])

In this sense, one can only call a 'norm' the 'ought' that objectively binds its 'addressee, that is, the individual at whom it is directed',[5] not only from his point of view and that of 'the one who performed the act of will', but also from the point of view of 'a third individual not involved in the relation between the two' (1967: 7–8 [1960: 7]). What he calls 'objective meaning' is precisely the dimension of 'validity' of a given norm. That is why, in his conceptual enterprise, he takes 'validity' as 'the specific existence of a norm' (1967: 10 [1960: 9]). In other words, for him, a norm exists if and only if it is a valid norm. It is true that not every scholar asserts validity to be an essential element for the existence of a norm,[6] but, before going deeper into this important matter, I will carefully examine the second line of reasoning, for it shall provide us with an initial conceptual framework of the basic degrees of noncompliance.

(1993 [1903]), known as a 'naturalistic fallacy'. Others tried to take the challenge to bridge the two worlds; see, for instance, in different fields Searle (1964) and Jonas (1979: 92–94); the latter even treated this distinction as one of the two 'most established dogmas of our time'. At another corner, in the field of sociology of law, claiming that there was 'no attempt of sociological analysis of the ought', Luhmann (2014: 33–34 [1987: 43–44]) argued that the 'meaning of the ought [*Sollen*] is no less factual than the meaning of the is [*Sein*]' and, hence, 'the usual opposition of the factual and the normative should be therefore abolished' for it is a 'conceptual misconstruction'; instead, as he suggests, to the 'normative' one should oppose the 'cognitive'.

[4] Here I decided to translate from the original in German: 'Er ist unserem Bewußtsein unmittelbar gegeben'. The English translation from Max Knight – 'We are immediately aware of the difference' – seemed to me not only a bit distant from a literal translation, but also misleading in regard to the depth of the assertion. Moreover, the English edition does not include the footnote written by Kelsen at the end of the sentence, in which he further explains that, by saying that the distinction is directly given to our conscience, he does not mean that the content of the 'ought' can be directly recognised through a special spiritual faculty, and expressly quotes Moore (1993: 59), comparing the concept of 'ought' with what Moore said about the concept of 'good' (see also n 3 above). This leads me to think that in this point Kelsen meant that the distinction between 'is' and 'ought' is given *a priori* and the same cannot be said of the content of the 'ought' – as well as it cannot be said of the content of 'good' or likewise 'yellow' ('simple notions' in the terms of Moore) – which can only be known *a posteriori*, that is, recognised after being determined (in the case of the 'ought') by an act of will.

[5] That is the '*subject*' of a norm in von Wright's (1963: 77) terminology.

[6] For a didactic exposition with references, arguing in favour of a distinction between existence and validity, see Alexy (1986: 47–50). In the same sense, but also with references to Brazilian scholarship, see Neves (1988: 39–49).

Provided that the validity of a given norm expresses the existence of a given 'ought' and not an 'is', that is, that a certain behaviour ought to be performed and not that it is performed, Kelsen (1967: 10 [1960: 10]) states one shall distinguish the fact that a norm exists from the fact that 'the norm is actually applied and obeyed, the fact that human behavior according to the norm actually occurs'.[7] Therefore, the 'ought-fact' of a norm – its validity – must be distinguished from its 'is-fact', what he calls its 'efficacy'.[8] This does not mean, however, that they do not connect with each other. There are some implications to draw from the relationship between validity and efficacy, as well as a rich scholarship addressing it, and I intend to explore them in the course of this work. For now, it is interesting to observe how this distinction provides a fruitful point of departure to our analysis. Even though Kelsen has not dedicated a sole study to the dimension of efficacy, a theme that only appears as important to the extent that it serves to back up his understanding of validity, he has, nonetheless, called attention to two distinct forms through which a given norm acquires its efficacy: when it is applied and when it is obeyed. It is true that on this plane he did not say much about efficacy, except that application is done 'by the legal organs (particularly law courts), which means, that the sanction in a concrete case is ordered and executed' and obedience 'by the individuals subjected to the legal order, which means, that they behave in a way which avoids the sanction' (1967: 11 [1960: 11]), nor did he conceive of other forms of efficacy. And there is always a risk in using a theory to handle problems for which the theory was not intentionally designed – a gap yet to be faced. As rightfully observed by Bulygin (1965: 39), more than a half-century ago – and it remains to a certain extent true today – the concept of efficacy has always received little attention from the traditional legal-philosophical literature, for 'one is often inclined to regard this term as clear and unproblematic. Even in those relatively rare cases where it is explicitly discussed, it falls short of the apparently much more important problem of validity.'[9]

[7] Such an approach neutralises questions about the conscience of the complying behaviour, that is, it does not matter if the individual is aware or willing to comply when complying with the norm.

[8] The original term he uses is *Wirksamkeit*, which was converted in the English edition by Max Knight to 'effectiveness'. But the translations are not linear nor consistent. In the General Theory of Law and State, originally published in English, both terms, 'effectiveness' and 'efficacy', were used – I would say – interchangeably; see Kelsen (1949: 118–22). 'Effectiveness' was also used in the Pure Theory of Law to translate *Effektivität* (1967: 208 and 211 [1960: 212 and 215]), which Kelsen associates to another level of *Wirksamkeit*, that is, when it reaches the whole legal order. In order to avoid misunderstandings, I prefer to convert *Wirksamkeit* into 'efficacy', which was Hart's translation when referring to Kelsen's work (HLA Hart 1994: 294) as well as when discussing the specific problems of validity vis-à-vis efficacy (HLA Hart 1994: 103).

[9] In the same vein but almost 15 years later, Raz (1979a: 42) when talking about the tests for identity and existence of a legal system, stated that 'efficacy is the least controversial of these conditions. Oddly enough it is also the least studied and least understood.' I would say that these warnings include even those who advocate the equivalence between validity and efficacy. In this sense, see Ross (1959: 34–35), for whom the valid law is precisely the efficacious law, and this is the law that is applied in courts in general, which includes police, prosecuting authorities, and judges. But this kind of approach, as I see it, is too restrictive and, for this reason, does not capture important aspects of efficacy as a more comprehensive phenomenon. As Ross conceives norms as directives for decisions to be taken by judges (and public authorities in general), the phenomenon of application would be,

As we shall see, there is much to be explored at this level, perhaps even more than Bulygin himself could imagine at the time.[10] Application and obedience might serve now as a starting point to build a comprehensive framework to understand the phenomenon we are trying to capture. That a norm is applied and obeyed shows, for our purpose, the basic forms of compliance with a norm. That a norm is neither applied nor obeyed shows forms of noncompliance with a norm. As these categories refer to daily operations of the legal system, I shall refer to them as examples of operational degrees of compliance and, conversely, noncompliance.

4.2. PRIMARY NORMS, SECONDARY NORMS, AND ILLEGALITY

It is important to be careful in handling Kelsen's theoretical framework, as it entails a set of presuppositions that need clarification, some of which I will slightly diverge from. His notion of obedience is strictly linked to the distinction he makes between norms according to which 'a certain individual "ought" to observe certain conduct', what he called 'secondary norms', and the ones which state that 'another individual ought to execute a sanction in case the first norm is violated', deemed the 'primary norms'. He does advocate that the law is essentially a system of primary norms, since they make secondary norms 'superfluous' (1949: 60–61), especially because, once a sanction is attributed to a certain behaviour, secondary norms will not be needed to explain that the opposing behaviour will not trigger the predicated sanction; in this sense, secondary norms are contained within primary norms and are dependent on them (1967: 54–58 [1960: 55–59]).[11] In any case, as both kinds of norms rely

in his line of reasoning, an obedience of the directive by the judge (and public authorities in general), making it the only criterion for the measurement of efficacy regardless of the behaviour of the individuals; that is, he actually excludes the whole dimension of compliance with a norm by individuals. For a thorough criticism of Ross in this regard, see Kelsen (1959: 9 ff). It seems unfair, however, to include into this criticism the legal pluralism scholarship; I will expand on this later (see ch 6, n 16), because they entail another approach to the problem we are facing. Studies of efficacy that have been developed in other fields are noteworthy; see, for instance, Calabria (2018: esp chapter 2) with respect to the concept of efficacy at the level of international law and human rights.

[10] In his conceptual enterprise, he clearly restricts efficacy to the use of norms for judges 'to justify their decisions' (Bulygin 1965: 52). This approach suffers, hence, from the very same restriction as the approach taken by Ross, since it hides, instead of facing, the complexity of a much bigger and pervasive phenomenon.

[11] Others employed a reversed reasoning in regard to whether a norm should be called 'primary' or 'secondary', such as Vilanova (1997: 111–12), to whom 'the non-sanctioning norm should not be considered superfluous', for 'without it the sanctioning norm lacks meaning'. In the same vein, see Geiger (1964: 138–49), but taking the legal sanction as a species of social reaction and developing the reasoning in terms of 'action norm' and 'reaction norm'. Cossio (1964: 661–62) proposed the concepts of 'endonorm', which conceptualises the behaviour to be performed, and 'perinorm', which conceptualises the sanction; this way, it would be possible to avoid the 'chaos' provoked by the often opposed meanings of 'primary' and 'secondary' as well as making it clear that they are 'one single norm and not two norms'; see also his criticism of Kelsen's reversed reasoning, which leaves the notion of 'legal duty' with a 'very modest theoretical role' and causes the notion of 'legal

on regulating behaviour, words like 'illegality', 'delict', 'breaking', or 'violating' the law shall not be understood as 'negation of the law' but rather a 'condition of the law', that is to say, they are words used to refer to those behaviours that specifically trigger the application of a given sanction.[12] In this sense, they are the condition of a sanction and, only in this sense, can be called 'unlawful behavior' in opposition to those behaviours that avoid the sanction, the 'lawful behavior' (1967: 112–13 [1960: 118–19]). And this rationale has two important consequences for our study.

If one calls a behaviour illegal – or a delict, a wrong, unlawful, noncompliant, etc – meaning the behaviour to which a norm specifically attaches a sanction as a consequence of its performance, it becomes very difficult to rely on any concept of informality that tries to set a boundary between the illegal and the informal, as for instance is done by the ILO and in a major part of informality scholarship.[13] For any behaviour to which there is a sanction as a consequence of its performance designates per se an illegal behaviour; there is no special feature that designates illegality other than a sanction as its consequence, nor is there any grade of illegality that could delimitate intermediary zones. Therefore, informality necessarily describes a set of illegalities or illegal behaviours. In order to make the concept of informality analytically fruitful, one should select the set of illegalities that might fall under the label 'informal',[14] and not rely on a sheer separation between informality and illegality.

Furthermore, by making this distinction between primary and secondary norms, Kelsen (1949: 60–62) comes to the conclusion that an individual 'can "obey" or "disobey" only the secondary norm', whereas the primary norm is subject to the organ which '"applies" or "does not apply"' the norm. As he is almost entirely focused on primary norms, which he considers as the 'genuine legal norm', one cannot avoid noting that this excessive emphasis diverts a

faculty to lose all meaning' (1964: 106 fn 25). The discussion over the nomenclature, however, is not important for our purpose here. What matters is to distinguish how forms of compliance and noncompliance vary depending on the type of norm.

[12] With the same understanding, see Cossio (1964: 658–60). Naturally, sanction is to be understood in this context as punishment. For a broader criticism of such restrictive use, suggesting that sanctions encompass both punishment and reward, see Bobbio (2007).

[13] See section 1.2. Charmers (2019: 2), however, goes in the opposite direction to say that that there is instead 'the tendency to equate informality and illegality'. But one can hardly say that he has a grounded notion of what legality means from the point of view of legal scholarship. This becomes clear when he asserts: 'informality has remained a confusing concept for most observers and policymakers, who commonly mix underground, parallel and criminal activities with traditional, spontaneous and non-registered – but legal – activities, which play a major role for poor populations to earn a living' (2019: 1). In an earlier work, he even states that 'non-compliance with the official regulations is far from meaning that these activities are illegal' (Charmes 2012: 105). If there are legal norms commanding the registration and establishing sanctions for not doing this, then the non-registered activity is by definition illegal. He does place the discussion in a historical backdrop, but this does not preclude the complexity of defining what an illegal behaviour is in general and a criminal behaviour in particular. I will deal with this further in this part of the book.

[14] This clearly is the solution adopted by Feige (2016a). I will comment on this again in the concluding remarks.

major part of his theoretical concern to an important but comparatively scant part of the legal phenomenon, that of the application of norms. Apart from the already notable criticisms,[15] this raises two concerns. On the one hand, as I shall demonstrate (see section 5.2), under 'application' he brings together two considerably distinct phenomena from the perspective of efficacy: that the sanction is 'ordered' and 'executed' (Kelsen 1967: 11 [1960: 11]). On the other hand, obedience is important as it is the opposite of disobedience, which in turn refers to the behaviour that triggers the application of a norm. Kelsen (1967: 11 [1960: 11]) further argues that when a norm acquires its efficacy by the fact that it is always obeyed by its addressees and, for this reason, is rarely brought to a court or to public authorities, this constitutes 'the ideal case of validity of a legal norm'.[16] This is to say that to a large extent his whole theoretical enterprise is built to explicate the application, or the 'law-applying act', which is, except from the borderline case of execution (1967: 234 [1960: 240]), essentially an act of norm creation. Specifically, it is 'authentic interpretation' of the law in the sense that the interpreter binds others to their will (1967: 354–55 [1960: 351–52.]). That leaves a very specific role to be played by the private individuals whose behaviour is commanded by the norm, since they are generally not in charge of creating norms, unless one is dealing with cases in which the norm itself instead of commanding a behaviour either empowers[17] the individual to create a norm (eg, contracts or declarations of last will and testament), or permits a certain behaviour (eg, self-defence), that is, cases in which

[15] Bulygin (1965: 42) criticised the fact that, actually, 'a very significant part of the legal order consists of such dependent norms [ie, secondary norms]', that is, norms which do not prescribe sanctions, but 'confer public or private legal power, regulate the creation, modification or abolition of norms imposing obligations and sanctions; therefore, almost all constitutional and procedural norms and a significant part of other public and private law'. For the proper argument according to which they must be understood as secondary norms, see Kelsen (1967: 54–58 [1960: 55–59]).

[16] It seems to me that it would be more consistent to speak of an ideal case of efficacy, since validity as an 'ought' should not be in principle affected by the way a norm is followed or applied, unless it is never obeyed nor applied, which would make the norm lose, in Kelsen's (1967: 213 [1960: 220]) understanding, its validity. That the norm is always obeyed consists of an 'is-fact'; therefore, it sounds somewhat imprecise to say that this is an ideal case of validity, a dimension which consists, on the contrary, of an 'ought-fact'. For a deeper assessment of Kelsen's position regarding the relation between efficacy and validity in terms of obedience and application in courts, see his criticisms of Ross (Kelsen 1959).

[17] Here Kelsen uses the verb *ermächtigen*, which was translated in the English edition to 'authorizing'. However, it seemed to me that this translation could be misleading in this regard, since it is very close to the English word 'permitting', which was used to translate *erlauben*. It takes time and a certain knowledge for a reader to depart from the ordinary use of the language to make a difference between permission and authorisation. For this reason I prefer 'empower', which seems not only a more direct translation but also a more precise way to say that a norm confers 'upon an individual a legal power, that is, the power to create legal norms' (Kelsen 1967: 56 [1960: 57]) and is closer to the translation used in the Portuguese edition, 'conferir poder ou competência' (Kelsen 1998: 16). In any case, Kelsen (1949: 31) uses both terms interchangeably in the General Theory of Law and State. In order to avoid misunderstandings, the term 'authorisation' will be used here in the sense of a norm that empowers.

the individual 'applies' the norm (1967: 15–16 [1960: 15]).[18] In other words, obedience or disobedience only takes place when the norm commands someone to behave in a certain way, either by performing a certain action (the action is mandatory) or omitting such action (the action is forbidden). Therefore, norms which either empower or permit cannot be obeyed or disobeyed.[19] This stark differentiation in Kelsen (1967: 4–5 [1960: 4–5]) is a result of how he conceives the deontic modalities of a norm, ie, the possible ways according to which an 'ought' can be expressed.[20] I shall demonstrate later that this differentiation can be strongly affected by the way that the 'ought' is pragmatically performed, changing the modality of the norm despite its modal expression at the syntactic or semantic level. For now, I begin with the first notion according to which obedience plainly means to behave according to the norm.

[18] However, in regard to permission, Kelsen is inconsistent. In an earlier part of the book, he says that 'making use of a positive permission may also be designated as the observance of law [*Rechtsbefolgung*]' (1967: 15–16 [1960: 15]). It also seems a bit inaccurate in terms of authorisation to describe both what a public authority does when creating norms and what individuals do when making use of them to create private norms. In respect to the latter, one could instead speak of 'offers of regulation' (Blankenburg 1977: 36–38), which may or may not be used; and which are not properly understood in terms of punishments and rewards (Friedman 1975: 79). I will return to these kinds of norms later (see ch 8, text following n 33).

[19] 'Offers of regulation' (see n 18 above) could also be included here, since they are not properly obeyed nor disobeyed.

[20] For a more detailed study on the basic deontic modals, see von Wright (1963: esp 7–8 and 100–02) and Alexy (1986: 182–85).

5

Conceptual Architecture

5.1. THE FIRST DEGREE: OBEDIENCE VERSUS DISOBEDIENCE

When a norm prescribes a behaviour (action or omission) that ought to be performed, obedience happens when the expected behaviour is performed. Disobedience, on the contrary, occurs when the opposite behaviour is performed. I will call this first notion the first degree of compliance because it is the most direct form of compliance in the sense that the norm is directly followed by the individual addressed by the norm – in Kelsen's (1967: 14 [1960: 13]) terminology, 'the individual that ought to behave', that is, the element that constitutes the 'personal sphere of validity' of a norm. To behave in conformity with a norm reflects the most intuitive meaning of compliance and is by far the most usual sense used by non-legal scholarship. For this reason, especially for laymen, the content of a norm is usually given by a mere reading of its linguistic support, normally the legal text in form of legislation. Such a reading almost never takes into account the interpretation conveyed by courts or public authorities which densifies a norm, sometimes expanding, reducing, or creating exceptions to it. In the majority of cases a reading may not even occur as texts are usually unavailable, difficult to access, highly complex, or written in a technical language. Thus, norms at this level are mainly spread through daily interactions or internalised as habits, without further considerations regarding other elements that belong to a proper legal hermeneutics.[1] Because of this, the first degree of compliance corresponds to a first, superficial level of a norm, which is usually construed by the norm addressees.[2] It is this

[1] For a similar understanding, see Blankenburg (1977: 36–37) and Geiger (1964: 87). The latter, however, distinguishes 'to effectively act in *conformity* with the norm' from 'to *obey* the norm'. For 'the binding nature of the norm' is not always 'the motive behind every complying action'. From the standpoint assumed here, as a matter of fact, the reasons or motives to comply with the norm are irrelevant to characterise obedience; *cf* Kindermann (1989: 258). Such understanding rejects the derivation of norms from moral rules. For a broader notion of how the law is communicated to legal authorities and the public, see Friedman (2016: 7 ff) with a long list of examples and studies.

[2] There are, nonetheless, those who advocate that the addressee of a legal norm is not the individual who must perform the behaviour, but rather the judges and public authorities who are in charge of enforcing such norm. See, for instance, Ross (1959: 35–36) and ch 4, n 9. In the same vein, see Bulygin (1965: 56), for whom the efficacy of a norm should be understood as its capacity to be used by courts [*Gerichtsfähigkeit*] as fundaments for their decisions.

specific level that the term compliance usually refers to, and for this reason one may even refer to it as compliance in the narrowest sense. In order to illustrate this form of compliance I return to some previous examples, but this time applying more consistent terminology.

In Fortaleza, there is a set of statutes which together prohibit the use of public squares for itinerant commerce, unless the individual obtains the proper permit from the mayor and sells only specific types of goods (Articles 1, 2, and 7 to 13 of Decree 9,300/1994 combined with Article 107, § 1, of the Constitution of the Municipality). This norm (henceforth: *Norm A*) contains different commands, authorisations, and permissions:

(A.1) It prohibits the general use of public squares for itinerant commerce;

(A.2) It permits itinerant commerce if the individual fulfils two conditions: obtaining the permit and selling permitted goods;

(A.3) It empowers the municipality, through some of its organs (Article 3 of Decree 9,300/1994), to issue or not issue the permit;

(A.4) It commands the municipality, through some of its organs, to apply and execute the respective sanctions (Articles 27 and 28 of Decree 9,300/1994) in case of violation of A.1.

All these items constitute fragments of *Norm A*, since they are just pieces of it. Were I to separate the primary norm, which sets the condition for the sanction and the sanction itself, from the secondary norms, that is, all the others not concerned with the sanction, then we could say that fragment A.4 falls into the former, and fragments A.1, A.2, and A.3, into the latter. The secondary norms can be further distinguished between their addressees: whereas fragments A.1 and A.2 are directed to the individual who ought to behave, fragment A.3 is directed to the organ which has the power to grant the permission. Making use of our initial framework, obedience and disobedience are only possible to assess in the case of secondary norms which command individuals to behave themselves by performing a certain action or omission. This is clearly the case of fragment A.1, which prohibits the use of public squares for itinerant commerce: it is obeyed by every individual who refrains from exercising itinerant commerce on public squares (henceforth: *general form of obedience of Norm A*) and disobeyed by the ones who do. Fragment A.2, however, provides for a permission, which makes legal a behaviour that otherwise would be illegal. *In casu*, it sets the conditions under which the use of squares for itinerant commerce is permitted: obtaining the proper permit and selling permitted goods. In this sense, fragment A.2 makes the disobedience of fragment A.1 more complex: it can only be disobeyed by vendors who either do not have the proper permit or, despite the permit, sell forbidden goods. But, in general terms, the prohibition can only be more obeyed than disobeyed, since obedience refers to the whole population under the personal sphere of validity of the norm,[3] unless one conceives a very improbable scenario in which the majority of the population would be using public squares for the exercise of itinerant commerce. This assessment is too broad and has little to offer, since the main targets of the norm are not the population in general, but rather those specifically involved with itinerant commerce on public squares. Thus, it is only within the scope of itinerant commerce regulation that an assessment of the compliance with the *Norm A* makes sense, that is, the 'vendors who have the permit and sell permitted goods' versus 'vendors who do not'. This gives us the following settings to assess the first level of compliance of *Norm A*: the norm is obeyed when vendors use the square for itinerant commerce with the proper permit to sell permitted goods (*specific form of obedience of Norm A*); the norm is disobeyed when vendors use the square without the proper permit (*first form of disobedience of Norm A*) or when they sell forbidden goods (*second form of disobedience of Norm A*).

Naturally, this is a somewhat simple architecture of the norm, which could be further elaborated by more trained eyes to include other pieces that would place *Norm A* into the more intricate Brazilian administrative law (eg, to distinguish the permit as an administrative authorisation and not as a licence[4]), the Penal Code (eg, to prohibit the selling of substances harmful to health[5]), the Constitution (eg, to permit the use of public spaces for itinerant commerce of cultural goods produced by nomadic populations[6]), and so forth.

[3] Theoretically, the sphere of validity of a norm could be unlimited if it claims to be valid 'for all individuals', such as universal moral orders. From a national legal order perspective, unless it has such universal pretension, the personal sphere of validity is limited to 'the behavior of individuals who live within the state territory and of the state's citizens who happen to be abroad' (Kelsen 1967: 14 [1960: 13–14]).

[4] Whereas an administrative authorisation is a precarious act which can be at any time revoked according to the discretion of the public authority [*Verwaltungsakt mit Ermessensspielraum*], the licence is regarded as a bound act [*verbindlicher Verwaltungsakt*] which can be revoked only due to illegality. For the difference and its implications in regard to administrative acts in Brazil, see Meirelles and Burle Filho (2016: 138–42, 191–96, and 211–14).

[5] Art 278 of the Penal Code.

[6] This would be, of course, a more complex case. In Brazil there is a group of street artists (nomadic craftsmen) who are constantly targeted by public policies aimed at hygiene in public spaces. Street vending for them is not only a means of work, but rather a way of life. As they do not have fixed residence and are in constant movement from one city to another, sometimes even crossing country borders, it is almost impossible for them to obtain permits to use public spaces for the selling of their merchandise. If the constitutional framework is considered, more specifically the constitutional protection of manifestations of popular culture and the modes of living of groups which constitute the Brazilian nation (Arts 215, § 1, and 216, II, of the Constitution), this may lead to the conclusion that their activity of street vending is constitutionally protected. For more information, see the following amateur documentaries about the life of these street artists and the legal problems they face, especially in regard to occupation of public spaces: *A criminalização do artista – Como se fabricam marginais em nosso país*, April 2011, vimeo.com/27659191; and *Malucos de Estrada II – Cultura de BR*, August 2015, www.youtube.com/watch?v=E2xYfyEANMw. Both accessed on 23 February 2020.

These further developments toward a 'complete norm'[7] bring other scenarios to be further analysed. It seems that the more one moves out of the realm of obedience and into the realm of application, the more complex the norm becomes, even though the boundaries between the fragments of a norm that are closer to the dimension of obedience and those that appear during the norm application are somewhat thin. Before analysing these developments in detail, I will examine the second degree of analysis, which takes place when disobedience happens.

5.2. THE SECOND DEGREE: ENFORCEMENT VERSUS FAILURE, FORBEARANCE, AND ABUSE

As I have argued, the most common notion of noncompliance pictures just a single layer of a multileveled phenomenon. When one says that a norm was violated, breached, not observed, or not followed, what is highlighted is one form of noncompliance with a norm that is performed by the norm addressee. In such cases, the individual whose behaviour is commanded by the norm does exactly the opposite and performs an action which is forbidden or refrains from performing an action when mandatory. This form of noncompliance, called disobedience, by default consists of a condition of another norm fragment which attaches to the norm, as a consequence, a sanction to be carried out by a public organ or authority. Here the further degrees of this analysis begin, which take place in the realm of imposing the sanction or, in Kelsen's terminology, the realm of 'application' of the norm. However, there are some considerations to be made, as the concept of 'application' as conceived by Kelsen embraces considerably distinct phenomena, each of which entails specific forms of compliance and noncompliance.

To start I present what obedience and application have in common, and what distinguishes one from the other in Kelsen's terms. Both are behaviours that perform the content of a norm. On the one hand, obedience is the term used to describe the performance of the norm addressee in conformity with

[7] I do not mean complete norm in the sense of Cossio (1964: 333 and 661–69), that is, the combination of both the endonorm and the perinorm and all of its elements, but more in the sense used by Dworkin (1977b: 25–26): an accurate statement of a rule which takes into consideration all of its exceptions. However, I do not accept Dworkin's understanding according to which a complete statement of a rule is possible because, in theory, all exceptions could be enumerated, in contrast to what happens to principles, which, according to him, 'are not, even in theory, subject to enumeration'. As I shall demonstrate, the possibility of creating norm-fragments which add exceptions to a rule is, by different reasons, inexhaustible. In the same sense and against Dworkin, see Alexy (1986: 88–89 [2002: 58]), arguing that 'the exceptions incorporated into rules on the basis of principles are unquantifiable in theory as well'; also Alexy (1979: 68). Similarly, Neves (2021: 52–54 and 63–64 [2013: 60–63 and 77–78]), for whom only 'at the end of the concretizing process, after a possible balancing of the exception clause or condition clause with the competing principles, we have a complete rule, under which the case is subsumed by a concrete ought-decision' (2021: 83–84 [2013: 106]).

secondary norms of command. On the other hand, application describes the performance of the public organ in conformity with primary norms. In this sense, as Kelsen (1949: 61–62) says, the public organ is the genuine addressee of legal norms, for he conceives of law essentially as a system of primary norms, and thus, 'only the organ can, strictly speaking, "obey" or "disobey" the legal norm'.[8] In any case, obedience and application point out at least two different addressees of a norm: the one whose behaviour is directly regulated by the norm and the public organ in charge of imposing the sanction in case of disobedience by the former. If, as Kelsen (1967: 11 [1960: 11]) proposes, imposition is to mean ordering and executing the sanction, then one can actually speak of three different addresses: the direct norm addressee, the public organ in charge of ordering a sanction, and the public organ in charge of executing the sanction. It is in regard to the latter two that I will propose to distinguish between application in general, adjudication, and execution of a norm.

Furthermore, in order to perform its content, naturally one must understand what the content of the norm is. From the standpoint assumed by Kelsen (1967: 348 [1960: 346]), both obedience and application also entail an act of cognition of the norm, meaning both the individual and the public organ to whom the norm is directed must interpret the norm and ascertain its meaning to determine whether, when, and how they ought to behave.[9] As this activity of interpretation involves the cognition of a myriad of possible meanings, the cognition of a norm can only be 'a frame within which several applications are possible' (1967: 350–51 [1960: 348–49]).[10] Against this background, Kelsen (1967: 71–75 [1960: 73–77]) draws a very important distinction between the interpretation carried out by the science of law, which has – I would add – the same nature as the interpretation carried out by the individual who ought to behave, and the interpretation by the public organ that has to impose the

[8] In a different formulation, Garrn (1969: 168) states: 'Not only primary norms but also secondary norms can be obeyed. The application of primary norms by judges and administrative officials is obedience of the respective secondary norms.' However, I find these formulations a bit inaccurate because, as I will demonstrate in this section, 'obeying' and 'enforcing' (through application or execution) are quite different things. See also n 26.

[9] At this point of his work, Kelsen (1967: 348 [1960: 346]) seems to incur inconsistencies. In many passages, he says norms must be interpreted: 'he [the legal organ] must interpret these norms' – here the English translation puts the verb 'interpret' into quotation marks, which do not exist in the German original – 'But also the individuals who have to obey – and not to apply – the norm … and finally the science of law, when describing the positive law, must interpret its norms.' However, if the norm is a meaning, then it is by definition the result of an interpretation; see Kelsen (1967: 3–4, 5, and 7 [1960: 3–4, 5, and 7]). Of course, the interpretation process is strictly speaking never-ending, since the result can always be further thematised. Nevertheless, in order to be precise, let us assume that what is interpreted is the normative texts to which a meaning is attributed. For a more detailed study on the difference between texts and norms and the respective outcomes of the interpretation process, see Alexy (1986: 50–53), Müller (1994: 234 ff), and, with a special emphasis on Brazil, Ávila (2007: 5–8 [2011: 30–35]) and Neves (2021: 10–17 [2013: 1–11]).

[10] Curiously, he develops this line of reasoning, the law as a frame within which there are several possibilities of interpretation, with references only to 'the law to be applied'. However, it seems plausible to say that the same holds true of the law to be obeyed.

sanction. Whereas in the first case the result is a mere 'legal proposition',[11] that is to say, a statement about a norm that merely describes one possible meaning; in the second, the result is a legal norm itself, prescribing the meaning to be followed or applied. The application of a norm in such terms is hence *ipso facto* creation of law. Making use of the previous distinction between subjective and objective meanings (see chapter four, text following n 4), the following can be said: while in both cases the result of the interpretation is a subjective meaning of a norm, only in the second case does the result have an objective meaning. The objective meaning is what properly constitutes a legal norm by making the interpretation carried out by the public organ binding on others. It is in this specific sense that the interpretation carried out by the norm-applying organ is not merely an act of cognition, but also an 'act of will by which the law-applying organ chooses between the possibilities shown by cognitive interpretation' (1967: 354 [1960: 351]). Naturally, this entails that 'the establishment of a legal act', which is the resulting operation of the fixation of meaning, 'so far as it takes place within the framework of the legal norm to be applied, is free, that is, within the discretion of the organ called upon to establish the act'. In this sense, 'this act of will creates either a lower-level norm or is the execution of a coercive act stipulated in the legal norm to be applied' (1967: 353–4 [1960: 351]). One important consequence of this line of reasoning is that primary norms, even though consisting of commands to public organs to impose a sanction, essentially empower a public organ to determine who ought to behave, when, and how, either by creating individual and specific norms or by using force to constrain others to do as prescribed. On the one hand, this explains why primary norms cannot be obeyed or disobeyed in the same way as secondary norms, but instead are applied or not applied. On the other, it highlights how obedience and disobedience refer to one's own behaviour, whereas application and non-application refer to the behaviour of others.[12] The activity of cognition here is not merely cognition but rather demands a more intricate knowledge of the legal order so

[11] The original word used in German was *Rechtssatz*, which was translated to 'rule of law'. This translation is in many senses wrong. Rule of law is a theoretically loaded concept that, despite the profuse academic debate, has no proximity to Kelsen's intention with *Rechtssatz*. For examples of the context in which the concept of the rule of law is properly used, see Raz (1979c) and, discussing closer concepts such as *Estado de Derecho* and *Rechtsstaat*, O'Donell (1999: 315–19). Others have translated it to 'legal statement' (van Roermund 2013: 13), 'legal rules in a descriptive sense' / 'descriptive-ought statements' (HLA Hart 1983 [1968]: 328) and, as can be found in the Portuguese edition (Kelsen 1998: 80), 'proposição jurídica' (legal proposition). In the *General Theory of the Law and State*, originally published in English, Kelsen does refer to 'legal rules' in this descriptive sense (1949: 170). As I have been using the term 'legal rule' in another sense, I will prefer here 'legal proposition' since it is more commonly used in the same sense of *Rechtssatz*; see, for instance, 'norm-propositions' in von Wright (1963: viii).

[12] Later in his *General Theory of Norms*, Kelsen (1991: 31–32 [1979: 24–25]) tries to explain why only the act of will directed to the behaviour of others can be an 'ought', and an act of will directed to one's own behaviour cannot.

as to determine the content of the norm. Thus, the second degree of compliance corresponds to a more complex level of the norm which brings different fragments into consideration.

Here we have arrived at the limits of Kelsen's thoughts on the differences between obedience and application. I do not disregard that I have touched several sensitive points of his theoretical approach, some of which have raised a swath of criticisms.[13] In any case, his scholarship helps us with at least three things: it pointed out how noncompliance is necessarily a multilevel phenomenon; that each level has different addressees; and that these levels have a distinct nature. Nonetheless, there are indeed some shortcomings that cannot be avoided and need to be corrected in order to sharpen the conceptual architecture of noncompliance's definition. The first shortcoming refers to the previously mentioned distinction between application and execution, whose consequences are not properly examined by Kelsen, but are of utmost importance in order to understand the phenomenon of noncompliance. Indeed, he recognised 'the execution of the coercive act' as a 'borderline case', since it takes place in the end of the 'law-creating procedure' and, for this reason, consists of an 'application … without being itself the creation of a norm' (Kelsen 1967: 234–35 [1960: 240]). Yet this differentiation had no major impact on his conception of efficacy: 'the fact that the norm is applied and obeyed, that people actually behave according to the norm'. In this sense, he assumes efficacy to be achieved through obedience by the norm addressees and application by legal organs. As application by legal organs – Kelsen adds, 'particularly legal courts' – means 'that the sanction in a concrete case is ordered and executed' (1967: 10–11 [1960: 10–11]), both ordering and executing a norm remain relatively undistinguished phenomena under the broad umbrella of application. I would like to discuss the accuracy of this in two steps: first, by examining whether and to what extent an 'order', particularly from legal courts, is capable of making people behave according to the norm in the same way an 'execution' does; and second, by investigating how noncompliance takes place in both cases.

If one is to understand efficacy as the fact that people behave according to a norm, either by autonomous observance of the norm or through impositions, then one is led to admit that ordering people to behave and forcing them to do so are quite different factual phenomena.[14] They are each a distinct form of an 'is-fact', and thus, the performance of an order and the performance of

[13] A general critical appraisal referring to many points can be seen in Müller (1994: esp 24–30), to whom the theory 'cannot offer any contribution to a useful theory of interpretation' (1994: 27). See also Müller (2013b).

[14] That might explain one of Garrn's (1969: 169) reservations about Kelsen's description of efficacy: 'because it sees the efficacy of a norm in case of its violation when the violation is answered by a so-called sanction'. It sounds, indeed, rather confusing to state that a norm has efficacy in case of violation. However, such a description is understandable if one assumes that the assessment of efficacy of secondary norms can only be done as part of the assessment of the corresponding primary norm, that is to say, either one or another; a 'disjunctive' association as Geiger (1964: 70) puts it. Curiously, Geiger does not assume the validity of a norm (ie, in his terms, the norm's bindingness) to

an execution realise different things and hence mobilise different resources to bring the norm into compliance. Considering the chain of norm-application, an order is indeed a specification of a norm and as such constitutes a new norm in the sense that it establishes an 'ought' to be followed or executed. From this standpoint, one cannot clearly disentangle the creation of law from an application (Kelsen 1967: 234 [1960: 240]). For every act that creates law is an application of a superior norm that empowers the lawmaker to do so, and conversely, every act of application creates law by fixing the meaning of norms to be applied. This is perhaps the reason why for Kelsen (1967: 353 [1960: 351]) there is no qualitative difference between court decisions and legislation, but only quantitative: 'the legislator is much freer in creating law than the judge'. This rationale does explain with some level of accuracy the relative indistinctness between norm-creation and norm-application and what judges usually do in courts.[15] Although taking different paths and using divergent frameworks, this qualitative indistinctness is somehow found in the work of several other scholars.[16] What seems clear, nonetheless, is that norm-applying acts, such as court decisions, are less factual impositions and more norm-creation in the sense that the result of such an act is always another norm, regardless of how concretely and individually specified it is. An execution, to the contrary, is not merely part of the norm-application chain, but its culmination – as Kelsen (1967: 234–35 [1960: 240]) correctly puts it, 'the final act' – that is, the moment in which the sanction turns into actual enforcement.[17] Such a differentiation leads to the understanding that strictly speaking the imposition of sanctions occurs only with the execution. For it is not always the case that orders will incur de facto sanctions: a crime might not be discovered, a person affected by the illegal action of another may tolerate it, the application could be delayed, or a defendant may evade prosecution.[18]

have the same disjunctive character, even though it could be measured as it corresponds to a 'factual context' [*Tatsachenzusammenhang*] (208). In contrast, advocating that the structure of the norm is a 'disjunctive judgment', see Cossio (1964: esp 216 and 664 ff).

[15] This should not be taken to imply that both legislator and judge perform the same activity. It is only in terms of prescribing meanings that they have something in common. I will return to this point later (see section 5.3).

[16] Müller (1994: 264) is perhaps the most strident example so as to even invert the intuitive sense of lawmaking. According to him, realistically seen, legislators do not issue norms, but texts of norms, which have no 'normative effects themselves'.

[17] In a similar formulation, Garrn (1969: 166 and 169) distinguishes them as follows: 'norm-application is the determination of a concrete norm based on abstract norms', and 'norm-execution is any realization of the content of the norm by the application of coercive means'. One could argue that norm-application does not always end in an individual and concrete norm, such as happen with the abstract judicial review; in this sense, see Neves (2021: 13–14 [2013: 7]). Borrowing von Wright's terminology, I could also say that application consists in '*normative action*' (1963: 116–17), that is to say, it is an act that by its very nature always '*results*' in prescriptions. Eventually, if the addressees behave in accordance with the prescription, then one may say that application changes the state of affairs, not as a '*result*' but by way of '*consequences*'. Execution, on the contrary, *results* in changes to the state of affairs.

[18] See Geiger (1964: 70). For a more detailed study on the selective mechanisms that result in nonenforcement in daily interactions between enforcement agencies and norm addressees, see Luhmann (2014: 206 ff [1987: 267 ff]).

Of course these are contingent examples of how 'the difference between execution and application (police and other enforcement agencies versus judges or courts and other officer or bodies in charge of applying law) can give rise to discrepancies between these two moments in the concretization of law' (Neves 2022: 30–31 [2011: 45–46]). In this particular sense and in slight contrast to Kelsen, efficacy is properly assured only through either obedience or execution,[19] for norm-applying acts in the same way as general norms may not be de facto enforced nor bring certainty to the public organ in charge of execution.[20] Naturally, in some cases, it becomes hard to distinguish application from execution, because both activities may be concentrated into the same agent. For this reason, despite being distinct activities, it can be said that they are nonetheless part of a 'process of increasing individualization and concretization' (Kelsen 1967: 237 [1960: 242]), whereby general and abstract norms become individualised in concrete cases.[21] Either way, this process entails different forms of bringing a norm into efficacy, be it autonomously by obedience or heteronomously by law enforcement.

This conceptual distinction makes it possible to identify an important feature of arenas of noncompliance: they are to a considerable extent constituted not only by high grades of disobedience but also by a significant distance between law creation and law enforcement or, likewise, norm-application and norm-execution. This is clearly seen when we observe the phenomena that emerge in between, such as the systematic difficulties in imposing court decisions, the negotiations between enforcement agents and norm addressees to overcome rulings, the use of courts as means of lawfare, the competition between different organs over regulation of specific issues, and so forth. What is remarkable is that, in those arenas, these forms of noncompliance are not merely contingent; they are rather structural. As this assertion entails other presuppositions, I will return later to this point (see chapter six). For now, I will delve deeper into the distinction between application and execution to observe the respective forms of compliance and noncompliance.

Even though Kelsen had extensively described obedience, its opposite (ie, disobedience), and application, he did not dedicate any of his studies to the forms of noncompliance regarding application. Indeed, most scholarly

[19] See n 14 for the notion of disjunctive association.

[20] This insight that uncertainty can take place even in the execution regardless of the certainty produced by a 'decision norm', in the sense of Müller (1994: 264), can be found in Neves (2021: 3 fn 9 [2013: XIX fn 8]).

[21] *cf* the process of 'normative concretization of legal texts' (Neves 2022: 31 [2011: 46]). Such a form of understanding the norm-concretisation is broader than the ones restricted to court activities that assume the judges' decision to be the 'final product of the concretization work' (Müller 1994: 264), that is, the 'case's final solution' (Müller 2013a: 180). In a more recent work, however, Neves (2021: esp 13–14 [2013: esp 7]) takes out obedience and execution from this process, which would end with the 'norm of decision'. Obedience and execution, therefore, would not be forms of 'concretization' but rather 'realization' of the norm. Nonetheless, this distinction has no practical significance for our purpose here since what matters is to observe the forms of inefficacy of each moment.

contributions to the subject hardly touch the problem, although it is difficult to outline the reasons for this. Perhaps the focus on noncompliance merely as disobedience derives from the empirical and theoretical challenges of assuming a reality where public organs do not comply with the law in a systematic manner, court decisions are to a considerable extent disregarded in practice, regulations barely change a certain state of affairs, and all of this occurs with the legal system maintaining its validity through daily operations. Apart from speculation, the challenges need to be faced, and the questions to be posed are: What behaviours constitute noncompliance of primary norms that prescribe a sanction to be applied or executed? Or in what conditions can one say that a norm was in fact not applied or not executed? How can one accurately determine whether a sanction was not executed by a public officer? In what cases can it be said that a court decision did not apply a norm?

It is tempting to answer such questions intuitively, as if they were of easy assessment by experience. But, once one pays attention to the different logical categories they entail, the matter becomes much more difficult to apprehend. Here we face a question similar to that posited by von Wright (1963: vi–vii) in order to determine how an act can be negated: 'Does it signify the *not-doing* of the thing … Or does it signify the *undoing* of that thing, *i.e.*, the doing of something which results in an opposite state of affairs?' In contrast to obedience, which is defined by its opposite (ie, disobedience), there is no opposite to application and to execution. It does not make sense to speak of 'dis-application' or 'dis-execution', therefore, noncompliance in the realm of application is not to be found in acts that 'undo', but rather in acts that 'not-do'. In this vein, there is a certain imprecision in approaches that treat application and execution as cases of 'obedience' of another norm. Naturally the non-performance of an application or execution might constitute a condition of another norm which attaches a sanction to it, but unlike in the case of obedience, this is not necessary. If our endeavour can profit from von Wright's (1963: vi–vii) investigation, more specifically from his doubt whether 'not-doing' can refer to 'the mere fact that a certain thing is not done' or to 'the forbearance of some agent from doing this thing', then it seems that inefficacy of primary norms can be only thought of as a particular state of affairs in which there is no application or no execution, or that an agent forbears applying or executing a norm. This, however, becomes problematic in the realm of application, especially when it comes to adjudication, for such acts do not result in mere changes to the state of affairs but rather in prescriptions of how certain state of affairs ought to come into being as a result of action, a mode of action von Wright (1963: 75) called '*normative action*'.[22] To explain the fact that a norm comes into being through application – that

[22] See n 17.

is, it starts to '*exist*' – is, as von Wright (1963: vi–vii) confessed, 'extremely difficult'. However, as Kelsen's (1967: 233 ff [1960: 239 ff]) solution suffices for our purpose I will move on for now. The problem becomes more acute in the case of adjudication and cannot be avoided. As such, I will dedicate the coming section to this discussion. Before that, the reasoning so far can be illustrated.

Considering again *Norm A*, its fragment A.4 states a primary norm which commands the municipality, through some of its organs, to impose a definite set of sanctions in case of violation of fragment A.1. In this case, as we have seen, the violation of A.1 occurs either when vendors use the square without the proper permit (*first form of disobedience*) or when they sell forbidden goods (*second form of disobedience*). In order to perform what A.4 demands, upon identifying any form of disobedience the municipal organ has to issue a fine, seize the equipment and the merchandise, suspend the activity, or revoke the vending permit, depending on the concrete situation of disobedience (eg, the kind of merchandise being sold, whether the seller is recidivist, the terms of the permit, etc; see Arts 29 to 40 of Decree 9,300/1994). In such cases, *Norm A* obtains efficacy not by obedience, but by application (the public organ fines the seller, suspends the licence for some days, or revokes the licence) and its respective execution (the public organ seizes the goods and equipment, or takes the licence back). As we have seen, efficacy cannot be assured by application itself, meaning that the sanctions applied need to be either obeyed by the norm addressee (the fine is paid, the selling is ceased)[23] or factually imposed (bank account is frozen, the vendor is removed, the goods are seized). Either way, these are mediate forms of compliance with *Norm A*, which becomes heteronomously efficacious despite the disobedience (*enforcement of Norm A*). In such cases, the determination of the concrete situation of disobedience, as well as the procedures to properly apply or execute the norm, demands a more extensive knowledge of other pieces of legislation. This is due to the fact that the sanctions vary according to the kind of merchandise being sold, whether the seller is recidivist, the terms of the permit, etc, and the public organ must comply with other fragments of the norm, which in principle do not need to be known in detail by the norm addressee, such as the one that commands the filling of the appropriate seizure report (Article 34 of Decree 9,300/1994).

[23] Here it seems appropriate to distinguish obedience (in a *strong sense*) as the first degree of compliance from obedience (in a *weak sense*) of an order applied, as the latter takes place only after a norm was already disobeyed. In terms of voluntariness, the second is actually the unfolding of a law enforcement process. This distinction makes the analysis of compliance more precise, since it measures how important or unimportant law enforcement is for a norm to achieve its efficacy and, hence, the need for execution. However, this distinction might get blurred when we leave the domestic level and observe the dynamics of obedience and application between nation states and international courts concerning international treaties. There is a body of studies concerning this specific point. For a list of references, see Kapiszewski and Taylor (2013: 805). For a more detailed study of these dynamics, see Calabria (2018).

Were one to construct a complete *Norm A*, the following fragment could also be added:

(A.4.1) It commands the enforcement organ to follow the respective procedure according to the sanction being applied or executed (Article 29 to 40 of Decree 9,300/94).

Obviously, for each kind of sanction to be enforced, one could specify the fragment above into other series of fragments of prohibitions, commands, permissions, and authorisations. Moreover, the activity of street vending could also be subject to other pieces of legislation, which should likewise be known by the enforcing organ. If the vendor, for instance, is selling imported goods without proper clearance, or pirated CDs and DVDs, the public organ must know that, beyond the administrative punishments, the vendor may be sentenced to imprisonment, since the selling of such goods constitutes the crime of improper clearance (Article 334, § 1, III, of the Penal Code) or copyright violation (Article 184, § 2, of the Penal Code), respectively. In such terms, *Norm A* could not be comprehensively understood without referring to other legal texts that affect its spheres of validity and, consequently, attach more fragments to it, such as:

(A.2.1) The selling of goods forbidden by the Penal Code cannot be permitted by administrative regulations.

From this standpoint, the application and execution are bound not only to *Norm A* alone, but also to the intricate system of norms that regulate the behaviour of enforcing authorities. In this perspective, second-degree forms of compliance may constitute first-degree forms of compliance with other norms. For instance, in the case of crimes the Code of Penal Procedure states that 'any of the people may and police authorities and their agents shall arrest anyone found in flagrante delicto' (Article 301 of *Decreto-Lei 5.452/1943*). This would add the following fragment to A.4:

(A.4.2) If the commerce is of forbidden goods according to the Penal Code, the organ shall also arrest the vendor.[24]

That a primary norm is applied and executed means that the agent performed the expected behaviour of enforcing the sanction when identifying the disobedience. However, primary norms can also be violated, if violation is taken to mean that the expected performance did not occur, that is, the application or the execution did not take place. There seems to be four distinct situations leading to this. It might be the case that the municipality is not able to deploy enforcement measures for all the cases of disobedience of *Norm A*. In such circumstances, the noncompliance with A.4 is a result of a more encompassing

[24] It could be discussed here whether municipal agents, such as inspectors, could be deemed to be a 'police authority', since in Brazil only the federation and the states can have security forces. However, there seems to be more or less a consensus that, for the purpose of the Code of Penal Procedure, municipal agents have the obligation to arrest somebody if they are caught red-handed.

state of affairs in which enforcement fails due to a lack of resources or apparatuses, which points to a more structural form of noncompliance with *Norm A*. This form is better analysed in the context of structural noncompliance (see chapter six). It might happen, however, that despite having the proper enforcement task force, the norm addressee successfully escapes the sanction (*failure of enforcing Norm A*). Running from the inspectors is an example of this. Furthermore, it might also be the case that the public organ forbears applying or executing the respective sanction. Forbearance in this case has to be understood in a strong sense: 'an agent forbears only such action as he knows he can perform on the occasion in question' and 'he knows he can perform but *decides* (chooses, prefers) to leave undone on the occasion in question'. In such terms, 'forbear' means 'abstain or forsake' (von Wright 1963: 45–46).[25] Thus one form of non-complying with A.4 is forbearing to apply or execute the respective sanction when disobedience of *Norm A* is identified. The public organ can apply and execute the respective sanctions but decides not to, ultimately assuring the inefficacy of *Norm A* (*forbearance of enforcing Norm A*). Of course, as previously mentioned, this kind of forbearance might constitute an element of another norm which attaches a sanction to it. If the agent, for instance, receives money to forbear, the agent commits the crime of passive corruption (Article 317, § 1, of the Penal Code). If the forbearance is to satisfy personal interest or feeling, the crime is that of prevarication (Article 319 of the Penal Code). In such cases, the public organ also disobeys another norm, but this is merely contingent and does not characterise the second degree of noncompliance, since it does not change the fact that *forbearance of enforcing Norm A* occurred, making *Norm A* inefficacious at this level, regardless of whether the disobeyed norm will be duly enforced and the public organ will be punished.[26]

There is yet another sense in which a public organ does not comply with A.4. It is not properly by forbearing to apply and execute the sanction, but by doing this while abusing the power conferred to do so. In this case, there is some sort of overenforcement, for the public organ acts in excess by doing more than expected (*abuse of enforcing Norm A*). The sanction is not properly carried out as it should be, imposing more harm than the norm addressee should bear. Consider the following fragment:

(A.4.1.1) In the case of seizure, the enforcing authority shall make a seizure notice containing: the full name, address, and identity of the offender; specification of the equipment or goods; date and place of seizure; deadline for removal of the seized equipment or goods; and indication of the breached article.

[25] It corresponds to the sense of '*forgoing a command*' used by Winter (1985: 221) when an agency – or, as I would say, agent – is not only empowered but also mandated to do so. This includes, as I see it, the '*forgoing the denial of a permit*' when the agent is mandated to deny it.

[26] This argues once more in favour of not describing application or execution in terms of obedience. See n 8.

If for instance, the public organ does not specify the equipment or goods seized, the vendor who suffered the sanction will be unable to recover them. In a sense, the vendor experiences greater harm than legally expected. This kind of over-enforcement is to be understood as noncompliance with A.4.1.1, since one of its commands was violated; therefore, it is also noncompliance with A.4.1, A.4, and, ultimately, *Norm A*. By definition the performance of the public organ does not correspond to the behaviour prescribed, making it illegal. Thus, instead of making *Norm A* efficacious by enforcement, the public organ actually uses *Norm A* merely as a token to exert a burden that is not prescribed by the norm as a consequence for disobedience. In this precise sense, one does not say that *Norm A* was enforced, but rather abused.

All these forms of noncompliance give us a glimpse at how complex and challenging it may be to achieve efficacy in a context where enforcement of norms is to a considerable extent prone to failure, forbearance, and abuse. In this respect, law enforcement cannot be taken for granted as the natural unfolding of lawmaking. On the contrary, one is forced to expect that, in arenas where second-degree compliance is compromised, the intended impacts of law- and policymaking will be *pari passu* uncertain. For the interactions between enforcement agencies and norm addressees are subject to specific dynamics that in such circumstances hardly can be controlled through legislative initiatives. In this sense, the regulated reality is always much more complex than can be captured by simple measurements of autonomous efficacy, such as measurements of obedience or compliance in the narrowest sense. Without a proper grasp of both levels, one cannot even be sure to what extent legal norms can actually guide expectations or orient behaviour in a given context so that they will be perceived as legally binding and capable of defining what is legal or illegal. In such circumstances, the organisations that lie in between lawmaking and law enforcement have the complex challenge of handling this distance in order to maintain the legal system as operational, and courts are perhaps the most striking example of that.

5.3. THE THIRD DEGREE: CONSISTENCY VERSUS INCONSISTENCY

It is true that in Kelsen's (1967: 234–35 [1960: 240]) framework, application is an umbrella term covering every single legal act apart from the borderline case of the basic norm. Except for execution, it is characterised as 'the creation of a lower norm on the basis of a higher norm'. However, when examining such acts from the perspective of their efficacy, three forms of application became relevant. Two of them, which constitute law enforcement acts, have already been examined in this chapter: application as a general act of compliance with primary norms whose result is another norm (usually individual and concrete) and execution as a strict form of imposition. The third form of application, which is generally delegated to courts, is that of adjudication. There are three reasons for making adjudication a special case. First, acts of adjudication cannot be assessed in terms of noncompliance with primary norms in exactly the same way that general acts of application or execution can be (that is, failure, forbearance, or abuse). Second, they entail a very specific cognitive process of norm-creation – the most complex one within a legal system – which eventually involves a further distinction between norm as principles and norms as rules (each with specific forms of efficacy).[27] Third, they are usually performed by a court, which is a type of organisation that has a very specific position within a legal system. I shall discuss each of these reasons in order to understand how acts of adjudication can be assessed in terms of compliance and noncompliance.

Considering the 'process of increasing individualization and concretization' as conceived by Kelsen (1967: 237 [1960: 242]), the creation of norms by courts through judicial decisions is at the 'transitional stage' that begins with lawmaking (establishment of the constitution, legislation, statutes, customs) and ends with the execution of sanctions. Its function is to ascertain, in a concrete case, whether the conditions of a sanction exist. This implies the ascertainment that there is a norm attaching a sanction to these conditions, and to order the respective sanction to be applied if this is the case. As judicial decisions by their very nature consist of the application of law, not only the order issued but also the ascertainment of facts have a 'constitutive' character; that is to say, even when dealing with facts, it is an 'error' to see judicial decisions as having a 'merely declaratory function' (1967: 237 [1960: 242]). It is constitutive in the sense that, regardless of whether the fact occurred, the opinion of the court is what brings the fact into legal existence. The court constitutes not only when and how the fact occurred, but also the legal effects that will be produced as a consequence of that fact, ie, whether an individual ought to be punished or acquitted for that fact, or the case should be dismissed, or a certain sanction must be executed. This relatively broad discretion, of course, does not mean that a judicial decision cannot be reformed if the parties find the ascertainment of the court to be erroneous. For 'the *subjective* meaning of the act of such decision need not yet be accepted definitely as its *objective* meaning' (1967: 240 [1960: 246]). Only when the decision becomes *res judicata* – final and unappealable – does it acquire a definitive objective meaning. Even if others find that 'the judicial decision was rendered by a court incompetent to sit, or in a faulty procedure' or 'the delict was committed by an individual other than the sentenced one or that the delict which he actually did commit was different from the one for which he was sentenced', the court decision is in all cases to produce its effects and, unless there is another procedure to reverse the decision, what the court has decided 'must be accepted as a fact *in itself*' (1967: 241 [1960: 246–47]). Such reasoning has important consequences that must be accounted for. On the one hand, despite considering that such

[27] See in this regard Ávila (2007: 54 ff [2011: 97 ff]).

acts are 'usually predetermined' by 'general norms of formal and material law' (1967: 242 [1960: 247–48]), one cannot avoid the highly constructivist implication that ultimately what governs the application of law by courts is its competence to state the facts as well as the law to be applied. On the other hand, there is in a sense room for manoeuvre whereby the court always applies the legal order when deciding a concrete case, either to ascertain that 'the defendant or accused has committed the delict' or that 'the defendant or accused has not committed the delict' and their respective consequences, namely that it 'finds for the plaintiff or condemns the accused or dismisses the action or acquits the accused' (1967: 242–43 [1960: 248]).

Against this background, it becomes difficult to analyse the performance of a court in terms of compliance or noncompliance with a given norm, a problem which in Kelsen's terms would turn out to be irrelevant in the same way as it is 'to consider the decision subjectively as being in conformity or contrary to law' (1967: 270 [1960: 274]), unless the consideration is made by an authority with competence to change the decision. In contrast to enforcement acts, which are more factual impositions than law creation and can therefore be assessed in terms of correspondence between the performance of the enforcement agent and the expected imposition prescribed by the norm, the performance of adjudication entails a decision about the facts as well as the selection of the norms relevant to govern these facts. If one goes to the extreme of that assertion, as Müller (1994: 263–65) does, one could say that the 'legal norm' is actually created 'in the middle' of the process of adjudication and does not even exist before that.[28] According to such a rationale, 'legal norms would not be predetermined, finished and "applicable" to cases', and, as counterintuitive as it may seem, 'the legislator, realistically seen, has not issued norms but only the norms' texts'. I do not intend to assume all of the linguistic presuppositions or the practical implications of this approach, some of which are hard to agree with.[29] What matters here is to demonstrate how adjudication involves a considerably complex procedure of norm-creation that accounts not only for the facts and the norms brought to litigation but also for a more comprehensive notion of the legal order, which has to be taken into consideration as a system of legal norms.

[28] That is why according to Müller the theory of the norm is also a theory of application or, to use his words, concretisation. As he puts it, his approach 'offers a general structural model of legal norms and also a theoretical framework for the structuring of legal decision-making processes' (Müller 1994: 233).

[29] As Neves (2021: 98 [2013: 126–27]) rightfully questioned, 'if legal norms arise only at the end of the concretizing process, judges and other officials in charge of interpreting and applying the law would not be subject to any legal norm in their activity of law concretization'. The attempt to extract elements of decision from the facts of the case also seems problematic; or, in Walter's words, 'he is not able to justify the possibility of this approach'. Indeed, the reformulation of a large number of legal problems in a 'not very clear language and a highly inappropriate systematics' also does not help (Walter 1975: 444).

This procedure is at least twofold: it creates the individual and concrete norm (as happens with application in general), but at the same time it builds the abstract legal norm from which the former is derived. In Müller's (1994: 266) terminology, this is explained in the relation between the 'legal norm' [*Rechtsnorm*] and the 'decision norm' [*Entscheidungsnorm*].[30] The creation of the 'legal norm' in the process of adjudication means that the norm, or any of its fragments, may gain quite different contours from what one could expect by observing the interpretations carried out by the norm addressee or even the enforcing authorities. This is especially true when adjudication involves constitutional reasoning, out of which there is always the possibility of a 'derivative norm' (Alexy 1986: 60) to appear.[31] Norms that might seem prima facie capable of solving a case might, during the adjudication, be overruled, distinguished, or limited by other colliding norms which are equally valid. But it might also be the case that, if there is no legal framework to guide adjudication, 'it must simply be invented' (Luhmann 2004: 288 [1995: 317]), once the *non liquet* is prohibited. Apart from the specificities of this judge-made law, whereby 'the court itself "creates" the law that it "applies"' (Luhmann 2004: 281 [1995: 306]), such legal reasoning is not relevant on the plane of the mere daily obedience and bureaucratic application[32] in which the legal order as a unity in principle neither emerges as a key point of reference nor has to be dealt with in terms of argumentation. Given that the interpretation of the norm at the level of adjudication is carried out by a very specific process of legal argumentation,[33] we may call this a third degree of compliance with a norm, which refers to the norm in its most complex formulation.

Out of such a framework, in which interpretation is in essence the creation of individual and concrete as well as the general and abstract norm (or, if one prefers, the fixation of its frame and meaning), it may be tempting to think of

[30] The former being the norm which is co-constituted by the linguistic data of the legal text (what he calls the 'program of the norm') and the input of the case which the norm intends to solve (the 'field of the norm').

[31] I do not disregard that Alexy and Müller offer different and, to a certain extent, opposing theoretical approaches. See in this regard Alexy (1986: 63–70). For a proper criticism of using both as if they were compatible, focusing especially on the Brazilian context, see Silva (2005: 136–39). However, it seems to me that what Alexy calls a 'derivative norm' is in practical terms a kind of 'legal norm' in Müller, even though he points out some similarities instead with the decision norm (1986: 69).

[32] *cf* Neves (2021: 64 and 76–78 [2013: 78 and 95–98]), referring however to the discussion about principles and rules. For daily obedience and bureaucratic application, 'the verbal meaning of the text suffices' (Luhmann 2004: 306 [1993: 340]). Of course, when concerned parties question the norm to be obeyed or applied, they may problematise the norm and eventually enter the level of 'argumentation'.

[33] By this I do not mean that decisions must have an extensive, convincing argumentation in order to create the law to be applied in a concrete case. Courts are naturally constrained by different kinds of pressure (time, workload, media coverage, etc). How courts came to handle the 'pressure of compulsory decision-making' and 'argumentation' is another problem; see Luhmann (2004: esp 288 [1993: 315]). What is at stake here, in Luhmannian terminology, is the argumentation at the 'level of second-order observation' (2004: 306–07 [1993: 340]).

judge-made law as the ultimate source of law.[34] However, this kind of interpretation cannot be properly understood without the distinction between legislation and jurisdiction. Apart from the historical movements toward the differentiation within the legal system,[35] such distinction was made possible through the differentiation of 'proceedings', in the sense that 'it depends on the evolution of norms of competence and their restrictive conditioning' (Luhmann 2004: 277 [1995: 302]), enabling some sort of double contingency between the judge and the legislator. Whereas the former 'must attempt to recognize the intentions of the legislator and how they observed the world', the latter 'must also anticipate in which forms cases are brought to the courts and how they are seen and managed there' (2004: 278 [1995: 302]).[36] This allows courts to avoid the circularity between creation and application by resorting to methodologies for 'interpretation of the intentions behind legislation' (2004: 278 [1995: 302]), by presenting its decisions as if they were a result of '"finding" of law' (2004: 281 [1995: 306]); that is to say, by creating asymmetry between legislation and jurisdiction. And as Luhmann insightfully noted, this must be done under a very singular and specific condition: deciding the case without the possibility of not deciding it.[37]

The 'prohibition of denial of justice' is, in Luhmann's account, the socio-historical condition that seems to differentiate courts from every other institution of the legal system and, ultimately, the kind of interpretation they realise.[38] As he observed, 'contracts need not be concluded and statutes need not be passed (unless specified otherwise in the constitution), but courts have to decide every case submitted to them' (2004: 284 [1995: 310]). Indeed, individuals are not obliged to contract with each other (even though this is done every day), lawyers do not have to advise or to litigate, and public officers may be equipped with discretion, but courts have no choice but to decide when cases are brought to them. The pressure to decide also ends up being the pragmatic excuse to cut the otherwise never-ending process of interpreting the facts and the legal texts. And the practical difficulties that come as a by-product are mitigated by 'more or less formal decisions', grounded for instance on 'rules on the onus of proof, failures to observe time-limits, rules about standing, rules of procedure' (2004: 286 [1995: 313]). Moreover, the tension between

[34] Perhaps the most striking example is the American legal realism originated in Holmes (1997). For its influence, see Burton (2000). Some strands of Scandinavian legal realism are in the same vein, as can be seen in Ross (1959: 75 ff, 2019: 89 ff).

[35] For a historical account, see Luhmann (2004: 275 ff [1993: 299 ff]). Parsons (1962: 63) also tried to explain the specificity of 'authoritative interpretations' from courts, which were made possible with the achievement of '"judicial independence" from political pressure, professionalization of the judicial role, and institutionalization of the decision-making process'.

[36] See also Neves (2021: 74–76 [2013: 92–94]).

[37] For the meaning and consequences of 'compulsory decision-making', see Luhmann (2004: 284–99 [1993: 310–19]).

[38] Parsons (1962: 163), although in a different framework, also noted how courts are a 'very special type of social organization' that 'institutionalizes the process of arriving at decisions'. See also n 35.

the need for a compelling argumentation and the compulsory task to decide paves the way for the different legal forms to handle this tension. Justification through 'legal principles' to solve 'hard cases',[39] the binding force of the *ratio decidendi* of precedents,[40] and the institution of *res judicata* are some examples of how argumentation can be facilitated to frame cases for which no apparent legislated solution is available, to transcend singular cases in order to avoid (or solve) future litigation, or to protect the decision against further complaints in case of material or procedural errors. In contexts like the Brazilian one, the prohibition of denial of justice is even further fortified into a 'non-obviation of jurisdiction' (Article 5, XXXV, of the Brazilian Constitution), which makes courts the last resort for reviewing violations and hence for deciding what is to be deemed to be legal or illegal, even when it comes to legislative or governmental acts.[41] By doing this, courts are tasked with providing consistency to the legal system by supervising other 'legal decisions (for example, those of statutes, contracts, judicial decisions)'. And they do this through the singular way that they interpret law: 'argumentatively and in order to present the *ratio* of their own decisions' (2004: 297 [1995: 327]).

This task of providing consistency reveals another face of the prohibition of denial of justice. Courts not only have to decide, but they also have to deliver justice while deciding. Evidently, in a modern, complex ('polycontextural'[42]) society with differentiated legal practices, it is hard to advocate a universally accepted conception of justice to be applied within legal procedures.[43] In a context where 'the conditions for an idea of justice based on natural law have vanished' and 'all legal norms and decisions, all reasons and arguments can take a different form' (2004: 215 [1995: 221]) than the form they actually took, justice can only be formulated contingently in each operation, as a '*formula for contingency* of the legal system' (2004: 214 [1995: 218]).[44] This implies that justice has to be generalised to the extent that every operation and structure of the system are expected to be just and, at the same time, re-specified to provide orientation for individual cases. Historically, the generalisation, as accounted by Luhmann (2004: 217 [1993: 223]), was achieved through the identification

[39] See in this regard Dworkin (1977a).

[40] For a study of precedents in Brazil, see Lopes Filho (2014).

[41] There is a worldwide trend towards courts taking an increasing role in addressing a varying range of subjects, especially those of moral and political nature. For a general account of this so-called 'judicialization', see Hirschl (2008).

[42] For the notion of 'poly-contexturality' and how it describes a morally fragmented society, see Luhmann (1997: 75). For the 'threatening' effects of this fragmentation, see Günther (1979) and with an assessment in terms of justice see Teubner (2009 [2008]).

[43] Such an assumption naturally regards as problematic the adoption of concepts of justice as conventionally discussed within the debate 'liberalism' versus 'communitarianism'. See in this regard Neves (2001b). For a more general criticism, *cf* Taylor (1991). For an account of how justice goes from the notion of perfection toward handling contingency, see Luhmann (2015b: 378 ff).

[44] It is important to note here that the English term 'justice' is being used in a slightly different context, namely in the sense of the German *Gerechtigkeit*. Before, the term was being used in the sense of *Justiz*, which is more related to the judiciary.

of justice with '*equality*', that is, 'something akin to regularity or consistency'. For the legal system, this means treating similar cases alike. In the same way that equality as a two-sided form also refers to its other side – inequality – justice entails 'the postulate that different cases be treated differently' (2004: 218 [1993: 223]). Justice is thus translated in 'the rule by which equal cases are decided equally (and consequently: unequal cases unequally)' (2004: 220 [1993: 227]). In an increasingly complex society, this brings about another task: courts also have to adapt the legal system to its environment, to handle its complexity, to have 'irritability' (2004: 219 [1993: 225]), or to be – if one wants to put it in other terms – 'responsive' (Nonet and Selznick 2017), and 'reflexive' (Teubner 1983). For this reason, justice is presented in systems theory as an '*adequate complexity* of consistent decision-making' (Luhmann 2004: 218 [1993: 223]). Against this background, the difference between legislation and jurisdiction can be presented in terms of variety/redundancy. Whereas decision-making in courts has to follow a principle of consistency in order to repeat previous decisions from similar cases and make law thus redundant, lawmaking aims to change the programmes and criteria according to which cases have to be decided, stimulating variety instead of redundancy. In this sense, 'legislation is necessarily adverse to the consistency of decision-making since it constantly changes the law' and, furthermore, 'makes it possible to decide equal cases unequally and unequal cases equally, depending on whether a decision is made before or after the passing of a statute' (2004: 222 [1993: 229]).

This notion of justice is of utmost importance to this analysis. It helps by providing the criterion of consistency for assessing the performance of adjudication according to the justice delivered in a given case and, consequently, whether a court complies or not with a given norm by the way this norm rules similar cases.[45] As a by-product, this criterion also drives out the need for pursuing normative theories for this assessment.[46] In addition it enables a further

[45] With the approach I am proposing here, it becomes easier to understand the problem often posed in very general terms that, in contexts of high informality, there is a lack of consistency in the application of norms. This is, for instance, the case of ILO, which long since urged: 'National governments and local authorities should promote efficient bureaucracies that are corruption and harassment free, are transparent and *consistent in the application of rules and regulations*, and that protect and enforce contractual obligations and respect the rights of workers and employers.' (ILO 2002b: conclusion 30, emphasis mine).

[46] This is seen in theories that advocate, for instance, one 'right answer' (Dworkin 1985: 119 ff) or a 'correct justification' (Alexy 1986: 61) to determine the accordance between the decision's result and the right answer or correct norm. In such terms, it is possible to say of a court decision whether it complies or does not comply with a norm, but this would not solve the problem faced here. In addition to the difficulties in generalising normative solutions in a society constituted by a shattered morality and structured by dissensus (ie, where people intensively disagree on what is to be taken as right, just, or correct), such approaches are exclusively focused on determining the dimension of validity of a norm and have – to say the least – little to offer for the study of efficacy. Our concern does not lie in the righteousness, justness, or correctness of a norm or of a behaviour, but rather in the assessment of whether a behaviour performs the content of a norm; in other words, whether it complies or does not comply with a norm. For a more detailed study about the management of subject-related dissensus through procedural consensus, see Neves (2001a: esp 136 ff); see also Neves (2006: 136 ff).

characterisation of arenas of noncompliance: they are marked by high grades of inconsistency in judicial decision-making. Often courts produce different norms to decide similar cases (what I shall call *horizontal inconsistency*) and also different norms to decide the same case if the case is brought before other instances of adjudication (*vertical inconsistency*). In this sense there is a very low grade of redundancy in courts. As a backlash to this high level of variation in judicial decision-making, it is common to see the enactment of laws to provide consistency to the legal order, repeating contents otherwise to be found in provisions, statutes, ordinances, and normative acts that had already been enacted but that had not found resonance in the courts.[47]

When it comes to the assessment of adjudication, there is still a subtle distinction to be made. As already seen, an act of adjudication brings about two different outcomes in a judicial decision: the legal norm construed through argumentation to be applied in the case – to avoid misunderstandings, henceforth called the *adjudication norm*[48] – and the decision norm, which is the result of the application of the former, constituting in a narrow sense the solution of the case. There are two distinct modes of assessing these outcomes. The first takes the decision norm as a paradigm of analysis, that is as an order directed to individuals who ought to behave according to the ruling. In this sense, decisions have the same character as any other normative text (such as statutes, ordinances, etc), issuing commands, permissions, or prohibitions. Therefore, one can assess whether the court decision was in fact obeyed, applied, or executed; in other words, whether it was efficacious. In this mode of assessment, however, the act of adjudication itself is not being assessed, but rather the obedience by the concerned parties or the enforcement by the concerned authorities; and everything presented in the previous sections about obedience and application holds true to assess the efficacy of the decision norm. The second mode of assessing court decisions is specifically concerned with the adjudication norm and thus with its creation by the adjudicating authority through argumentation. It is this assessment that the third degree of compliance refers to. The question to be posed here is whether the adjudication norm is being applied in the same case or in similar cases, that is, whether it finds vertical and horizontal consistency in the legal system – or, if one wants to be more precise, in the courts. Naturally such a question gives rise to considerable challenges, as it demands a qualitative analysis of the argumentation employed by the adjudicating authority in order

[47] This phenomenon can be in part described in terms of 'symbolic legislation', more specifically as a kind of 'alibi legislation' (Kindermann 1989: 269–70; Neves 2022: 24–27 [2011: 36–41]).

[48] It corresponds to what Müller calls 'legal norm'; see n 31. It could also be called a 'derivative norm', as it is to a certain extent similar to Alexy's formulation except for two things: on the one hand, it is not necessarily a result of a 'correct justification' (Alexy 1986: 61); on the other hand, it does not need to be bound to fundamental rights, but any norm subject to a more complex interpretation (that is, unfolding of fragments) during adjudication. It refers, in Neves's (2021: 11 [2013: 3]) terminology, to 'norm statement' but exclusively produced by adjudicating-authorities.

to be sure of the contours of the adjudication norm. I shall illustrate below how this assessment may be carried out.

Considering fragments A.2.1 and A.4.2 previously mentioned, it is prohibited for street vendors to sell forbidden goods according to the Penal Code under the penalty of arrest. As argued in the last section, these fragments are derived from statutes that affect the spheres of validity of *Norm A*. Since the activity of street vending is intersected by different norms that happen to regulate the use of public space for itinerant commerce, those fragments could be further unfolded as there are norms apt to be applied accordingly. For instance, taking the following norm (henceforth: *Norm B*):

B The selling of imported goods without proper clearance is prohibited (Article 334, § 1, III, of the Penal Code).

In the case *MPF v Zhu Min Pan and Wang Cui Qin*,[49] two street vendors selling goods on a sidewalk in Fortaleza were arrested by the federal police because they were selling imported goods without the proper receipts, disobeying *Norm B*. In the first instance, the judge decided to dismiss the charge due to the low value of the goods (R$ 389.00).[50] According to him, this value would be irrelevant for tax purposes, let alone criminal. Furthermore, he understood that there was no criminal intent, since the selling was taking place during daylight in competition with other sellers; that 'the large-scale trading of foreign products without proper documentation is usually tolerated in the eyes and with lenience of society and the authorities responsible to fight against smuggling'; and that there was absolutely no 'social danger in the alleged crime' (pp 1–2 of the sentence). It was also interesting how, among his arguments, he backed up his position with an attempt to adapt the norm to a very specific social reality:

> … the accused, as a general rule, seek an answer, in this informal trade of goods of low value (some of them of foreign origin), to the inherent necessities of life, given the continuous limitations of the formal labour market (in contrast with the growth of the active population); [criminal charges like this] represent an extra burden on the shoulders of a Justice distressed with the queue of individual and socially more expressive and urgent cases. In other words, the state can no longer worry about facts of little juridical relevance, otherwise important events will lose space for those, thus drowning the already troubled legal order of the country.

All the argumentation employed to dismiss the charge could be summarised in an adjudication norm that prescribes the 'principle of insignificance' (or 'bagatelle') to rule the case. This norm permits a behaviour that *prima facie* is criminal, but due to the small damage resulted it shall not be considered a

[49] For the purpose here, this case is formed by lawsuit no 0008345-89.2001.4.05.8100 TRF5/JFCE, appeal 'RSE 526/CE' before the TRF 5, *Habeas Corpus* 40.384/CE filed before the Superior Tribunal of Justice (STJ), and appeal 'RHC 94.905/CE' before the Supreme Federal Court (STF).

[50] Applying the rates used by the valuation expert consulted in the case at the time, which was 1 USD = 2.5 BRL, the amount was about U$ 155.60.

crime, deeming it as a trifling matter. In this concrete case, the adjudication norm is constructed as a fragment of *Norm B*, having the following deontic expression:

(B.1') The selling by street vendors of low value imported goods without proper clearance is permitted.

I used the apostrophe in B.1' to mark the fragment as an adjudication norm, ie, a norm specifically built through argumentation in case law. It was exactly the possibility of application of this norm that stood in the centre of the appeals that followed the first ruling. On the appeal brought by the MPF before the TRF5, the second instance for federal jurisdiction, the ruling was reversed on the grounds that the principle of insignificance could not be applied when 'the practice of trading goods of foreign origin without the corresponding tax documentation was habitual'. The appellate court decided thus that the permission provided by B.1' does not apply if the practice is habitual. Even though its decision norm was to reverse the dismissal, consequently moving the charge against the vendors forward, its adjudication norm (which could be further developed into a fragment, say B.1.1', in order to dispel B.1' in case of habitual practice) rendered the behaviour of the two street vendors illegal. The appellate court's ruling was later affirmed with one dissenting opinion on a *Habeas Corpus* filled before the Superior Court of Justice (STJ), but with a slightly different justification: considering some precedents of the court, Article 20 of Law 10,522/02, which at the time prescribed that court claims for taxes lower than R$ 10,000.00 should be dismissed,[51] could not be invoked to regulate the relevance of tax debts in criminal matters; only Article 18 of the same law, which provides for the extinction of tax debts equal or lower than R$ 100.00,[52] could be invoked for criminal purposes.[53] On appeal, the Supreme Federal Court (STF) ordered the first-instance judge to dismiss the criminal charge based on precedents that considered that the principle of insignificance should be applied in smuggling cases whenever the sum of the goods was lower than the value established by Article 20 of Law 10,522/02. In practical terms, B.1' was affirmed, despite the slightly different justification, with a significant change: the permission holds even if the selling is habitual and as long as it does not surpass the limit that enables a court claim for taxes. In practical terms, the behaviour of the vendors was adjudicated as not disobeying *Norm B*.

[51] Applying the rates mentioned in n 50, that amounted to U$ 4,000.00. Since 2019, this Article has been amended, and the amount of the tax debt is now determined by act of the Attorney General of the National Treasury.

[52] Respectively U$ 40.00 at the time.

[53] Awkwardly, the leading opinion considered that 'the amount of the tax not collected, R$ 389.00 (three hundred and eighty-nine reais), exceeded the limit by which the state expressed its disinterest in the tax collection, so there is no talk of applying the principle of insignificance' (pp 2–3 of the Justice Hamilton Carvalhido's opinion), as if the tax to be collected was the same as the price of the goods.

This example, on the one hand, shows how the judiciary ultimately plays an important role in defining what is legal and illegal in a given context.[54] Without a proper examination of judge-made law, one cannot ascertain adequately which norms (and the respective fragments) are at stake in the regulation of a certain activity. On the other hand, it shows how adjudication, instead of diminishing uncertainty and hence providing specific legal orientation, can actually diminish consistency and increase variation. One could argue that courts are designed to review other decisions, and this does not signify that courts are inconsistent, otherwise their function would be par excellence to provide inconsistency to the system. Indeed, the variation of adjudication norms does not per se reveal inconsistency. However, if the example is carefully examined, one can notice that each court invoked 'precedents' to ground their ruling and thus the respective adjudication norm.[55] In a context where 'precedents' on the same subject are summoned to ground opposing solutions, it seems fair to say that, strictly speaking, there is no precedent at all. Therefore, inconsistency describes the failure of adjudication in providing equal treatment to similar cases without adequate justifications. It is in this sense that one can say that there is noncompliance with a norm in courts. Naturally, the problem does not lie in occasional, sporadic conflicting interpretations, but rather when a long swath of varying decisions are taken in the same or similar cases, to the extent that one cannot predict, based on the decisions, the chances of success if a similar case were brought before the judiciary.[56] The understanding of the norm (even with hindsight) at this level varies in such a way that, ultimately, one cannot say with confidence whether a certain behaviour will be deemed to be legal or illegal.

The variation of adjudication norms should not in principle be a major issue for the legal system. It is common to see procedural mechanisms specifically designed to overcome inconsistencies and unify varying interpretations.[57] It becomes particularly problematic though in arenas of noncompliance, where the inconsistent norm is to a large extent disobeyed and also not enforced. Under such circumstances, judge-made law tends to be overwhelmingly disconnected from the reality of the norm addressees and the practices of

[54] Of course, that does not mean that the codification between what is legal or illegal belongs to courts. Such codification is the *proprium* of the legal system as a whole and encompasses every legal communication. See Luhmann (2004: 98 ff [1993: 66 ff]).

[55] TRF5 invoked the HC 33.455/RS, a case already ruled by STJ. In the STJ, the winning opinion summoned the Resp 685.135/PR, HC 38.965/RS, Resp 742.895/PR, HC 32.576/RS, and HC 41.700/RS; the dissenting, by *apud*, the cases in Ackel Filho, JTACrimSP 94 (1988). The STF, in turn, invoked the cases HC 100.365/PR, HC 96.819/PR, HC 97.096/MG, HC 100.316/SC, HC 94.058, RHC 96.545/SC, HC 96.309/RS, and HC 92.364/RJ, RHC 89.624/RS, HC 88.393/RJ.

[56] In this sense, previous decisions and arguments do not diminish the 'surprise value' of future arguments and decisions in similar cases. *cf* Neves (2021: 146 [2013: 196]), however, focusing on the constitutional level.

[57] In Brazil, this is usually done through procedural mechanisms such as *Recursos Repetitivos*, *Súmulas*, and *Súmulas Vinculantes*.

enforcement authorities, and this disconnection does not come without major consequences. Decision norms become prone to inefficacy. Adjudication itself tends to present high degrees of inconsistency. Courts, instead of providing solutions to filter conflicting interpretations, frequently increase the difficulty in determining the legality of a behaviour. In such cases, noncompliance ceases to be a purely operational problem and reaches structural levels. Instead of being occasional events of nonfulfilment of a norm, either by individuals or state authorities, it becomes a somewhat permanent state of affairs in which courts are not able to solve conflicts, and people start to expect (and even rely on) failures, forbearances, or abuses of enforcement – sometimes doubting whether a certain illegal behaviour is, in fact, illegal. Naturally, this degree of noncompliance corresponds to a much deeper assessment of the phenomenon, for it involves not only the daily operations of the legal system, but also the formation of more or less stabilised structures, institutions, organisations, and networks which must be dealt with.

Part III

The Impacts of Noncompliance

Once noncompliance becomes pervasive and entrenched in society, that is, it achieves considerably high levels in all of its operational degrees, one can observe a series of impacts on the legal system. This part is dedicated to those impacts. In chapter six, the focus lies on the impacts on time and space and how they constitute action and experience in arenas of noncompliance. The concept of an arena will be presented as a modelling tool in chapter seven, that is, as a conceptual framework to organise the findings of the previous chapters. As a way of examining the material dimension of the arena, the last chapter will set out the impacts on this dimension, namely the spiralling deflation of political power and the emergence of a bartering rationality over law enforcement, which decentralise power, downgrade the state to a mere stakeholder in regulating arenas of noncompliance, and make the law flexible.

6

On Time and Space

6.1. FROM EVENTS TO STRUCTURES OF NONCOMPLIANCE

THUS FAR, I have been insisting on describing noncompliance as a multileveled phenomenon, in particular because it takes place in different forms and to varying degrees. The previous chapter was dedicated to presenting the set of operational degrees which encompass behaviours and decisions performed in violation of legal norms. They consist of events whose meaning was examined here through a very specific perspective, that of the legal system. Thus, they consist of legally relevant events, and for this reason, they are absorbed within the legal system as part of it. Once observed and communicated about in a legal framework, they reproduce the logic of the legal system, which ultimately means the reproduction of the legal system itself. It is in this sense that noncompliance at this level was described before in terms of operations or – more specifically – operations of the legal system. However, the phenomenon can reach a structural level, leading to much broader consequences. In order to examine these consequences, certain presuppositions ought to be clarified. First, I will start by contrasting events with structures.

Events have a very specific nature with regard to time. To use Allport's (1954: 292) terminology, they are a sort of macroscopic 'happening'. If one resorts to von Wright (1963: 26), 'events are facts which *happen*', but 'the happening of events is a *taking place* and not a *going on*'.[1] In any case, once events happen, they cease to exist. As Luhmann (1995d: 287 [1991: 389]) summarised, an event 'is the (socially smallest possible) temporal atom', forming the most basic element a social system can observe and deal with. Seen under the perspective of the legal system, events are internally processed as legal events and, hence, serve to update and simultaneously actualise the system, making the system itself also observable to the extent that further events can be attributed to previous ones as consequences, or – from our standpoint – legal consequences. That is why one can say, when observing this succession of events, that the legal

[1] Von Wright (1963: 35–36), however, does not call 'acts a kind or species of events'. For he conceives events as a '*change*' (1963: 28), and thus action may or may not bring about a change. Nonetheless, this particular distinction is not important here, but rather the insight according to which the event (and action likewise) is instantaneous, that is to say, it 'is momentary and immediately passes away' (Luhmann 1995d: 287 [1991: 389]).

system is 'in movement', 'functioning', 'working', or 'operating'. But what is important to note here is the connection between the events, or rather how a connection can be established so that the attribution of a line of 'causality' or 'continuity' between different events becomes possible. It is at this point that the concept of 'structure' comes into play.

Apart from the varying uses of the concept across different disciplines,[2] what is behind the notion of structure is that 'it defines how elements relate across temporal distance' (Luhmann 1995d: 282 [1991: 383]). This does not mean that structures are 'relations between elements'[3] nor that they 'can be materialized in every kind of element', but that unlike an event they endure in time and hence allow for the creation of multiple relations between elements. In those terms, they also define the possible relations between elements and create interdependencies between them, and thus constrain the meanings of the events that can be taken as elements by the respective structure. It is through constraining that a structure provides a system with 'internal guidance', 'invariance', and 'redundancy' (1995d: 283–85 [1991: 384–86]). Ultimately, all these features, if one sticks to Luhmann's (1995d: 285–86 [1991: 387]) reasoning, 'can be subsumed under the selection of a constraint'. Structures, then, are mechanisms through which constraints are selected and exerted upon actions, decisions, and communications. That is the reason why structures also have a constitutive character for a social system: they are the constant that enables the system to reproduce itself from one event to the next and to bear the changes each event brings about without losing its identity.[4]

If a social system is to report to actions as elements of its self-reproduction, it 'must then develop structures capable of connecting action-events together' (Luhmann 1995d: 287–88 [1991: 390]). And this connection is only possible if one can expect that a future action is going to happen, anticipating it, and orienting one's own behaviour accordingly. Therefore, structures for such systems can only consist of expectations of actions or – if one prefers – expectations of behaviour. Structures of expectations can not only connect actions but also, from a temporal perspective, bind them as if an action could 'escape its momentary transitoriness' (1995d: 289 [1991: 392]). In order to achieve this and keep the system reproducing itself through each event, 'the meaning of

[2] It is hard to account for the whole body of literature concerned with the concept of structure. For theoretical-comparative studies in social sciences that summarise some uses of the concept, see the book organised by Greshoff and Kneer (1999). Perhaps the most known contribution is provided by Lévi-Strauss (1963 [1958]) especially on the field of anthropology. But the concept itself has a longer history in linguistics with Saussure (1959 [1995]). For a brief account with regard to the 'structuralism' of Lévi-Strauss and the 'structural functionalism' of Parsons, see Luhmann (1995d: 278–82 [1991: 377–82]). I will follow the use as proposed by Luhmann.

[3] *cf* Maturana (1980: xx and 138).

[4] In systems theory, the relation among elements of a system is presented as its '*basal self-reference*'. The identity, however, is only achieved through two other levels of self-reference: 'reflexivity (processual self-reference)' and '*reflection*' (difference between system and environment). See Luhmann (1995d: 442 ff [1991: 600 ff]).

an action' has to be 'constituted within a horizon of expectation that anticipates further actions – whether by expecting that a meaningful sequence will continue (as with the next digit in the sequence when dialing a phone number) or by expecting complementary behavior of various sorts (as in opening the door when one hears the doorbell ring)' (1995d: 289 [1991: 392]). On the one hand, this implies that actions are 'always oriented by expectations' (1995d: 294 [1991: 400]). On the other hand, it is the existence of an expectation that creates further alternatives of behaviour, that is, reactions to what is expected. One either fulfils the expectation or disappoints it. This bifurcation can likewise be anticipated, and hence, considering that 'expectations are either given up when they have been disappointed or they are retained', one may opt in advance for the reaction, predetermining 'one's expectations as cognitive in the first case and as normative in the second' (2004: 149 [1995a: 133–34]). In other words, one either learns with the disappointment, and in this case the expectation serves to differentiate 'knowledge' from 'ignorance';[5] or one maintains the expectation notwithstanding, allowing the differentiation between 'compliant and deviant behavior' (1995d: 322 [1991: 439]). In any case, disappointment 'is a problem inherent to expectation' (1995d: 332 [1991: 452]) and 'consequently immanent in all structures' (2014: 32 [1987: 41]).

The capacity of an expectation to absorb disappointment is of utmost importance here since it underpins the very comprehension of normativity in society and is the key to understanding the passage from operations to structure. It is precisely this feature that allows one to observe, following Luhmann (2014: 32–33 [1987: 41–43]), the 'mechanisms for the handling of disappointments' that make behavioural expectations 'counterfactually stabilized' and thus recognisable as 'norms'. Through mechanisms of repair and maintenance, structures become institutionalised and gain the capacity of being 'independent of actual fulfilment or non-fulfilment', which is expressed by an 'unconditional validity', meaning one can with some security expect that certain behaviours ought to be performed even though in fact they might not be.[6] Naturally, the legal system plays a major role in generalising and securing such expectations, and – as it seems – it is the only social system capable of doing so in modern society (Luhmann 2014: 73 ff [1987: 94 ff], 2004: 142 ff [1995a: 124 ff], 2015a). The legal system functionally selects which norms in society are to be equipped

[5] The original German terms are *Wissen* and *Nichtwissen*. In the Spanish edition of *Social Systems*, the latter was translated to *no saber* (Luhmann 1998: 294), which amounts to 'non-knowledge'. The same translation was made, although in a different context, in *A Sociological Theory of Law* (2014: 216 [1987: 281]). For more details on how knowledge is achieved through generalisation of cognitive expectations, see Luhmann (1995d: 328 ff [1991: 447 ff]).

[6] As I briefly mentioned in ch 4, n 2, when summarising some concepts of norm. With the explanations provided in this section, it becomes easier to understand Luhmann's criticism of the traditional difference between *is* and *ought* as reported in ch 4, n 3. Cognitive and normative are both factual expectations and, in this sense, do not differ in quality from each other. The difference lies rather in the reaction to disappointment.

with the binary code of legality, transforming them into legal norms. This in turn orients which expectations one can rely on to predict the legal advantages and disadvantages of acting in conformity or with deviation. This kind of structure in turn makes it possible to observe compliance and noncompliance as operations of the legal system, that is to say, as events of fulfilment or nonfulfilment of expectations of behaviour. Granted that the norm is a structure that absorbs disappointment, the legal system is able not only to provide mechanisms to handle the disappointment, but also mostly to assure that, regardless of continuous disappointments, the expectation will stand, and one can count on it (2014: 40 ff [1987: 53 ff]). In such terms, noncompliance in principle should not represent a major issue for the legal system. On the contrary, it only makes sense to speak of law where deviant behaviour is a reality,[7] and the converse is also true: deviance can only be clearly distinguished if there are generalised expectations of behaviour.[8] In this sense, the distinction between compliant and deviant behaviour is a '*system-internal differentiation*' (2014: 96 [1987: 124]).

Undoubtedly, the law has this function of selecting 'which [normative] expectations will meet social approval and which not'. This enables one to 'take on the disappointments of everyday life with a higher degree of composure; at least one knows that one will not be discredited for one's expectations'. Meaning that 'one can afford a higher degree of uncertain confidence or even of mistrust as long as one has confidence in law' (Luhmann 2004: 148 [1995a: 131–32]). Given that selectivity embraces law enforcement as well, one must also reckon with a considerably 'high non-enforcement quota of formally valid law'. The difficult 'flow of information to official instances', the various rules for '*complaint mechanisms*', the performance of '*enforcement agencies themselves*', and the existence of '*trifling matters*' are some examples of filtering mechanisms that law enforcement goes through (2014: 207 ff [1987: 267 ff]). It is in this sense, for Luhmann (2014: 30 [1987: 38–39]), that the function of law would not lie primarily in 'securing behavior that conforms expectations' or in the 'certainty of fulfillment of expectations', but rather in the creation of 'security of expectations',[9] and this incurs decisive consequences.

At the outset, one has to settle for the fact that law is not primarily structured to steer behaviour. Such a task, even though valuable to 'influence the behavior of certain people and give them a different direction' (eg, through contracts and statutes), is not compatible at every level with 'securing expectations' (Luhmann 2015a: 73–74). As the fulfilment of an expectation cannot be certain, since the behaviour can always be deviant, legal structures also cannot assure

[7] *cf* Kelsen (1992: 59–60 [1934: 68–69]).

[8] See Luhmann (2014: 96 [1987: 123]).

[9] *cf* Luhmann (2015d: 118). That law has '*only one* primary function' does not mean of course that it cannot be specified in a number of 'sub-functions'; in this regard, see Luhmann (2004: 148 [1993: 132]), referring among others to a list made by Raz (1979b). See also Luhmann (2004: 151 [1993: 135–36]), mentioning the existence of too many functional equivalents to 'steering behaviour' in contrast to 'contra-factual stabilization of expectations'.

conflict resolution. In the attempt of being secured, they may actually create or catalyse even more conflicts. As Luhmann (1995d: 330–31 [1991: 451]) correctly put it, 'law is not only a means of solving social conflicts, but first and foremost a means of creating them: a support for demands, claims, and refusals, even and especially where resistance is anticipated'.[10] In any case, legal norms are to a large degree capable of absorbing disappointment and enduring nonenforcement in order to protect the expectation against its destruction, but this does not mean that there is no threshold. Luhmann (2014: 216 [1987: 281]) has indeed realised that 'a generalization of disappointed experiences could then come about instead of the generalization of norms'. More than that, he suggested that a 'rapidly changing society' would have to 'develop mechanisms that can discover the chance of new structures even in deviant behavior' (2014: 101 [1995a: 130]). And he insightfully observed: 'Where law is no longer respected, or is no longer enforced as far as it is possible so to do, the consequences extend much further than what amounts to breach of law, and the system has to retreat to much more basic forms of securing confidence' (2004: 148 [1995a: 132]).[11] Which consequences come from the generalisation of disappointment, which mechanisms discover the structures in deviant behaviour, and which forms of securing confidence develop under these circumstances, however, are questions left unanswered, and the most Luhmann (2004: 488 [1993: 582]) had to offer in this respect was 'to throw doubt on the functionality and the differentiation of orientation by law' with some suspicions that this is due to problems of exclusion.[12] I shall discuss this hypothesis in detail in section 6.2.

Apart from the discussion about how well the legal system is capable of implementing its function of securing expectations,[13] what matters here is to

[10] See also Luhmann (2004: 153 [1993: 139], 2012: 281 [1997a: 468]). The first part of this book (see esp sections 2.2 and 3.3) demonstrated this. For another case study in this regard, see the criminalisation of homelessness in Connecticut in Frankel et al (2016), which shows how people may be 'forced into breaking the law'. But that hardly is a sole problem of the legal system. Modern society as a whole seems to be more and more often confronted with 'the problems that it itself has created' (Luhmann 1995c: 19), and there are no guarantees that societal structures, in the course of their development, will 'remain compatible with each other' (1997b: 76). For the orientations of law in terms of function (to generalise expectations congruently), performance (to regulate conflicts), and reflection (to mitigate the tension between its function and performance), see Teubner (1982: 48). In a slightly different direction, understanding the 'resolution of conflicts' and not its 'regulation' as the 'legal system's most generic performance', is Neves (2022: 109 [2011: 159]). I will discuss later how conflicts develop in arenas of noncompliance (see ch 7, text accompanying n 12).

[11] Parsons (1962: 71), too, realised that law cannot flourish in a society where the 'enforcement problem' is 'too seriously acute' and, likewise, where forces – be them even informal – do not reinforce 'conformity with at least the main lines of the legally institutionalized tradition'.

[12] Regarding the basic forms of securing confidence, some hints can be found in a later text about the south of Italy; see Luhmann (1995c: esp 24–25), mentioning how official norms, the question of validity, and the capacity of enforcement can be submitted to 'conditions of personal interaction'. For the background on how Luhmann started to problematise exclusion, see Ribeiro (2013).

[13] See Neves (1992) and Villas Bôas Filho (2009) with a special emphasis on Brazil. In regard to Latin America in general, see Mascareño (2012: esp 100 ff, 2015: 148–51). Luhmann (2004: 490 [1993: 586]) himself in the end seemed to dispute his own thesis by casting doubt on the proper 'functioning of the legal code', as if it was an 'European anomaly'. I will come back to this point (see text accompanying n 36).

account for the crossing of the threshold in which operations of noncompliance become so recurrent and pervasive – 'law is no longer respected, or is no longer enforced' – that they form social structures; that is to say, structures that emerge from deviance or, within the conceptual framework proposed here, structures of noncompliance. Disappointment, instead of being absorbed, is learned, and once learned it is counted on with certain confidence and anticipation. Disobedience, failure, forbearance, abuse, and inconsistency enter the horizon of expectations not only as simple events of deviation but also as guiding principles of action and behaviour. As the disappointment cannot be duly and regularly handled through the legal mechanisms established for this purpose, the norm loses not only part of its characteristic counterfactuality but also its relevance for guiding everyday life situations.[14] Instead of keeping 'distance from reality',[15] the norm appears as if it aims towards 'another reality'.[16] Even when it comes to situations where the norm becomes relevant and has to be thematised, the structures of noncompliance impose learning pressures toward adapting the norm to the legal system's environment, paving the way for expectations of lenience or tolerance. Thus, the maintenance of the norm by means of full enforcement tends to be processed as ignorance of the 'local reality', and usually results in resistance from those affected, frequently under discourses of injustice being practised

[14] *cf* Neves (2005: 68–69 [1994: 261]).

[15] *cf* Grimm (1991: 14–15, 2016: 18), but referring to the constitution. The difference between norm and reality, however, becomes much more problematic when it comes to historical contexts such as the ones that have long since been denounced by traditional Brazilian scholarship: 'Constitutions written for noncompliance and laws enacted for violation – all for the benefits of individuals and oligarchies – are a current phenomenon in the history of all of South America' (Buarque de Holanda 2012: 182 [1995: 149]). For the respective effects on legal-constitutional practice and doctrine, see Neves (2021: 141–43 [2013: 189–91], 2022: 62 ff [2011: 90 ff]).

[16] Some try to interpret the distance between enacted law and its lack of enforcement as if there are two opposing legal systems. The most famous contribution on this regard is perhaps the one provided by Ehrlich (2017: 493 [1913: 399]) and his widely known distinction between the official law 'enforced in courts and other tribunals' and the 'living law'. In the same vein, but referring to Brazil, Santos (1977) spoke of 'the law of the oppressed', a sort of unofficial law developed especially in *favelas* to deal with – sometimes in confrontation, sometimes in an adaptive manner – the official law of the state (or, in the commonly used expression of the inhabitants of these communities, the 'asphalt law'). For a more extended version of his work which includes the original theoretical chapter of his doctoral thesis, his personal impressions of the field work, and interviews with some inhabitants of the *favela* he researched, see Santos (2014). In a more general context, Friedman (2016: 79–83), for instance, argued that there is actually 'the law on the books' and 'the law in action', forming a kind of 'dual system' which is a result of 'widespread violation' or a 'chasm between official and living law'. However, it seems to me that none of these approaches will accurately describe the impacts of noncompliance I am depicting here. The main reason is that structures of noncompliance are in essence cognitive and not normative structures. This means that neither emerging normativities nor autonomous legal orders can be found (or at least not in the cases examined in this research). It is not possible to speak, therefore, of a legal pluralism, for the only legal order in place is the state one, even when lacking compliance. When structures of noncompliance are established, what are observed are learning strategies to deal with the general lack of compliance and to behave successfully in arenas of noncompliance; or, to put it another way, to deal with the '*social miscellanea* of codes and criteria of conduct' (Neves 2003: esp 130 [1995: esp 12]).

against them. Injustice, in these cases, can circumstantially be understood as unequal treatment: as the rule is general noncompliance in all of its degrees, the act of compliance becomes exceptional. Regardless, if the enforcement is to be carried out at all costs, then it is not sufficient to merely apply the sanctions established by the norm. The public authorities quite often have to resort to overenforcement, sometimes in the form of extreme violence, to achieve legally determined results. In turn, this reinforces the structure of noncompliance, as violence beyond the established sanctions, that is, abuse of enforcement, is itself a form of noncompliance. To avoid major conflict from both sides (ie, the norm addressees and norm enforcers), the disappointment has to be dealt with less as deviance and more as the fulfilment of external social constraints that cannot simply be avoided and hence must be endured, if one wants to take part in the arena governed by structures of noncompliance. In such a state of affairs, as all the evidence points out, one will find neither a completely lawless land – and Luhmann (2004: 488 [1993: 583]) was right to assert that 'one cannot say that under such circumstances there is no longer any law (there never have been societies without law)' – nor a *hic sunt dracones*.[17] We are basically dealing here with spaces where the law does exist, but in which action and experience are structured instead by noncompliance.

As this topic entails on the one hand a notion of space and on the other a central debate in systems theory, that is, the problems of inclusion and exclusion, I shall delve into this notion and debate in more detail. In possession of the analytical framework to be provided by the discussion, I will be able to draw with more precision the concept of the arena of noncompliance and point out the impacts of noncompliance therein.

6.2. TERRITORY AND CONTROL

To deal with the notion of space is no easy task. There is a vast body of literature to conceptualise its various dimensions.[18] Within the legal scholarship,

[17] How Luhmann treats the unknown does not go unnoticed here. For some reason, he usually – sometimes subtly, sometimes not – portrays areas where the law's function is heavily undermined as almost necessarily violent spaces: '… places where one cannot enter without special protection, for instance the favelas of the big Brazilian cities' (2004: 481 fn 40 [1993: 573]). The problem becomes even worse when he implies that such areas of undifferentiated law are blatant to the eyes: 'Anybody who dares a visit to the *favelas* of South American cities and escapes alive can talk about this [mass exclusion and misery beyond description]. But even a visit to the settlements that were left behind after the closing of the coal mines in Wales can assure one of it. To this effect, no empirical research is needed. Who trusts his eyes can see it, and can see it so impressively that all explanations at hand will fail' (2008: 44 [1995b: 147]). It is as if he has attached a label to such areas: there are dragons here! I will come to this point again; see n 38 below.

[18] There are entire fields of knowledge dedicated to this. The variation of approaches is so great that one could say, as Schroer (2008: 232) did, that 'to this day it is by no means clear what can be understood by space'. Schroer (2012, 2019) himself made comprehensive attempts to analyse the concept across the different disciplines and uses.

space is usually conceived as determining the sphere of validity of a legal norm that designates the territory where the norm ought to produce its effects.[19] This first notion is important, and I shall discuss it in detail. But when seen as 'territory', space has a much more comprehensive aspect that cannot be left behind. Parsons (1962: 61), for instance, observed that 'it is only within territorial limits that enforcement of universalistically defined rules can effectively be carried out'. Indeed, it is undeniable the historical role it played in the early development of 'higher forms of law and its coordination with decision-making competence and use of sanctions'.[20] In this sense, 'it was only within territorial boundaries that the normativeness of expectation, and therefore the disjunction of conformist and deviant behaviour, could be enforced and formulated in detail' (Luhmann 2014: 99 [1987: 127]). Nonetheless, when it comes to the systems theory of Luhmannian provenience, the framework we are particularly interested in here, space, which is also conceived in its pure physicality, that is, as *territorium*, has no prominent role in the overall conceptual architecture.[21] As Luhmann (2012: 6 [1997a: 25]) himself made clear, any definition of society grounded on 'territorially defined entities' would be impregnated by, in the terminology of Bachelard (2002: 24 ff [1947: 13 ff]), 'epistemological obstacles'. In contrast to old forms of societal differentiation, in which space still had a pivotal role,[22] the transition to modern society has been marked by the decreasing relevance of territorial and physical boundaries. This can be seen, on the one hand, in the technological developments which accelerate society,[23] diminishing the resistance of space, for example 'in the eighteenth century by the improvement of roads and carriages, in the nineteenth century by the rail road, in the twentieth century by flight, and in the twenty-first century presumably by replacing travel with telecommunication' (Luhmann 1995d: 385 [1991: 526]). And, on the other hand, in the increasing number of modes of

[19] In this sense, see Kelsen (1967: 12–13 [1960: 12]). Criticising how the contemporary political and legal theories 'focus almost exclusively on *borders*, that is, on the spatial boundaries which demarcate the territory of a state or other collective', Lindahl (2013: esp 40 and 43) speaks of 'spatial boundaries' as one form of 'limit', the kind that constitutes the 'ought-place' of the legal order. The state, in his line of thought, would be just a 'distribution of ought-places'.

[20] *cf* Parsons (1963b: 241), arguing that 'there is thus an inherent relation between both the use and the control of force and the territorial basis of organization'.

[21] For a more detailed argument in this regard, see Schroer (2012: 145). That Luhmann conceives space in a physical sense seems clear when he postulates that 'space is constituted, for example, by the assumption that two things cannot occupy the same place at the same time' (1995d: 385 [1991: 525]).

[22] See Luhmann's description of 'segmentary societies' (2013: 27 ff [1997a: 634 ff]), societies divided into 'center and periphery' (2013: 42 ff [1997a: 663]), and 'stratified societies' (2013: 50 ff [1997a: 678 ff]). A summary specifically focused on space can be found in Schroer (2012: 132–42).

[23] The acceleration of society paves the way for a plethora of analyses of new regimes of time. Perhaps the most famous contribution in this regard is offered by Koselleck (2004 [1979]), pointing out the dissolution of the very topos of history, that of *historia magistra*. For an analysis in terms of regimes of historicity, see Hartog (2015 [2003], 2016). For a more comprehensive study on social acceleration, its mechanisms, manifestations, causes, and consequences, see Rosa (2013 [2005]). Other studies, ranging from classical perspectives to political consequences, can be found in Rosa and Scheuerman (2009).

communication at a distance, that is, communication without the need for the physical presence of participants, creating some sort of a 'given reachability, in principle, of everyone' to such an extent that, for instance, 'a successful song could be heard by everyone, a certain economic good (eg, a mobile phone) could be bought by everyone, a sporting event could be observed by everyone as part of the audience, a certain religious belief system could impress everyone as an offer for conversion' (Stichweh 2017: 550).

Indeed, if one concurs with Luhmann (2012: 48 [1997a: 90]) in conceiving society as *all* communication and communication *only*, it becomes easier to understand why these kinds of boundaries have no major relevance today for society to reproduce itself, as communication is not bounded to territorial constraints. In this sense, space not only 'loses its constitutive condition for the social' (Schroer 2012: 144) but is also eliminated from the definition of society, whose 'unity as a social system' cannot be explained 'in terms of territorial borders' (Luhmann 2012: 86 [1997a: 149]). Provided that the whole of society can no longer be restricted by geographical categories – and this entails the fact that any regional comparison can only be made if one assumes society as a comprehensive world system – then it is almost unavoidable to conceive modern society as 'world society' (Luhmann 2005a, 2012: 83 ff [1997a: 145 ff], 1997b).[24] Against this background, space is relegated to account for only those old forms of differentiation which still remain in modern society, such as the segmentary differentiation of the political system into the territorial form of nation states (2000a: esp 190 and 222),[25] and the systems still dependent on corporal presence for their constitution, namely interaction systems, which can only emerge in a concrete space where reciprocal perception is possible (2005b). In the first case, the segmentary (regional) differentiation works as a secondary form of differentiation since it is subjected to, and a by-product of, the functional differentiation of society (1989: 85 [2008a: 110]). Thus, in practical terms, it seems that a constitutive relevance of space – at least within systems theory – is confined to simple systems of interaction. Therefore its importance would be retained, in a world society, only as a 'substrate for interaction' (2005a: 75).

Naturally, one can criticise with valid reasons the role space plays in the theory,[26] but one cannot discount how Luhmann tried, in his later work, to

[24] In the same vein, see Stichweh (1995, 2017).

[25] En passant, questioning the capacity of space to establish social boundaries, see Luhmann (2005a: 76).

[26] Schroer (2012: 144), for instance, argued that 'the internal differentiation of the functional systems is hardly conceivable without the localization of the organizations which belong to them'. That is to say, there are specific buildings which allow the 'concentration of specific functions in one place' as well as 'the stabilization of communications otherwise improbable'. In this sense, 'the constitution and reproduction of the family is ensured not least by the spatial centring in the house, that of religion by church and monastery, that of politics by agora or parliament, that of economy by the market, that of law by the courts'. And this kind of 'spatial presence of organizations' is another way of creating 'visibility of functionally differentiated societies', something that, in the criticism of Schroer, goes unnoticed by Luhmann. Yet regarding the market, banks would seem a better example of organisation.

reconcile with the notion of space, which somehow appeared to occupy a kind of unforeseen position within the theory, more specifically – be it coincidence or not – in his attempts to tackle problems of exclusion.[27] Space here enters the scene to describe certain places where exclusion 'exists on a massive scale and in such forms of misery that are beyond description'. Apart from the rather problematic notion of something being 'beyond description' to the effect that 'no empirical research is needed',[28] Luhmann always made geographical references in order to localise such places: '*favelas* of South American cities', 'settlements that were left behind after the closing of the coal mines in Wales' (2008b: 44 [1995b: 147]), and 'ghettos in large cities', especially in the United States (1995a: 260).[29] In this sense, they would be a kind of spatialisation of 'zones of exclusion', in which he argued (1995a: 260) that the very 'logic of the functional differentiation' is in 'contradiction with the facts of exclusion' in such a way that the 'codes' of the functionally differentiated social systems would be 'valid and not valid in the same society'. This ambivalent condition, despite being an apparent contradiction, could be explained through the 'supercodification' (1995a: 260) of society in terms of the distinction between inclusion and exclusion, meaning

> that large parts of the population are excluded in a very stable way from any participation in the areas of performances of the functional systems and that in the opposite zone, that of inclusion, unforeseen forms of stabilization are set which parasitically use the opportunities of these performances and form their own mechanisms of inclusion and exclusion for the maintenance of this network. (Luhmann 1995a: 250)

Announcing this overarching differentiation between inclusion and exclusion as the new 'primary differentiation of society' (1995a: 261) – which earlier was presented as a 'pre-ordered, primordial difference' (1992: 3), and afterwards as a 'kind of meta-code' (2004: 489 [1993: 583]), and then as a 'metadifference' (2013: 25 [1997a: 632]) – Luhmann indeed took a rather controversial step in his theoretical enterprise, bringing about a whole set of different implications.[30] In this turnaround, he conceded that space, in contrast to his previous argument (ie, its decreasing relevance in a world society), might play an indispensable role, for 'the differentiation of inclusion and exclusion requires a spatial

[27] I have already brought forward this discussion above. See nn 12 and 13.

[28] A criticism of Luhmann's 'impressionistic seeing' of ecological problems of exclusion and human rights violations is made by Pedro Henrique Gonçalves de Oliveira Ribeiro in his ongoing doctoral research at Frankfurt University.

[29] As Mascareño (2015: 155) puts it, these spaces would be a form of 'container from which no one can escape and which makes attempts at intervention from outside impossible'.

[30] As a matter of fact, Luhmann clearly put a core postulate of his theory into question, which has rendered him subject to a lot of criticism. See, for instance, Neves (2018: 390–401), speaking instead of a 'concurrence' between the two forms of differentiation. As Schroer (2012: 152 fn 65) rightly noted, this new approach of Luhmann 'seems to have found no sympathizers even among his closest followers'. However, what Schroer fails to recognise is that this thesis arises from the earlier criticism of Neves (1992), someone who could arguably be among Luhmann's closest followers.

substrate, and thus spatial boundaries by which the movement of bodies can be controlled' (1995a: 260). The spatial reference, or rather the spatial segregation, in this context is not only a prerequisite for the exertion of control but also comes as a result or an effect of cumulative exclusions:

> For the factual exclusion from a functional system – no work, no income, no papers, no stable intimate relationships, no access to contracts and to the legal protection of the courts, no possibility of distinguishing between electoral campaigns and carnival events, illiteracy, inadequate medical care and food supplies – limits what can be achieved in other systems and defines larger or smaller sections of the population, who are often set apart residentially and hence kept out of sight. (Luhmann 2013: 24 [1997a: 630–32])

Furthermore, if the difference between inclusion and exclusion is accepted as an overruling difference, its main role being 'to mediatize the codes of functional systems', then the most striking consequence is that each and every functional code might be submitted to that of inclusion and exclusion. In practical terms, this means that the performances of a given social system are filtered by the mechanisms which create the criteria of access to such performances and the respective advantages. However, this should not necessarily be a problem per se. In Luhmann's (2004: 490 [1993: 584–85]) line of reasoning, the problem emerges when 'the inclusion of some depends on the exclusion of others', which ultimately would undermine 'the normal functioning of functioning systems'. Of course, one could fairly ask for more empirical evidence about this sort of person-related dependence, for such dynamics cannot simply be taken for granted.[31] The question of which social conditions are required for this dependence to happen, or rather how it comes to emerge and change in the course of history, poses considerable challenges which cannot be overcome solely with Luhmann's writings. At least in the general case of Latin America there are, for instance, some theoretical approaches that may offer different directions.[32]

[31] Luhmann (1990: 34 [1981a: 25]) first formulated the concept of 'dependence' as part of the concept of inclusion: 'The concept of inclusion means the encompassing of the entire population in the performances of the individual function system. On one hand, this concerns *access* to these benefits and, on the other, *dependence* of individual modes of living on them.' So, it referred to system-related dependence on social performances. In the later work, however, he came up with a kind of person-dependent form of inclusion, in which one can only be included at the cost of the exclusion of another. All in all, the argument related to the latter form of dependence can be traced back to Neves (1992: 147–60), referring to the Brazilian case. More recently, Neves (2018: 396) corroborated it as a necessary connection at the structural level: 'It seems to me inconceivable the structural under-integration, the exclusion of those who are below the functional systems, being usable or disposable according to the context, without the privileges of over-integration.' Elsewhere, I tried to provide more empirical evidence to support this claim in the case of traditional fishing communities and entrepreneurs in Brazil (Araujo and Moita 2018).

[32] From the once famous identification of 'structures of dependence' (T dos Santos 1970), passing by the examination of negative effects of the race toward 'encountering development' (Escobar 1995), to the 'absence of citizenship' due to relations of 'under-integration and over-integration' (Neves 2005 [1994]), there are certainly many ways of tackling the problem, which, depending on the direction taken, almost always end up in discussions about inequality, poverty, or exclusion. To place these approaches under scrutiny would take us, however, far beyond the scope of

Shortcomings aside, Luhmann did provide fruitful insights into the understanding of those spaces in society in which the logic of functional differentiation is heavily impaired. Two are particularly important to note. The first, as he suggested (2004: 489–90 [1993: 583–85]), is when the difference between inclusion and exclusion becomes problematic, it 'affects law above all, for the legal system is based not only on the sanctions of the system, on sentencing and punishment, but also on the society-wide resonance of breaches of law, which is an additional motivation for obeying law'.[33] Therefore, one can definitely say that 'the difference between legal and illegal certainly exists and there are legislative programmes (statutes) that regulate how the values of legal or illegal are attributed to facts'. But as a matter of fact, 'this question is of little importance to the excluded group of the population compared with what is imposed on them by this exclusion'. How they are legally treated and what accordingly determines their behaviour are rather dependent on 'their situation and opportunities' (2004: 489 [1993: 583]). And naturally, the same would apply for those who are included.[34] In this way, 'the difference between coding and programming does not function or functions only at a reduced rate because other preferences come first',[35] meaning that 'legal or illegal behavior can be chosen regardless of the "label" on both sides of this schema (even if in a very different, "fatal" way)'. If one considers the integrative effects of exclusion, that is, 'exclusion from one functional area prevents inclusion in others', this likewise creates different 'opportunities for the violation of law and for corruption' (2004: 489 [1993: 584]). All in all, the consequences stand out:

> There is nothing to lose in the highly integrated area of exclusion, apart from control over one's own body. In the poorly integrated areas of inclusion, the consequences of legality or illegality are not conveyed, and there is nothing to be gained from paying attention to such values according to law-specific programmes. In (the not so rare) extreme cases it is even irrelevant to politics and politicians' reputations whether they act legally or illegally. The organization of the administration of force, that is, the police, is also guided primarily by status, which is provided by inclusion or exclusion and not by law. (Luhmann 2004: 490 [1993: 585])

This is indeed a painful diagnosis, which undoubtedly undermines a theory that was at the outset conceived to explicate the functional differentiation of society as its guiding principle. Not by coincidence it forced Luhmann (2004: 490 [1993: 586]) to recognise at the end of his masterpiece on law that 'the prominence

this work. Even though not directly facing the theories of dependence, Luhmann (1995a: 250 fn 38) always showed himself sceptical about their descriptive capacity.

[33] I slightly changed the English translation here, which converted 'vor allem' to 'especially'. In my perspective, considering the context of the discussion, Luhmann meant that the system which suffers the most from the cumulative exclusions is the law.

[34] See also Luhmann (2013: 25 [1997a: 632]). For a more detailed development of this line of reasoning, speaking of over-inclusion and under-inclusion, see Neves (2005 [1994]). See also n 31.

[35] *cf* Neves (1992: 148), speaking of 'functionality, dysfunctionality and inadequate functioning'.

of the legal system' and the dependence on a 'functioning legal coding' were nothing but a 'European anomaly'.[36] It also made him suggest much more drastic consequences for the lives of those who live in spaces of exclusion. As the communication media of functional systems tend to lose their capacity to propel the symbolic recursion of their symbiotic mechanisms,[37] one can then expect the rise of unrestrained 'physical force, sexuality, and the elementary, compulsive satisfaction of needs' (2013: 26 [1997a: 633]) – a so-called civilisational detour. Under such circumstances one must endure living with 'more contingent social expectations' and being 'guided by short-term time horizons, by the immediacy of situations, by the observation of bodies', that is, one cannot rely on 'time-extending reciprocity expectations' (2013: 26 [1997a: 633]). Given the difficulties in describing a society marked by such features,[38] to develop a solution for all of this is, as one might imagine, another tremendous challenge. Luhmann (2013: 26 [1997a: 633]) even mentioned the possibility of a 'secondary functional system … at the level of social welfare or development aid.' But he was sceptical about it himself, as the 'resource-dependence of these efforts' would be 'so strong that it is doubtful whether we are dealing with an extant social subsystem or with scattered endeavors at the level of interactions and organizations'.

There is also the second insight. Amidst his forays into the drastic consequences of living in spaces of exclusion, Luhmann (1995a: 251–52) gave some hints about the mechanisms which would emerge to cope with such excluding social structures. They could be seen as some sort of 'disturbing' circumstances or as 'useful transitory "survivals"' of old social formations, which are now embedded in the functional differentiation of society so as to provide 'mediation services' between the performances one can obtain from social systems. The mechanisms assume the form of 'reciprocity chains, useful friendships as network friendships, patron/client relationships and the like' which are constituted to manage the 'resources of functional subsystems' for building 'interconnections' and caring for the 'maintenance of the network itself'. And they work mainly on the basis of their 'legal/illegal capacity to act', which in turn is provided by 'positions in organizations' and, in this way, 'can be

[36] See n 13.

[37] For the function of symbolically generalised communicational media, see Luhmann (2012: 190 ff [1997a: 316 ff]). For the notion of symbiotic mechanisms, see Luhmann (1981b). I will discuss the notion of symbolic generalised media when dealing with resources in arenas of noncompliance (see section 7.3).

[38] Bringing back the discussion initiated previously (see n 17), I do not want to assume all the thoughts developed by Luhmann. For it seems to me a bit hard to take for granted without further empirical specifications some of the features appointed by him, as if they could be generalised for each and every case in which one finds spaces of exclusion. I refer especially to the abovementioned non-symbolically restrained symbiotic mechanisms of physical force, sexuality, and the elementary, compulsive satisfaction of needs. Mascareño (2015: esp 152 and 156) improves this overgeneralisation slightly by differentiating the relations of 'superposition' and 'decoupling', limiting those unrestricted mechanisms to the latter as its 'coordination form'.

demanded'. In doing so, they create a kind of 'network of granting favours and shifting benefits' which, in a society functionally differentiated, 'begins to operate parasitically', that is, against the own logic of the functional differentiation. Its 'basal resource', as it appears to Luhmann, consists in 'knowing someone who knows someone', supposing that there is a state of affairs in which 'asking for favours is so wide-spread that, if one has the opportunity to help in any way, one cannot refuse it without being excluded from the network of mutual services within a short time'. In this sense, the network 'generates its own mechanisms of exclusion, which can cause one to become a nonperson that no one knows, and which for this very reason, despite all the formal rights, cannot find access to the functional systems'. This way, as the network is fundamentally based on contacts, it is structured by 'interactions face-to-face',[39] allowing for 'particular but not universalistic and diffuse but not specific orientation of themes'. For the same reason, in order to profit from the network participants distributed in different organisations, it presupposes 'personal acquaintanceship', which can also be intermediated by others (extending the 'principle of exchange'), and relies on 'oral communication' (1995a: 254), which makes it clear that the general form of addressing, even if at the level of organisations, is from person to person.

This parasitic dynamic reveals the intriguing aspect of this kind of network: it presupposes the functional differentiation, because it requires organisations capable of offering positions to intermediate system's performances, but at the same time it also presupposes that the differentiation will not function as it is supposed to. As Luhmann (1995a: 254–55) puts it, the functional differentiation 'is constantly short-circuited, and this is what enables the network of useful friendships to work and ultimately decide on inclusion and exclusion'. Naturally, the operations of such a mechanism can be seen in every social domain within the network's coverage: 'Thus, *qua* inclusion, one gets seats in already fully booked airplanes, preferential treatment in tenders, passing school and university exams, political protection and vice versa, political careers earned through protection – but all this at the expense of opportunities for rationality specific to the functional system.' When it comes to the state's bureaucracy, the situation becomes even more paradoxical. The bureaucracy reacts by placing an 'increased emphasis on authentic documents', which in turn leads to a kind of scapegoat in the sense that they can always refer to external references as

[39] In this passage, Luhmann (1995a: 252) still makes one caveat: 'which does not exclude the use of telephone if someone is known'. He wrote his piece on inclusion and exclusion in 1995. Of course, at that time, it was difficult to predict the intense and pervasive change the world would see with the advent of the new modes of communication, especially through social media, and the worldwide use of high-speed internet. One could, in this sense, hedge even more on the need for face-to-face interactions. But this naturally would demand a deeper study on the possible new forms of interactions that do not require face-to-face presence.

something beyond their will ('We cannot help it!') but which, in the observer's perspective, can be recognised as 'self-reference' – as something they could actually do, but needs to be decoded in a sort of 'game in a game'. In this way, 'the bureaucracy paralyses itself, so that there is all the more reason to get things moving again via the network of favours'. In such a state of affairs, one can say that there is 'a self-created incapacity of the official order', which not only serves the network well but also deprives the official institutions of the 'ability to mobilize support themselves'.

This mode of operation also explains, still following Luhmann's (1995a: 256) account, why illegality becomes a valuable resource to this kind of network. Considering the many ways through which social performances like social benefits can be managed through favours, 'joint ventures between politics and crime' may be found quite frequently. Illegal acts may function as an 'entry ticket to the organizations that use these advantages: one makes oneself vulnerable – and therefore reliable', since the illegal act can at any time be exposed. Under such circumstances, illegality mediates the forms of access to benefits of social systems. That is why the success of 'deviant behaviour' (and the criminal organisations alike, such as the mafia, drug cartels, and militia) is due to 'the fact that effective work can only be motivated in the medium of illegality'. And even those 'legally acting organizations' cannot avoid the 'side-effects', especially toward a tendency to 'hypercorrecting', that is to say, they 'react to illegality all the more by requesting records, documents, evidence'; but this requesting might trigger in turn a kind of 'competent illegality', by which the desired social performance can be mobilised once again through the network. Of course, 'there are grey areas between unequivocal legality and unequivocal illegality' as well as 'ways of placing illegality where it is not suspected in order to gain enforcement competence elsewhere' (1995a: 256 fn 50). To this extent, illegality becomes a manageable resource. It serves not only to facilitate obtaining access to social performances but also to assure that no consequences will follow. In this sense, the 'guarantee of consequence-free illegality' also 'becomes a service that one can bring in and for which one can demand something' (Luhmann 1995a: 256).[40]

I do not disregard the fact that this long foray has encountered different discussions and entails a vast array of issues.[41] However, what is important to observe, in such a state of affairs, is 'the high degree of deviation – deviation from what is expected from the opportunities for rationality, the promises of performance, and the structural and ideological premises of the functional systems' (Luhmann 1995a: 256–57). That deviation in high degrees affects the

[40] I will try to demonstrate later how similar guarantees of consequence-free illegality are instilled in the very programs of law by means of bartering arrangements, turning illegality itself into a bargaining chip (see section 8.2).

[41] Just the variations in the use of the conceptual pair 'inclusion/exclusion' in the span of 20 years have rendered a field of investigation of its own. See in this regard Farzin (2006), but lacking references to Neves' work, which played a major role in the development of Luhmann's approach.

way functional systems work and offer their performances is hard to deny, whether one agrees or not with Luhmann's approach on inclusion and exclusion. This can be empirically researched through different perspectives. As this book is particularly concerned with the legal system, I shall stick to the impacts that the high degrees of deviation – or, in our terminology, noncompliance – have on it. I have previously shown how events of noncompliance can lead to structures of noncompliance. Additionally, I have addressed how space plays a role as a substrate for interactions, enabling the control of bodies, and how parasitic mechanisms may be formed to benefit from the legal system's performances. In chapter seven, I will discuss how structures of noncompliance materialise into what I have been calling arenas of noncompliance.

7

Arenas of Noncompliance

IN ORDER TO avoid mixing incompatible theoretical frameworks, I must point out that the concept of arena is extraneous to systems theory. Moreover, it is hardly a popular sociological concept in general, especially when compared with the overwhelming usage of other concepts that reflect, or at least resemble, to a greater or lesser extent, the notion of space.[1] Some ascribe its descriptive potential to micro-levels of society in actor-oriented approaches. In this sense, it appears in the socio-anthropology of development, as can be seen in Olivier de Sardan (2005 [1995]), along with the concepts of 'conflict' and 'strategic groups'. An arena is then presented as a kind of 'social space' marked by 'confrontations and competitions', that is, 'a space in which real conflicts between interacting social actors occur around common stakes' (2005: 189–90 [1995: 178–79]). Its importance lies in 'identifying the actors and mapping out the issues, resources and discourses entailed in particular situations of disagreement or dispute'. In contrast to the idea of 'forum', which 'carries with it the implication that the rules for debate are, in a sense, already agreed upon', the 'contestation in an arena usually denotes discontinuities of values, norms and practices' (Long 2001: 59).[2] Others in turn carry out – although in a scattered way – meso-level analyses. This is the case, for instance, of those who undertook the challenge of building a theoretical framework to describe the development of public policies in 'arenas of power' (Lowi 1964, 1975, 1970, 1972)[3] or, rather,

[1] Perhaps the most noticeable in this regard is the concept of the 'social field', which nonetheless appeared a relatively long time ago in certain sets of sociological analyses. See, for instance, its use by the so-called Manchester School in Barnes (1954: 42 ff), Epstein (1968: 232), and Long (1968: 9–10). In any case, it became popularised worldwide, although within a different theoretical framework, by Bourdieu. For his concept of field, including a brief difference between field and systems in the sense of Luhmann, see Bourdieu and Wacquant (1992: 94–115). For the relationship between space and field, see Bourdieu (2018).

[2] A more recent application of this approach can be seen in Hilhorst and Jansen (2010), analysing 'humanitarian space' as arena on the basis of a study of two humanitarian operations: a protracted refugee camp in Kakuma, Kenya, and the tsunami response in Sri Lanka.

[3] These four articles set out Lowi's approach, which is basically designed to account for the development of domestic public policies. The model consists of four categories (or arenas) of public policy according to state power/coercive force employed: distributive policy, regulative policy, redistributive policy, and constituent policy. It assumes a very particular perspective: '*policies determine politics*' (Lowi 1972: 299) or 'policies cause politics' (Lowi 1978: 178). A biography of the arenas along with a collection of key essays on the subject can be found in a book published decades later (Lowi 2009). For a critical account of this model, see Kitschelt (1980: 13–17) and, including a review of Lowi's book when it first came out, Kellow (2009).

'political arenas' (H Kitschelt 1980),[4] and of those who proposed in a more general scale to account for the rise and fall of social problems in 'public arenas' (Hilgartner and Bosk 1988).[5] In this vein, arenas 'are neither geographical entities nor organizational systems. They describe the political actions of all social actors involved in a specific issue' and may contain, just like a theatre, many different stages, or 'manifestations of the same arena within different institutional context, such as litigation or policy making' (Renn 1992: 181).

It would lie beyond the scope of this work to analyse in detail each of these arena models, especially since they deal with phenomena considerably distinct from the ones being dealt with here. But despite the enormous variations in their conception and application, there seem to be certain notions that are common to the concept of an arena, revealing commonalities that elucidate some of its core aspects. Four are particularly important here: a specific issue around which conflicts emerge, evolve, and are eventually solved; the configuration of the arena into stages where the conflicts take place; the existence of actors playing an (un)defined role according to their position within the stage; and the resources at stake that enable actors to achieve goals. I propose in the following sections a reconstruction as well as an application of these four elements aiming at one specific end: identifying the impacts of high grades of noncompliance on the legal system.

7.1. THEME

The first point I would like to make is that, by having a specific end, the concept of arena that will be constructed here does not aim to capture a reality without which it could not be observed. Its main purpose is to serve as a 'modeling tool to interpret and structure empirical data' (Renn 1992: 193),[6] organising in an intelligible manner the set of descriptions developed so far around one specific

[4] In contradistinction to Lowi, but with the same purpose of analysing public policies, Kitschelt (1980: 18) formulated his concept as follows: 'By a political arena I mean the political space of action in which certain classes of social problems are politically addressed and which exhibits certain structural characteristics and "constraints" of the processes of problem formulation, decision and implementation. These features relate to the type of political actors, the political institutional system and the forms of political conflict resolution.'

[5] The model proposed by Hilgartner and Bosk (1988: 55) aims at '"arenas" where social problem definitions evolve, examining the effect of those arenas on both the evolution of social problems and the actors who make claims about them'. 'A social problem' in this context is defined 'as a putative condition or situation that is labeled a problem in the arenas of public discourse and action'. An arena is then the locus 'where social problem definitions evolve', and the resource in dispute therein is 'public attention'.

[6] Of course, this does not eliminate its potential to serve 'as a structural tool to conduct exploratory studies' (Renn 1992: 193), that is, as one type of 'exploratory concepts, allowing for the production of new and comparable data which have nothing to do with pre-programmed overinterpretations' (Olivier de Sardan 2005: 31 [1995: 15]). In any case, I will depart from the frameworks of Renn and Olivier de Sardan.

subject matter. In this particular sense, the concept of arena becomes by definition a theme-oriented concept. In the case analysed here, the main theme is noncompliance. Therefore, all the elements of the arena are to a greater or lesser extent connected to it, and for this reason the term 'arenas of noncompliance' has been used throughout this book. On the one hand, this clarifies the perspective of analysis, that of the legal system. On the other hand, as noncompliance is also an overarching theme, it allows, for the same strategic reasons, further specifications. That is why noncompliance was targeted here in the light of informality and, more specifically, of its most common, visible, and representative case, that of street vending. If this line of reasoning has been made clear, then it becomes easier to realise that the type of arena of noncompliance under examination here is the arena of street vending. And this thematic orientation brings together a set of analytical gains.

The first gain is the provision of a criterion for selecting the legal norms that are at stake in the arena. Of course, this will be an easy task when the norm, at the level of its signifier, is already constituted around the theme. This is the case, for instance, for Decree 9,300/1994 (discussed in chapter three), which regulates the exercise of itinerant commerce activities. The task, however, becomes more complex when it is necessary to resort to abstraction in the interpretation of the spheres of validity of the norm or to refer to actual enforcement procedures. The crimes of improper clearance (Article 334, § 1, III, of the Penal Code) and copyright violation (Article 184, § 2, of the Penal Code), for example, regulate behaviour in general, regardless of street vending; they only become relevant in the arena when their personal and material spheres of validity cross this activity, that is, when the behaviour they regulate is being performed in the context of street vending. The same happens with norms such as those ascribed to Article 672, VII, of the COPM, which prohibits 'embarrassing or impeding by any means the free transit of pedestrians or vehicles in public places'. Once the embarrassment or impediment is done in the context of street vending, this norm enters the arena. In sum, the theme allows a specific type of connectivity among norms that, in principle, would not be connected. It creates a kind of non-intended legal ordering, which is composed of norms that take part in the arena, regulating – at least under the perspective of the formally valid norms – the behaviour of the actors therein. By implication, it is also possible to put together administrative procedures and court decisions that, similarly, deal directly or indirectly with the theme.[7]

The analytical gain in this regard is not restricted to the pertinence-test of a norm in terms of its spheres of validity. It also enables its efficacy to be assessed in a more contextualised manner. In this sense, from the fact that the

[7] This enables interesting analyses. I have been gathering, for instance, court decisions that mention 'street vendors'; see ch 3, text following n 51. As a preliminary result, it can be noted that the role of street vendor is usually associated with 'illegal activities' but it is, for different reasons, 'socially acceptable'. A further development here would, nonetheless, exceed the scope of this work.

prohibition of import without proper clearance and of copyright violation are to a considerable extent inefficacious when it comes to street vending, one cannot conclude that both norms are generally inefficacious. Efficacy in this context can be thematically measured; some norms, or even an entire set of norms, may have their efficacy compromised only in respect to an activity or a given set of activities. This context-related measurement makes, for instance, Kelsen's (1967: 211–13 [1960: 215–20]) approach to efficacy more complex, for one is not limited to assessing the efficacy either of 'a legal order as a whole' or of 'a single legal norm' in all of its generality. Both the legal order and a single legal norm may have completely different assessments when seen from different viewpoints. A norm may be in general efficacious but, within a specific arena, it may be by and large disobeyed, not enforced, tolerated, abused, and inconsistently adjudicated. The same happens with the 'legal order as a whole'. In this case, however, the situation becomes more complicated, for it affects the very function of the legal system. Putting this in systemic-theoretical terms: whereas the legal system is able to congruently generalise expectations of behaviour for the whole of society (see chapter six, text following n 6), in arenas of noncompliance it is not. There is instead an 'insufficient functioning' of the legal system, which 'results from the insufficient or deficient concretization of positive legal norms, which, according to their abstract content, could contribute, in an appropriate manner to the environment, to secure expectations and steer behaviour in a hypercomplex society' (Neves 1992: 148).

Against this background, one can observe a *diffuse functioning of the law inside the state*, as if there were several legal orders taking place,[8] which makes the legal experience in states like Brazil overly complex and almost unbearably contingent.[9] The reliance on legal norms to guide behaviour – and on the respective enforcement/adjudication procedures – is dependent on whether one is inside or outside the arena. Therefore, identifying whether an arena of noncompliance exists is a kind of factual need in order to orientate oneself.[10] For those who take part therein as actors, this means the need to learn or build strategies to act in accordance with the structural constraints in effect. They have to be at least aware of the current structures of noncompliance forming the experience in the arena. Naturally, given the social positioning and the corresponding role to be played, the strategies may vary and when it becomes a matter of survival and individual or collective subsistence, they might even constitute

[8] This feeling that the law functions differently according to the context is what perhaps explains the option of a certain scholarship to advocate a legal pluralism in Brazil. For my criticism of such an approach, see ch 6, n 16.

[9] *cf* Neves (2018: 381 and 14–15), referring to the hypercomplexity of peripheral countries; originally in Neves (1992: 16–17).

[10] *cf* Luhmann's (1995a: 260) insight on the factual need to pay attention to the distinction between inclusion and exclusion in a 'supercodified' society (see ch 6, text following n 29).

'survival strategies'.[11] In the arena of street vending, the 'game of cat-and-mouse' (see chapter two, text accompanying n 16 and chapter three, text following n 34) is perhaps the most common one. In summary, one needs to know 'the game in place' and 'know how' to play it, but being aware that the 'rules' are neither positivised nor can be congruently generalised, for the arena is built upon one constitutive contradiction: legal rules, the only kind of expectations capable of being generalised and changed through political procedures of collective decision-making, are constantly violated, including by the very enforcement agencies in charge of handling the violations.

This contradiction is what paves the way for a latent, but permanent state of conflict: if conflict exists 'when a contradiction is communicated', that is, 'when expectations are communicated and the nonacceptance of the communication is communicated in return' (Luhmann 1995d: 388 [1991: 530]),[12] every player is entitled to reject legal rules on the basis that nobody else follows them (a claim for justice!). In principle, the possibility of conflicts is not a problem at all. In a highly complex society, rejection and nonacceptance are part of everyday life: 'The wealthy man can reject a communication anyway; but the poor man can now also do so, if he *is in the right*' (Luhmann 2012: 281 [1997a: 468]). This is one of the reasons why, as previously discussed (chapter six, text between nn 9 and 10), the law's primary function entails the 'intensification of conflict possibilities'. But this function, under conditions of a functioning legal system, is performed in ways 'that do not endanger social structures'. The conflict, under these circumstances, is defused 'through social regulation and the influence of third parties on the outcome of disputes' (Luhmann 2012: 281 [1997a: 468]). It is absorbed through legal mechanisms, and the dissent behind the conflict can be properly handled, not necessarily to assure the conflict resolution (one can never be sure that the conflict will disappear!) but to repair and maintain the social structure behind it, that is, the legal norm (one can expect that there will be consequences for anyone who is reckoned deviant). In the case of arenas of noncompliance, however, the insufficient functioning of the law does not merely

[11] These appear mainly when informality is intricately linked to poverty and misery. In Bielefeld, especially during the 1980s, a group of scholars from the so-called *Bielefelder Verflechtungsansatz* (Bielefeld Interdependence Approach) carried out a series of empirical research worldwide to explore this link in terms of subsistence and market production. For an overall picture of the school and its essential elements, see Evers (1987). An in-depth application of the approach, focusing on the 'survival strategies' of fishermen in Port Morant, Jamaica, can be found in the doctoral dissertation of F Kitschelt (1984), later published as a book (F Kitschelt 1987). For the series of studies which targeted the 'survival strategies' in Brazil with special emphasis on Recife, see Augel (1985). Noteworthy, although within a different framework but similarly focused on poverty and misery, are Rabanal's (1991: 135) [also available in German (1990: 156)] findings of the psychological consequences of survival strategies 'that result in personality deformations', impairing one's 'autonomy'. Despite its age, I would argue, based on the evidence brought in part I of this book, that many of these findings are still valid.

[12] See also Luhmann (2015c, 2012: 280 ff [1997a: 466 ff]). A more comprehensive study of conflict and law can be seen in Gessner (1986 [1976]).

intensify the possibilities of conflict. It multiplies them to a much higher degree, for not only the abstract content of the norms is subject to rejection, but also state apparatuses of law enforcement and adjudicative proceedings are denied by default. The result is the weakening of social regulation and third-party conflict resolution mechanisms, which heavily impairs the underlying social structures dependent on a functioning legal system. Under such conditions, it becomes to a certain extent irrelevant to know whether one is 'in the right', for the legal mechanisms of law enforcement are themselves another driver of conflict. It is in this sense that the theme of the arena is conflictive by its own nature and presents itself almost as an unending problem among all of those who participate in the arena: vendors and enforcement agents constantly engage in physical contention, courts become a stage for the initiation of lawfare, and policy makers act to compensate for the lack of legitimation, especially at the symbolic level.[13] How the conflict takes shape will depend on the players and the resources available to each of them, which in turn varies according to the stage within which the arena takes form.

7.2. STAGES AND ACTORS

Stages are 'manifestations of the arena'.[14] They refer to 'where' the conflicts are localised. However, since conflicts can emerge, develop, and be solved at the level of organisations, the stage is not necessarily a geographical entity. It only becomes geographical when the conflict resides in systems of interaction, for which space in its territorial sense plays a pivotal role as the substrate. An open-air street market, hence, becomes an instantiation of the arena of street vending. But as judicial proceedings concerning the activity in this market are part of the arena as well, courts may eventually become another stage. Each stage has its own internal dynamics, yet the ones which are spatially configured have a particular importance for arenas of noncompliance, for they are mainly constituted by the face-to-face interactions of the actors. I shall focus on the spatial stage for the following reasons.

As previously described (chapter six, text following n 25), interactions are a kind of simple system dependent on corporal presence and reciprocal perception. The presence is what enables 'different techniques of social control', increasing 'the danger, but also the domesticability of the individuals' (Luhmann 2005b: 37–38). This is why conflict in spatial stages of the arena,

[13] The case *Feira da Sé* is a striking example in each sense. For the conflicts, see the media coverage in ch 3, n 36. How courts are used for lawfare and how legislators act on a symbolic level is shown in section 3.3 (an example of the latter can be seen at ch 3, in the text following n 41). I will return later to the discussion about the lack of legitimation (see section 8.1).

[14] *cf* Renn (1992: 181), referring to 'different (theater) stages within a single arena' instead of different arenas as used by Peters (1991: 115). Also speaking of arenas inside the political arena, Kitschelt (1980: 18 ff).

in contrast to conflicts located at the level of organisations, have a unique feature: they can easily result in contention and physical confrontation, directly exposing those at the fore of law enforcement to danger. The danger becomes even higher when the nonacceptance of enforcement proceedings happens by default. Under such circumstances, in which conflict can be anticipated, one must resort to strategies of either conflict avoidance or direct engagement. On the norm addressees' side, avoidance is the entry ticket to and condition of permanence in the arena. It is no wonder street vending is above all considered a 'supreme art of escaping, evading and skirting' (see chapter two, text following n 16). On the enforcement agents' side, avoidance comes mainly as another form of noncompliance: forbearance. This can happen through friendly oral admonitions (see chapter three, text before n 33) or even bribes (see, generally, chapter two, n 17 and, with regards to our case study, the complaint initiated by SINFECE at chapter three, n 35). Thus, avoidance may become at first a kind of win-win situation for both sides, a type of preferential behaviour offered by established structures of noncompliance.

However, depending on the 'issue amplifiers', that is, those 'who observe the actions on stage, communicate with the principal actors, interpret their findings, and report them to the audience' (Renn 1992: 183), avoiding may become untenable, and both sides are pushed into direct engagement. Mass media quite often perform this role through newspaper reports, turning the issue into a social drama, which in turn raises the pressure for action (see esp chapter two, n 12 and chapter three, nn 31 and 42). The issue amplification might also gain a complexity of its own in the public sphere and may eventually become a stage itself. The way in which magazines, journals, newspapers, TV programs, radio channels, and documentaries thematise informality in general and street vending in particular point to this direction.[15] This is especially due to the fact that typical offering of the information in the 'mode of news and reporting' (Luhmann 2000b: 26 [1996: 55]) tends, in an arena of noncompliance, to be parasitic of the state of affairs, 'feeding on the unsolved problems of the functional systems' and, hence, reactivating 'forms of contact (legal or illegal) with the functional systems' (Stichweh 2016: 62).[16] Evidently the issue amplification is, in the spatial stages, part of an equation that also involves other enforcement costs, such as 'police and bureaucrats' salaries, the political costs of forbearance or heavy policing, or the opportunity costs of using law enforcement resources in one area instead of another' (Hummel 2017: 1538). When enforcement is ultimately put into motion, noncompliance tends

[15] In newspaper reports (see generally the list of newspaper and online reports at p 159), there are various examples in which there is a tendency to present the issue as a 'surprise' despite the continuities, focusing on 'conflicts' and 'quantities' which are marked by 'local relevance' of 'norm violations', the typical selectors of news (Luhmann 2000b: 27 ff [1996: 58 ff]).

[16] Stichweh is referring to people living in exclusion areas. In the framework developed here, it could be said: actors located at the arena's spatial stages.

to be further expanded, but in the form of abuse: harassment, intimidation, abuse of authority, and embezzlement of the seized goods are some examples (see chapter three, n 35). In spatial stages of the arena these specific dynamics of conflictual interactions – structured by noncompliance – are what creates the considerable distance between lawmaking and law enforcement (see chapter five, text following n 21). Legislation and court decisions, especially when recently issued, often become tokens for strategic uses by the actors instead of immediately being obeyed or enforced. This happens sometimes even regardless of their abstract content or legal scope. On the vendors' side, they can be used by those who take the front in the representation to gather support among their peers, with the possibility of converting it later into electoral capital (see Figure 15). On the enforcement agents' side, they become a sort of commodity to exchange for certain behaviours or compromises (see the context of the TAC at chapter three, text following n 39). I will return to this later (chapter eight). For now, it is important to understand how legislation and court decisions become a kind of resource which can be primarily mobilised not for the purpose of compliance per se, but rather to achieve the goals of the actors directly engaged in the arena.

7.3. RESOURCES

Resources constitute another fundamental part of the concept of arena. Different approaches to identify what can be labelled as resources can be found,[17] but they all basically answer the question of 'what' is at stake in an arena, leading to struggle, competition, and bartering. One useful way to understand how resources work is to present them as 'generalised symbolic media', following a tradition that traces back to Parsons. In his framework (Parsons 1976: 95), 'money' was the example par excellence, especially due to its 'value in exchange', functioning as a 'measure of value' which allows comparability in terms of utility, and serving as a 'store of value' in the sense that its retainment does not lead to a loss (apart from inflation) but to a gain (in the form of interest). These traits of money paved the way for Parsons to come up with the general properties of media one could find in society. The first property could be found in the above-mentioned first function of money: to say that it has a value in exchange and not in use points out a 'symbolic character' of the medium. One does not eat money, but rather one uses it to acquire food; in other words, it has no value itself. Such property would be, as argued Parsons (1976: 96), close to that of 'linguistic symbols, eg, the word "dog," though signifying a species of mammalian quadruped, can neither bark nor bite, though the concrete dog can do both'.

[17] Lowi (2009: 188–89) speaks of 'resources of power', differentiating them from 'power itself'. Renn (1992: 184–89) proposes a functionalist approach to 'social resources'.

It is through this symbolic character that the other four properties can be addressed. Media are then characterised by a 'state of institutionalization' via nexuses of social norms. They must have '*specificity* of meaning and efficaciousness in both evaluation and interchange', be equipped with '*circulability*' in the sense of being 'subject of transfer of control from one acting unit to another in some kind of interchange transactions', and '*not have zero-sum character* attributed to it in all contexts', that is, the increase in the amount of the medium held by one actor does not necessarily mean the decrease in the hands of another actor (1976: 96).[18] It is in this line of reasoning that Parsons presented, beyond 'money', the media of 'power' (1963b), 'influence' (1963a), and 'value-commitments' (1968). These would be the primary generalised symbolic media of interchange apt to be mobilised as resources across the primary subsystems of society, which, in Parsons' tetradic paradigm (AGIL), correspond respectively to economy (adaptation), political system (goal attainment), societal community (integration), and the fiduciary system (latent pattern maintenance).[19]

Amidst all the presuppositions and consequences of this approach, what is important is to understand how generalised symbolic media enable different kinds of exchange processes to take place between subsystems of society; in other words, how they relate to the allocation of social resources.[20] Money enables the transfer of property and the performance of services, which makes contracts in a complex 'institutional nexus' of principles and rules the basic reference for 'legitimate exchange and possession' (Parsons 1976: 97–98). Similarly, power offers bindingness, which is institutionalised through 'authority', that is, 'the legitimized capacity to make and to contribute to the implementation of decisions which are binding on a specifiable collective unit or class of them', giving the 'holder of authority' 'some kind of right of speaking in the name of the collectivity' and the capacity to invoke 'coercive sanctions' against those who do not comply (1976: 98–100). Influence, on the other hand, triggers persuasion so that one can shape 'the attitude and opinion of others' (1963a: 37) without resorting to the threat of coercive sanctions; 'occupying positions of prestige'

[18] These properties of media are presented in different ways. *cf* Chernilo (2002: 435–36), Habermas (1987a: 264–67 [1987b: 395–400]), and Münch (1987: 77–79 [1982: 125–286). Yet the latter proposes some substitutions in the media's nomenclature; see Münch (1987: 219 fn 51 [1982: 123 fn 51]).

[19] For a schematic outline of the media and their specifications, see Baum (1976: 467). Parsons also tried to sketch other media operative not at the level of the social system but rather at the level of the general action system, such as 'affection', 'intelligence', 'performance capacity', and 'definition of the situation' (1970: 45–48 and 62–68); a further attempt to describe intelligence and affection can be seen in Parsons (1976: 104 ff). For a detailed summary in this regard, see Münch (1987: 91 ff [1982: 143 ff]).

[20] A graphical representation of the interchange possibilities can be seen in Parsons (1963b: 260, 1968: 138). Casting doubts onto the possibility of interchange between the subsystems of money and power, see Habermas (1987a: 267–70 [1987b: 400–03]). Luhmann (1976: 522), in turn, conditions the interchange on translation, coding, and recoding of inputs. For a brief reference in which media are treated as 'social resources', see Parsons (1968: 146).

facilitates this (1976: 103–04) as well as giving relevant information, which eventually dispenses with verifications if one has 'reputation' (1963a: 50). Lastly, commitments call for loyalty and appeal to the 'implementation of values', so that behaviour can be morally approved or disapproved; hence one has to keep up one's own 'moral authority' in order to get 'the privileges of association with others', in the same vein the association by having as many commitments as possible may become stronger 'both collectively and for its members individually' (1968: 148–49).

A detailed extensive incursion into Parson's framework is beyond the scope of this work, not only because many have already done this, but also because it has incurred throughout the past decades criticisms as well as further developments, many of which aimed at the much more comprehensive endeavour of explaining the development of society itself.[21] In addition to providing a point of departure from which to identify what kinds of resources are capable of being mobilised in society, it also helps with another insight: resources, in the form of symbolic generalised media, 'are ways of "getting results" rather than only of conveying information' (Parsons 1963a: 42).[22] If one wants to capture which results are pursued in an arena and which exchange processes take place among actors to achieve them, this framework indeed paves the way for a plethora of fruitful analyses.

One example is provided by Renn (1992: 184–85), conceiving an arena theory with an emphasis on how 'resources can be used to gain the attention and support of the general public, to influence the arena rules, and to "score" in competition with other actors'. In this sense, 'resources may be the ultimate goals of an actor', or 'more likely they are the means by which actors can accomplish their specific intentions'. Regardless of 'whether these intentions are egoistic or altruistic, overtly stated or hidden', the focus of an arena, in any case, would lie in grasping 'the success of resource mobilization'. As he aims at analysing political debates about risk issues, beyond the already described resources of money, power, influence, and value commitment, he also considers 'evidence', which is 'the claim of truth that social groups or special subsystems of society (in particular science) make based on methodological rules and accepted

[21] See part IV of Loubser et al (1976). A known development in the framework of the theory of action can be seen in Münch (1987: 73 ff [1982: 123 ff]). Yet the most famous critical appropriations specifically dedicated to constructing a theory of generalised symbolic media and their role in the evolution of society are probably the ones made by Luhmann (2012: esp 190 ff [1997a: esp 316 ff]), in terms of generalised symbolic media of communication, and by Habermas (1987a: esp 235 ff [1987b: esp 352 ff]), distinguishing steering and communication media vis-à-vis the distinction between system and lifeworld. A brief summary of the positions of Parsons, Luhmann, and Habermas can be seen in Chernilo (2002), who in turn proposes observing the theory of generalised symbolic media as a 'progressive research programme, in Lakato's terms'.

[22] *cf* Parsons (1960: 182) and Luhmann (2012: 120–23 [1997a: 202–05]). The latter even calls the symbolically generalised communication media 'success media' (*Erfolgsmedien*) (2012: 121 [1997a: 203]), which enhance the chances of acceptance of communication.

theoretical knowledge' and therefore, 'can be used to convince persons about the likely consequences of social action' (1992: 187 and 185).[23] All of these resources 'help actors to be more influential' (1992: 184). Hence, if one wants to influence how certain risks should be handled or policies be shaped, then one has to be prepared to enter the arena and mobilise the required resources to achieve success.

This task of achieving success naturally imposes some structural constraints. As observed by Renn (1992: 187), 'in modern democratic and pluralistic societies actors need more than one resource to be successful in an arena'. Indeed, one would hardly disagree with the fact that 'neither money nor power is sufficient to shape policies'. But Renn (1992: 187) further claimed that 'all actors, including the rule enforcement agency, need a minimal reservoir of each resource in order to be successful in a given arena'. On the one hand, he has a point in making the rule enforcement agency a 'particularly interesting example'. 'As many cases have demonstrated', he argued (1992: 188), 'citizens protests have successfully blocked the siting of unwanted facilities, although the responsible agencies had the power to override such opposition'. Therefore, agencies could not rely on only one resource in order to put forward a contested project. As a matter of fact, 'if situations arise in which rule enforcement agencies have nothing but power, they are more willing to share this power in exchange for other resources, such as evidence or value commitment' (1992: 188). I will show later why enforcement agencies are an interesting example in the context of this research as well, although for different reasons (see section 8.2.2). On the other hand, as he conceded, determining how much is the 'minimal reservoir' is a difficult empirical challenge. Easier to observe is the conspicuous result of the need to collect resources: it creates an 'exchange market for resources'. This way,

> Social actors with lots of money try to purchase social influence by paying highly reputable persons to join their cause. Groups that offer meaning and values use these resources for fund raising. High-prestige groups may use rewards to honor charismatic leaders, who in turn will provide value commitments. Other groups

[23] Renn does follow a mix of approaches, ranging from Parsons to Luhmann and Münch. However, it seems to me rather confusing how they come up together. This is seen, for instance, in the way he describes 'social influence' and 'value commitment' (1992: 186–87). In contrast to Parsons, he treats 'persuasion' as a 'generalized medium' of 'value commitment', whereas it should be of 'influence'. Moreover, he claims to use 'the term *power* in the classical Weberian sense' (1992: 185). But in this sense power is defined as 'the chance of a man or of a number of men to realize their own will in a communal action even against the resistance of others who are participating in the action' (Weber 1946: 180, 1947: 152 [2013: 210]). The problem is that, as was already noted by Parsons (1976: 99), in such a definition, which traces back to Hobbes, 'money clearly is a form of power, as also are influence and a number of other entities'; see also Parsons (1963b: 232). Furthermore, putting Luhmann and Münch together without proper caveats is also misleading, for both advocate frameworks that to a certain extent compete, namely, systems theory and action theory. For an overview of the lines of conflict and complementarity between both paradigms with special emphasis on the development of the discussion in Luhmann, see Stichweh (2000).

> may use their power or money to hire experts in exchange for receiving evidence. (Renn 1992: 188)

Of course, since exchange processes may not consist in zero-sum games, it is necessary to be aware of the inflationary and deflationary consequences of generating too many resources. In the same way that 'too many medals, for example, diminish the social value of each medal', excessive creation of money leads to a decrease in its value, and similarly making too many promises may undermine political leadership. Additionally, it cannot be overlooked that the 'use of resources outside their dominant application' may lead to problems of legitimisation, 'for example, the use of money for compensation may lead to a decline in social influence and value commitment because the transaction is perceived as bribery' (Renn 1992: 188).

This framework unlocks a number of different research agendas to explore. As Renn (1992: 193) rightfully realised, from the 'quantification of the resource reservoir' available in certain stages to the 'mobilization potential' of actors in order to be successful in an arena, there are invariably many empirical challenges to tackle. I do not address them all here since I am focused on examining one particular type of arena: those constituted of noncompliance. And when it comes to noncompliance, there is one resource that draws special attention: power.

8

On the State and its Law

8.1. THE DEFLATIONARY SPIRAL OF POWER

THROUGH THE MEDIUM of power, certain people – those possessing authority – are legitimated to produce collectively binding decisions. As Parsons (1976: 99) made clear, 'collective reference' and 'bindingness' are thus two essential ingredients of the concept. What I want to contend here is that, in arenas of noncompliance, the 'bindingness' element of the concept is hampered to such an extent that we are forced to deal with a deflation of power: authority exerted without bindingness, or – put into more careful terms – authority exerted despite bindingness. As this entails presuppositions and consequences that cannot go unnoticed, especially because both ingredients are discussed together in a very specific manner in Parsons' framework, I will examine the relationship between both in more detail, showing the impacts of structural noncompliance on the exercise of authority.

In the same sense that 'utility' is the reference value for economy, 'effectiveness' is that of the political system (Parsons 1963b: 234). Whereas money generalises at a symbolic level the measurement of utility, even though 'it does not itself possess utility in the primary consumption sense' (1963b: 236), power does something analogous to collective decisions. Under certain conditions of institutionalisation, power becomes 'the generalized medium of mobilizing resources for effective collective action' (1963b: 240). This presupposes that certain set of commitments and obligations can be made 'binding', that is, 'under normatively defined conditions their fulfilment may be insisted upon by the appropriate role-reciprocal agencies' (1963b: 237). Insistence here takes the form of sanctions, meaning that the fulfilment of binding commitments and obligations can ultimately be '"enforced" by the threat or actual imposition of situational negative sanctions, in the former case having the function of deterrence, in the latter of punishment'. In the same sense that the grounding value of money lies 'in the commodity value of the monetary metal', that of power is ultimately the resort to 'physical force as a means of coercion and, in the limiting case, compulsion' (1963b: 240). Of course, as Parsons (1963b: 240) rightly adverted, 'just as a monetary system resting entirely on gold as the actual medium of exchange is a very primitive one', being incapable of mediating 'a complex system of market exchange', would also be primitive 'a power system in which the only negative sanction is the threat of force'. Therefore, in the same way that 'confidence' in the monetary system is a factor of 'mutual acceptability and stability' for money to be used in interchange relations, 'legitimation' is that of power, which is only possible if power also achieves a symbolically generalised level at which it is no longer to be confused with the use of physical force to secure compliance (1963b: 238).

In this context, legitimation functions as a kind of collective agreement according to which those who come to occupy certain positions in society are entitled to make binding decisions. Thus conceived, it departs from a traditional understanding of power as coercion so that 'securing compliance with a wish, whether it be defined as an obligation of the object or not, simply by threat of superior force, is not an exercise of power' (1963b: 238). It is true that compliance can be pursued without resorting to the use of coercion by means of other generalised media of interchange. In this sense, different sanctioning strategies to bring about 'a change in what the actions of one or more other units would otherwise have been' are available, such as 'inducement', 'persuasion', and 'activation of commitments' (1963b: 238). This leaves coercion to be exercised only in those socially accepted cases where there is legitimation do so. The legitimate exercise of power – 'the power of *A* over *B*' – would then precisely mean 'the "right" of *A*, as a decision-making unit involved in collective process, to make decisions which take precedence over those of *B*, in the interest of the effectiveness of collective operation as a whole'. This 'right to use power' is exactly what Parsons (1963b: 243) called 'authority', following Barnard's take on the subject.

It should be noted that what Parsons meant was that the holding of authority does provide the capacity to legitimately use force if called to do so, but authority also – and perhaps more importantly – involves something else, connected with what Barnard (1968: 164) in another context called attention to: 'the acceptance or consent of individuals'.[1] Authoritative decisions are very often grounded not on sheer use of coercive sanctions, but on a kind of acquiescence of those upon which they will have effects. This creates a sort of mandate, whereby subordinates are bound to binding decisions and those to whom authority is granted are bound to the limits pertaining to the consent itself. At the level of a more comprehensive social system – I would add, in which consent can only be supposed[2] – the concept of authority presupposes the institutionalisation of a 'normative

[1] Although Barnard's *The Functions of the Executive* is mainly focused on organisations, management, and public administration, Parsons (1976: 100) considered it to be 'one of the classics of political theory'. It was from this particular perspective that Parsons seemed to draw much more comprehensive conclusions than the ones intended by Barnard. For a critical assessment of Barnard's concept of authority from the specific point of view of modern management, see Hoopes (2003: 173–75).

[2] For acceptance or consent of individuals at that level is a practical impossibility. See Luhmann (2004: 247 [1993: 261–62]). At most, one would be able to speak of procedural consensus; see Neves (2001a: 136 ff; 2006: 136 ff).

order' by which 'binding obligations can clearly be "invoked" by lower-order against higher-order agencies as well as *vice versa*' (Parsons 1963b: 243). Authority should then be distinguished from power in that 'authority is not a circulating medium', but 'the institutional code within which the use of power as medium is organized and legitimized'; it defines the 'right to acquire and use power' or at a more general level, it defines 'rights of participation in the power system' (1963b: 243–44). One particular consequence of this high level of institutionalisation is the multitude of offices involved in the exercise of power, ranging from the right to speak in the name of a collectivity to the right to insist on compliance by means of coercive sanctions. In a highly differentiated society, as Parsons (1963b: 244) rightly remarked, the result is a 'general division of labor' in which 'the holder of authority very often is not himself in a position to "enforce" his decisions, but must be dependent on specialized agencies for this'. Naturally such division reinforces the symbolic level of power, making its use to a certain extent independent of its capacity to effectively become coercive and trigger compulsory compliance.

It would be possible to call into question the accuracy of Parsons's description of power vis-à-vis money and focus on its shortcomings.[3] Further research could also be employed in order to grasp how actors in an arena acquire power, which strategies they use to keep hold of it, and what kinds of exchanges take place among them.[4] However, as I am more interested in understanding the impacts of structural noncompliance, there is one particular strand to account for. By way of summarising the previous discussion in the context of an arena model, it can be said that the resource of power grants at least three things to be exchanged: on the part of collective reference, power grants the capacity to speak in the name of the collectivity on the one hand and the making of collective decisions on the other; on the part of bindingness, power provides the offering of coercive means to dissuade and punish noncompliance. As I briefly advanced in the beginning of this section – and as the case study of street vending seems to make clear – when it comes to arenas of noncompliance, we must deal with a very limited capacity for collective decisions, which in respect to state organisations assume the form of legal norms, to be de facto enforced. This creates an asymmetry between the collective reference and bindingness in the exercise of power, which sets – paraphrasing Parsons (1963b: 256) – a 'deflationary spiral' of power. The consequences are a series of impacts of structured noncompliance on how power can be exchanged in the market of resources and how law codifies relationships between actors in the arena. I will explore this phenomenon of power deflation a little further, and then – instead of focusing

[3] Exemplary in this regard are Giddens (1968: 264 ff) and Baldwin (1971). See also the references mentioned in ch 7, n 21.

[4] In the case of street vending, it seems that all these questions are to some degree connected with processes of creation of organisations and collective action. See ch 2, n 19.

on the political system as Parsons did – I will analyse it from the perspective of the legal system.

Assuming that the creation and exchange of power are not necessarily a zero-sum game, that is, the mobilisation of power as a social resource makes it possible for surplus to emerge, the management of a resource is 'subject to fluctuations on a dimension of inflation-deflation' (Parsons 1963b: 256). Whereas the surplus in the case of money, in the analogy employed by Parsons, is mainly derived from 'credit-creation through commercial banking' (1963b: 251), in the case of power a conspicuous source is seen in democratic electoral systems. Specifically with the channelling of support by the electorate to back 'collective leadership', there is an element 'analytically independent of the routine power position of office' (1963b: 255). So in the same way that banks can mobilise credit provided that the expectation of future payment will be fulfilled according to the agreed terms – and this naturally entails a relationship of 'mutual confidence or trust' (1963b: 252) – leaders can 'mobilize the binding commitments of their constituents' given that once in office, they will make 'increments of effectiveness which are necessary to implement new binding policies', for instance the 'development of new agencies, procurement of personnel, new norms, and even changes in the basis of legitimation' (1963b: 255). This illustrates a typical state of affairs in which fluctuation in the quantity of power might occur, and the 'credibility of the assertion of the bindingness of obligations' (1963b: 256) may be undermined. This can happen in two directions, both being signs of 'crises which indicate a decrease in the ability of the system in question to fulfil its function' (Münch 1987: 86 [1982: 137]).

In the first direction, there is an overextension of 'power-credit' or 'new power-expectations' but without the 'necessary organization basis for fulfillment of expectations' or 'adequate provision for making them effective' (1963b: 256). Too much confidence is put on the power system in such a way that the extensive increase of symbols of power is not followed by the necessary increments of effectiveness. The result is power inflation, the practical consequence of which is that 'attempting to invoke the obligations will result in less than a full level of performance, inhibited by various sorts of resistance' (1963b: 256). In the second direction, the opposite process, that is, power deflation, takes place. There is a decrease of confidence in the system so that legitimate power becomes a scarce resource to mobilise collective action and activate obligations. The organisational basis for fulfilment of expectations is then contracted, subordinates tend to question their positions, and achieving compliance becomes *pari passu* more difficult, requiring progressively stronger means of coercion. As confidence is lost, legitimation is called into question. Evidently, deflations occur with varying frequencies in any power system, and different forms of coercion (from warnings to compulsion itself) can be used by authorities as mechanisms to re-establish confidence and assure compliance. If confidence cannot be restored or maintained, escalating deflation might eventually lead to 'loss of authority' or even 'revolution' (Johnson 1966: 29–32 and 91). In extreme cases, the use of force due to the lack of legitimation tends to turn into the naked use of violence.[5] Without going that far, it is suffice to say that in the course of power deflation, due to expanding noncompliance, the capacity to mobilise collectively binding decisions is impaired to the extent that they cannot be secured by legitimate mechanisms of enforcement. As noncompliance is eminently a legal phenomenon this process affects the legal system in many ways.

In possession of the conceptual architecture built so far, I now contend that the most comprehensive impact of structural noncompliance is the deflation of political power, making it a scarce resource. The chief consequence of this can be seen in the increasing difficulties in mobilising support, commitments, and decisions to effectively achieve collective goals and making them binding. This can be expressed not only by high grades of disobedience of institutionally binding decisions but also by the disengagement between offices in charge of making those decisions and the offices in charge of executing them, in other words, disengagement between law creation and law enforcement. That is perhaps the reason why lawmaking in general and public policies in particular have low capacity for solving structural problems in arenas of noncompliance. In conditions of power deflation where subordinates tend to question decisions taken at higher levels in the hierarchy, government-driven policies cannot be transmuted into administrative practices without major obstacles. And this should be understood not as a gain of autonomy of the administration vis-à-vis the government, contributing to the autopoiesis of the political system, but more as a break in the hierarchy system of authorities.[6] The issuance of more collective decisions (in the form of legislation, ordinances, decrees) as a reaction to power deflation, when not followed by a concrete expansion of the basis for their fulfilment, convert these symbols of power into mere tokens without value of interchange,[7] which in turn deflates power even more. It is in this sense that one can speak of a *spiralling effect of power deflation* in arenas of noncompliance, whereby the reactions to the loss of confidence bring about new deflationary processes that make power capable of mobilising resources increasingly scarce.

Generalised symbolic media are the mechanisms through which interchange can take place between actors in an arena, or – if one wants to put it in Parson's terms – between structural units of society (eg, a private business firm, an administrative agency, or a court of law). Such a way of facilitating interchange is a very specific evolutionary acquisition that, as Parsons (1963b: 259)

[5] Understanding the process of power deflation might actually explain not only 'why revolutions occur' but also, as suggested Baldwin (1971: 609–10), 'why world government does not'. Regarding the processes of power inflation and deflation, *cf* Johnson (1966: 29–30), Giddens (1968: 267), and Baldwin (1971: 608–10). An analysis of the economic phenomena of inflation and deflation that underlie Parsons' analogies lies beyond the scope and interest of this work. For the state of the art at that time, see Bronfenbrenner (1968).

[6] *cf* Neves (1992: 177–79).

[7] This does not preclude but rather tends to reinforce the symbolic use of legislation to achieve certain political ends to the detriment of its 'legal-instrumental function' (Neves 2022: 21 ff [2011: 31 ff]).

insightfully realised, 'precludes mediation of processes in terms either of ascriptive expectations or barter arrangements, or a combination of the two'. It seems that extending his insight *a contrario* would capture what happens when a symbolic medium becomes scant: the emergence of ascriptive expectations, barter arrangements, or a combination of the two to fill up the functional demands for resources to circulate. In the realm of politics, it would hardly be surprising to find that exchanges are made on the basis of quid pro quos or that offices are distributed according to family membership.[8] The effects of power deflation become however less conspicuous when seen under the perspective of the law, which works as a 'secondary coding' of power (Luhmann 2012: 213 [1997a: 357]). Here these barter arrangements are not only brought about during law enforcement but also instilled in the very programmes of law. I will now explore these reactions to, and effects of, power deflation, since they can be observed as further impacts of noncompliance.

8.2. THE BARTERING RATIONALITY

That bartering has been becoming a pattern in regulation is well known.[9] What seems to underlie the emergence of such arrangements is the fact that under conditions of scarce resources authority can still be exercised over norm addressees; however, due to the different costs involved, instead of pursuing coercive compliance the enforcement agent is prone to cooperative strategies. Of course this does not avoid the considerably difficult question of determining how scarce the resources available are and thus what kind of strategy should be adopted.[10] Apart from the empirical challenges and the construction of theoretical models to determine what is the best behaviour for each player in the arena, more important here is to account for the rationality behind these arrangements, which not only take the form of legal operations but also use legal statuses as bargaining chips.

[8] At least in Brazil it is not difficult to see how family for instance plays a central role in politics as well as economy. See in this regard: www.nexojornal.com.br/entrevista/2020/11/21/%E2%80%98A-estrutura-pol%C3%ADtica-no-Brasil-se-confunde-com-genealogias-e-fam%C3%ADlias%E2%80%99. Accessed on 13 January 2021.

[9] See, for instance, Jowell (1977), Scholz (1984), and Winter (1985). I will expand here on the latter.

[10] See Scholz (1984), building on the 'enforcement dilemma' and demonstrating why cooperative strategies are preferred. For a more recent study and specifically focused on street vending, see Hummel (2017). In an arena model, as previously noted (see the last paragraph in section 7.3), the problem can be framed in terms of determining the resource reservoir and mobilisation potential. What the literature seems to miss, at least if it were to be applied to arenas of noncompliance, is that noncompliance is not only a matter of disobedience but also of pervasive failure, forbearance, abuse, and inconsistent adjudication. In these conditions the enforcement dilemma does not hold, for it presupposes a commitment to law enforcement, either by cooperative or deterrence strategy. In this sense, for instance, one cannot even clearly distinguish 'good' firms from 'bad' firms as Sholz does.

An interesting point of departure is the prognosis provided some decades ago by Winter and which, for the reasons I shall delineate, lays the basis to explain the further outcomes of power deflation in arenas of noncompliance. Based on empirical and theoretical works produced at the time, he argued that there was a '"bartering rationality" coming to dominate the law of modern regulation' (Winter 1985: 220). Particularly noticed in the process of implementation of regulatory law between firms and regulatory agencies, the bartering was not only taking place in the 'law enforcement stage' but also 'being instilled into the program of the law itself'. This could be seen in the way the law was often being used as a 'mere bargaining chip', for instance, to accept 'partial compliance' under the 'agreement' not to go to court. And also in the movement by which the bartering was being brought 'from the "shadow of law" into the light of legality' when the law itself allowed 'substantive regulation to be traded for cooperation'. In some cases, the regulation was even legally designed to be broken down 'into pieces of rights (eg, to pollute) that the administrative agency may "sell" (eg, for the payment of charges) as a market mechanism for limiting disfavored conduct'. Two things seemed to be at stake in these trade-offs: the 'legal powers' at the disposal of regulatory agencies and 'the different ways that the regulated can obligate themselves' (Winter 1985: 220–21).

On the side of the agency the 'basic bargaining chip is its ability, either in law or in practice, to refrain from exercising its full authority' (Winter 1985: 221). As a kind of intended, conscious 'underexploitation of its authority' the agency may offer to forgo a regulation, a command, or the denial of a permit, or may offer to remove procedural obstacles (1985: 221–22). In exchange firms are asked to offer 'some sort of recompense', either in the form of '*partial compliance*', whereby the agency's primary goals are to a certain extent fulfilled, or in the form of '*extended benefits*', which include more performance than the agency may legally require, or 'some sort of *payment*', such as cash in lieu of compliance.[11] As Winter (1985: 228–29) pointed out, all of this was 'conducted largely at the discretion of the agency', including cases in which 'the agency's willingness to barter is in apparent violation of its legal mandate, and in other instances the agency uses bartering to secure behavior that it has no authority to demand'. This of course did not exclude cases in which similar practice was incorporated into the law itself with provisions of 'permissible barters' and 'trade-offs that condition the legality of an action on the receipt of specified returns'.

What appeared to underlie the phenomenon – at least in the cases Winter was analysing (ie, in the United States, United Kingdom, and Germany) – was a growing trend toward 'cooperation, negotiation, bargaining, bartering' instead of full enforcement in order to deal with 'regulatory problems' (Winter 1985: 237). Although most of these practices could indeed be found long before, the novelty

[11] Regarding the latter, see Winter (1975: 58–62).

was the emergence of a public discourse that describes and justifies them in a way that 'necessarily challenges *legal doctrines* about the binding force of the law' under the premise that the requirement of full enforcement is no longer a goal of 'the political process that legitimates regulation'. This obviously did not preclude the fact that, as Winter (1985: 240–41) carefully realised, 'without the clear power and duties to interfere with private interests, the administrative agency would not have a position from which to barter effectively'. In a kind of paradoxical way, the bartering acts on the assumption that full enforcement is a 'benchmark' without which 'the value of the legal rule as a bargaining chip would be diminished'. It seems that what this new discourse was attempting to ground was the mindset according to which compliance should not be necessarily disregarded as 'a per se societal good', but the starting point of analysis should be 'the existence of exceptional circumstances'; in other words, 'circumstances determine whether compliance is desirable' (Winter 1985: 237).

One could delve into the history of the phenomenon or seek its connections with a certain legal scholarship committed to values of efficiency or utility of regulation and regulatory agencies.[12] But such endeavours would divert far from the concerns here, namely, the bartering practices that emerge from power deflation in arenas of noncompliance. Before continuing, I will first update and expand the study done by Winter to the context of Brazil, in order to maintain the consistency of this empirical basis.

8.2.1. The Brazilian Case: Bartering in Reaction to Noncompliance

Among Winter's many predictions, one has clearly become true: the bartering rationality has come to dominate the law of modern regulation. Actually, it has been instilled not merely into the very fabric of regulatory and administrative law, but also into almost every sector of public law. In Brazil the trend has become entrenched in such a way that one could even speak of a turn in those branches of law for which the practice of bartering would in principle be extraneous. The paradigm shift seems to have started in the 1990s. A cornerstone was laid by Law 8,078/1990, which, beyond creating the Consumer Defence Code, substantially changed Law 7,347/1985, the Public Civil Action Act. Amid the modifications one was particularly important: the inclusion of § 6 in Article 5 of the Public Civil Action Act. The new text was clear regarding its purpose: 'Authorized public bodies may commit the interested parties to adjust their conduct to the legal requirements, by means of sanctions, which shall be effective as an extrajudicial enforcement instrument'. The provision formally created the

[12] Winter (1985: 235–37) himself provided fruitful insights. It seems that game theory approaches have been the dominant trend in this regard. Not surprisingly, there has been a growth of studies in which cooperative strategies gain prominence. Cooperation has even risen to the level of explaining the evolution of the 'constitutional society' itself; see Almeida (2020: esp 70 ff).

possibility for the parties to conclude what today is known as a TAC, which is an abbreviation for *Termo de Compromisso de Ajustamento de Conduta* (Terms of Conduct Adjustment Commitment). A TAC is an agreement that defines what is to be done by the parties and the respective consequences in case of violation. In practical terms the regime of compliance with certain legal norms, including the respective sanctions, is negotiated, and the resulting agreement substitutes the provisions of the enacted law.

It is true that few months earlier an almost identical provision was passed within the then newly approved Statute of the Child and Adolescent (Law 8,069/1990).[13] But its scope was restricted to the legal protection of individual, diffuse, and collective rights of those who fell under the protection of the statute: persons up to 18 years old (see Article 2). Its adoption within the realm of the Public Civil Action Act considerably extended the cases for which the agreement could be negotiated. Broadly speaking, the Public Civil Action is a kind of class action that aims at protecting any kind of diffuse or collective rights (see Article 1, IV), which makes the Act deserve the category of a 'trans-substantive statute' (Gidi 2003: 327).[14] Throughout the years, in addition to the already encompassing list, a couple of amendments further enlarged the scope of the action, which nowadays includes the liability for damages caused to the environment, to consumers, to assets and rights of artistic, aesthetic, historic, touristic, or landscape value, as well as the damages caused for violation of the economic order, urbanistic order, the honour and dignity of racial, ethnic or religious groups, and public and social patrimony (see Article 1). Despite the few express restrictions,[15] it goes without saying that under the scope of this action it is possible to fit, in a way or another, almost every possible conflict that involves collectivities in the public sphere, which consequently entails the legal possibility for the concerned parties to barter the terms of compliance of the respective enacted laws. This alone allows a glimpse into the extension of what can be bartered according to Brazilian law. But the instillation of the bartering rationality was much more pervasive, for it also came to cover matters not only of collective rights in general but also of individual rights within public law. The most sensitive case is perhaps that of criminal law.

In terms of criminal matters, a progressive scale can be observed. A seed of the trend was planted in the Constitution of 1988, which provided for special courts with jurisdiction to deal exclusively with civil causes of lesser complexity and less serious criminal offences (Article 98). One of the novelties, however, was the provision under the same article of the possibility of 'settlement' within their

[13] See Art 211. The only textual difference is the part 'by means of sanctions'.

[14] As Gidi (2003: 327 fn 27) explains, 'in American legal jargon, procedural rules applicable to the litigation of any mater, irrespective of the area of substantive law in dispute, are called "trans-substantive."'.

[15] The sole paragraph of Art 1, for instance, excludes individually determined matters that involve taxes, social security contributions, and retirement or other institutional funds.

jurisdiction. Apart from the discussions about the constitutional status of such a clause,[16] the creation of the special courts only came later with Law 9,099/1995. Its Article 2 made it clear among the purposes that the procedure should seek 'whenever possible … the settlement'. Initially considered to be less serious offences were all the misdemeanors and crimes whose maximum penalty did not exceed one year of imprisonment (Article 61). In 2006, the coverage was further extended, up to two years. Whereas these provisions referred only to cases under the jurisdiction of the member states of Brazil, a constitutional amendment from 1999 also included in the constitution special courts for federal jurisdiction (see Article 98, § 1, of the Constitution). And Law 10,259/2001, which regulated the creation of these special federal courts, repeated the same formula from the member states, but now extending the possibility of settlements for the same criminal offences under federal jurisdiction.

The criminal settlements were just the beginning. In the justification of the bill that resulted in Law 9,099/1995 (*Projeto de Lei 1.480/1989*), the then congressman Michel Temer spared no words to express the rationality behind what was coming:

> In fact, the idea that the state can and should criminally pursue, without exception, any infraction, without admitting, under any circumstances, a certain dose of discretion or availability of public criminal action, has shown with all evidence its fallacy and hypocrisy. In practice, several informal and politically chaotic selection criteria operate, including among the bodies of criminal and judicial persecution. It is not unknown that, in a very high percentage of certain crimes of public prosecution, the police do not initiate the investigation and the prosecutor and the judge act in such a way that limitation period is achieved. Nor is it unknown that the victim – with whom the state has so far cared little – is increasingly interested in redress for the damages and less and less in the application of the criminal punishment.

The intention expressly was to move away from a model exclusively governed by the 'principles of mandatory and nonavailable public criminal prosecution' and open space to the 'principle of regulated discretion' as a method of fighting the pervasive lack of compliance with criminal law. Law 9,099/1995 itself did not stop at settlements. In Article 89 it created a probation offer for crimes whose minimum penalty is equal or less than one year, even if they do not fall under the scope of the special courts; namely, the 'conditional suspension of the prosecution'. Whereas criminal settlements allow the accused and public prosecutor to negotiate penalties other than imprisonment and in exchange the alleged offender will be free of prosecution (see Articles 72 to 76 of Law 9,099/1995), the conditional suspension functions as a *sursis* before trial: the prosecutor offers

[16] It could be asked whether this implies a constitutional right to settle, since bartering makes it possible to avoid negative sanctions from the state, but that would depart from the scope of this book. For the discussion of whether the offender has a right to the bargaining and whether the prosecutor ought to offer the benefit, see Giacomo and Vasconcellos (2015: 1116–118) with references to the debate.

the benefit, and if the accused accepts the conditions[17] set by the judge, the criminal lawsuit will be suspended for a period of between two to four years, at the end of which the state will lose its right to prosecute.

In the following years the instruments and forms of bargaining only increased, both in coverage and discretion. The crescendo was arguably Law 12,850/2013, known as the Law on Criminal Organizations, which gave form to a kind of bargain that turns the criminal into state's evidence: the 'plea agreement' (Article 3, I). Among the highlights were the bargaining chips of judicial pardon, reduction of up to two-thirds of the sentence of imprisonment or its substitution (Article 4). Brought into force as an answer from former President Dilma Rousseff to the nationwide anti-corruption demonstrations, this law has been at the centre of the most important political affairs of the last years, including the one that played a major role in her impeachment.[18] A couple of years later, another law was passed amid a turbulent dispute over a tougher approach on crime,[19] namely Law 13,964/2019, which brought a different set of changes. One of them was to give more precise contours to the then extensively and in many cases controversially used plea agreement, especially in order to avoid the abuses committed in the preceding years.[20] Another was the creation of two more bartering arrangements, both in the form of 'agreement not to prosecute'.

[17] Namely, redress the damages, not go to certain places, not travel without authorisation, and appear in person before the court on a monthly basis to inform and justify their activities (Art 89, § 1, I to IV, Law 9,099/1995).

[18] This is the case of the now widely famous Car Wash operation, which was made possible mostly thanks to this law and the then newly formalised bargaining instrument. A day before the impeachment of President Dilma, a first-instance judge illegally disclosed a confidential wiretap between President Dilma and her ally, the ex-President Lula, who was then being threatened with arrest within the realm of the operation. Although there was nothing illegal in the content of the phone call itself, it sparked public protests against the President, creating the political environment for the impeachment to take place. For a journalistic cover of the events, see: www.washingtonpost.com/news/monkey-cage/wp/2016/03/26/how-the-release-of-wiretapped-conversations-in-brazil-threatens-its-democracy. Accessed on 30 November 2020. A newspaper even insinuated that the operation disclosed the biggest corruption scheme in the history of the world; see: www.theguardian.com/world/2017/jun/01/brazil-operation-car-wash-is-this-the-biggest-corruption-scandal-in-history. Accessed on 27 November 2020. At the time, Lula was the most popular candidate for the Brazilian presidency. The illegal conduct and schemes, especially in regards to the methods applied in order to get better bargaining positions against the accused, of the chief members of the prosecution office in charge of the operation and the judge Sergio Moro (who ordered the arrest of Lula in the middle of the election and later became minister of justice for the winning candidate, Jair Bolsonaro) were carefully investigated and published by The Intercept; see: https://theintercept.com/series/secret-brazil-archive. Accessed on 30 November 2020.

[19] The bill was initially part of the 'anticrime package' put forward by Sergio Moro as a minister of justice. A summary of his proposals can be seen here: www1.folha.uol.com.br/poder/2019/02/entenda-os-principais-pontos-do-pacote-anticrime-de-moro.shtml. Accessed on 30 November 2020.

[20] This was the tone of the criticism conveyed by many. See, for instance, the pronouncement of a Chief Justice of the Supreme Federal Court (STF) in this regard: www.conjur.com.br/2017-nov-16/abusos-podem-levar-extincao-delacao-premiada-gilmar. Accessed on 1 December 2020. In the same vein, lawyers and scholars who have worked with the bargaining denounced problems of application; see for instance: www.conjur.com.br/2017-dez-15/limite-penal-delacao-premiada-lei-evitar-atuais-abusos. Accessed on 1 December 2020.

The first form was related to criminal matters, meaning the inclusion of Article 28-A in the Code of Criminal Procedure, whereby powers were given to the prosecutor not to prosecute if the accused confessed, the criminal offence did not involve violence or serious threat, and the minimum penalty was less than four years. The punishment could then be agreed between the parties from a pool of different possibilities, ranging from simple payment to the victim (Article 28-A, I) to the fulfilment of any other condition established by the prosecutor (Article 28-A, IV). The second form provided legislative grounds to a bartering process that was already taking place in practice despite the uncertainty about its legality.[21] It applied to the agreements made in cases within the realm of the Public Probity Law (Law 8,429/1992), which establishes the civil and administrative liability of agents holding office, whether deriving from a mandate, position, employment, or function at public bodies and agencies. Even though 'transaction, agreement, or conciliation' in those cases were expressly prohibited (former § 1 of the Article 17, Law 8,429/1992), the National Council of Prosecution Services (CNMP), when regulating TAC made by prosecutors, admitted to its application in cases under the scope of the Public Probity Law (Article 1, § 2, Resolution 179/2017 of the CNMP). One could argue that, in view of the previous legislative changes regarding the different possibilities of agreement on criminal matters, agreements on issues of civil and administrative nature could be regarded as merely a corollary to those changes. However, it would be somehow hard to pose such an argument against clear legislative intentions: in 2015 there was an attempt to revoke the referred prohibition through presidential Provisional Decree 703/2015 (which provides for leniency agreements), but which was not converted into law by the Congress and therefore expired; in other words, the prohibition of transaction, agreement, or conciliation under the provisions of the Public Probity Law entered into force once again. Only with Law 13,964/2019 was the question finally settled, for it not only definitely revoked the prohibition but also provided in its place the possibility of 'agreement not to prosecute on civil matters' (at the time, it came as a new § 1 of the Article 17, Law 8,429/1992; currently the agreement is provided for in the Article 17-B).

I certainly could continue offering more examples, because the bartering rationality has also penetrated environmental law,[22] economic law,[23] regulation of the health system,[24] and virtually all kinds of matters that involve the

[21] Something similar could be said of the first agreement not to prosecute, which was regulated by the CNMP (see Art 18 of Resolution 181/2019) before Law 13,946/2019 came into being.

[22] See Art 79-A of Law 9,605/1998, providing for the possibility of TAC in cases of criminal and administrative liability for environmental damages.

[23] See the leniency agreements under Arts 86 and 87 of Law 12,529/2011 (Anti-Trust Law).

[24] See Art 29, § 1, of Law 9,656/1998 (regulates private health care plans and insurance) and Art 4, XXXIX, of the Law 9,961/2000 (creates the National Supplementary Health Agency).

public administration.[25] Underlying this shift in Brazilian public law are promises to shorten the caseload of courts, reduce costs spent on litigation, decrease social unrest, and fight high grades of noncompliance.[26] Whether those legal reforms are able to fulfil such promises is something worth examining, but the complexity of the matter and the necessary evidence for plausible answers hamper such an endeavour for now. What seems easier to assert is that they did pave the way for a system of 'bargained justice';[27] or, considering the perspective here, 'bargained compliance'. Additionally they brought about a set of impacts on the medium of power in the exchange market for resources in arenas of noncompliance and on the use of legal norms. I will give an account of such impacts.

8.2.2. Decentralisation of Power, Flexibilisation of Law

When Winter carried out his research, he was aware of the general consequences of the bartering rationality for administrative law. In contrast to an 'instrumental rationality' behind the 'traditional view of administrative regulation', in which agencies were conceived to implement previously established legislative goals by altering the behaviour of the regulated who were 'targets of the agency's actions' (Winter 1985: 241), the bartering rationality takes a different approach. It puts private actors, not in the position of an 'object to be altered through the unilateral exercise of power', but rather as 'a counterpart' whose 'resources and rights establish a bargaining position' and whose behaviour is hence driven by 'adequate offers'. From this perspective, 'the law's primary role' 'is to allocate bargaining chips to private actors as well as to governmental bodies.' And despite empowering 'agencies to work toward certain goals', it consequently assumes that agencies might 'work for ends that are not specified' and that 'specified ends' may not be 'fully obtained' (Winter 1985: 241). In such

[25] See Art 32 of Law 13,140/2015 (regulates the mediation between private individuals and the self-composition of conflicts within public administration) and Art 26 of the *Decreto-Lei* 4.657/1942 (Introductory Act to Brazilian Law) after the changes made by Law 13,655/2018. See also the leniency agreement under Arts 16 and 17 of Law 12,846/2013, known as the Anti-Corruption Law, for administrative and civil liability of legal persons that carry out acts against national or foreign governments.

[26] This shift also seems to be closely related with the expansion of a lobbying toward 'alternative dispute resolution', the so-called ADR, but further details in this regard would lie beyond the scope of this book.

[27] This expression, along with similar ones (eg, 'dialogic justice', 'consensual justice', 'negotiated justice') have gained widespread use, especially among scholars of criminal law, since the creation of the special courts. See, for instance, Grinover et al (2005: 47), Lopes Jr (2002), Giocamolli and Vasconcellos (2015), and Oliveira Neto and Cabral (2020). The criticisms of bartering practices in criminal law were vast, and Brazil is not the only place where such criticisms are heard. See in this regard Schünemann (2013) with special emphasis on the German case. Moreover, the discussion is almost always framed by comparisons with bartering practices of the American system of plea bargaining, whose structural problems have long been known; see, for instance, Schulhofer (1992).

a state of affairs, one could also speculate on the long-term consequences as Winter did,[28] or try to verify whether they came true in recent decades. In any case what seems hard to deny is that the bartering rationality brings about a 'commodification of legal powers' (Winter 1985: 247). If it is understood that 'the powers to inquire, to entitle, and to command constitute what is intended to be a political endowment and not a marketplace currency', then it becomes easier to realise that 'commodification destroys the political character of legal power as it transforms political endowments into commodities for bartering.' In this sense, in which 'the agency does not exert its powers but trades them', the commodification, as Winter (1985: 247) argued, 'also tends to privatize (in the name of the public, to be sure) the authority given the agency'.

Underlying this framework there is one line of reasoning I would like to shed light on by making use of the conceptual framework developed so far. It refers to a kind of unleashed expansion of authority in society. As defined in Parson's terms, authority is the right to acquire and use power, which is distributed among offices according to a general division of labour. When bartering arrangements are provided *de lege lata*, one immediate consequence is the distribution of authority in two distinct but intertwined directions. On the one hand, agencies that were previously restricted to law enforcement – and therefore to the strict function of insisting on compliance – are given the authority to barter the standard of compliance itself, which to a certain extent blurs the distinction between lawmaking and law enforcement. Depending on the agency's concrete interests, this may result in a practice of implementation that was already perceived by Winter (1985: 248): 'norms that cannot be altered openly may be rendered nonbinding in practice, thus making the law flexible.' This flexible law corresponds to, in the wording used earlier (see section 8.1), an exercise of authority despite bindingness. For the legal norm this has specific consequences in the conception of its structure, namely, the pragmatic passage from 'rules of conduct' to 'offers of regulation'. I shall discuss this shortly (see text accompanying n 33). On the other hand, by bringing the norm addressees to the table of compliance negotiation, authority is likewise expanded to private actors, who then become, in a certain sense, stakeholders in institutionally determining the scope and the meaning of certain regulations, which also entails turning enacted norms nonbinding. In the obverse of this double privatisation of authority (regarding agencies and norm addressees) lies another phenomenon: the decentralisation of political power.

By decentralisation I mean two things. First, a movement by which the regulation of certain matters, especially those under public law, leaves to some degree

[28] See Winter (1985: 242–46) for his insights in terms of 'strategies of seizing the battlegrounds', 'impeding structural reform', 'preserving inequality', 'concentration of divisible goods', 'stressing monetarizable goods', 'the loss of a critical public', and 'broadening the gap between the societal construction of reality and reality'.

the state's monopoly and moves toward the inclusion of private actors. In this specific sense, the state becomes a mere stakeholder in the regulation of public affairs, and, depending on the resources it can mobilise, its share in the regulation is increased or decreased. In arenas of noncompliance, where the state's capacity to produce collective decisions effectively and to enforce them is considerably impaired, the share is at the same rate lower. But even where it is higher, the state is still a stakeholder and has to deal with other stakeholders – not in the sense of traditional legislative processes but rather in terms of bartering arrangements to define the standard of compliance. Second, a tendency for the state to present itself as a fragmented constellation of different political interests, which vary from agency to agency, and from public body to public body.[29] Each of them becomes an actor to dispute its own share in the regulation. As resources of power are generally scarce, especially in arenas of noncompliance, one can observe in such conditions the emergence of competing agendas of legality, that is, each state actor pursues its own institutional goals with little reference to a unitary or unified common public interest. In this scenario of fragmentation, in which political power cannot be sufficiently distributed to equally promote all the state actors' goals, there is a tendency of politicisation of agencies and public bodies in general according to their proximity/distance to the agenda of the local, state, or national administrations. Power disputes are not restricted to electoral campaigns nor to the political parties involved in lawmaking. The process of law enforcement itself, which in this context implies a preference for a certain political agenda, is prone to be organised not primarily according to the scheme of lawful/unlawful, but that of government/opposition.[30] Thus conceived, the decentralisation of political power seems to result in another prediction of Winter's (1985: 248) regarding the justifications for bartering rationality: they 'tend to legitimate and promote a longstanding disguise for thwarting the popular will'.[31]

Concerning arenas of noncompliance, the legislatively designed bartering arrangements play a yet more specific role. Whereas for the whole of society they can indeed be presented as a functional answer to a general problem of effectiveness and lack of confidence in the polity, in arenas of noncompliance

[29] As it seems to me, this points out – though with different empirical grounds – a shift 'from the unitary state to the disaggregated state' (Slaughter 2004: 12 ff).

[30] I have already demonstrated how this takes place in practice. See the lawfare mentioned in section 3.3 (see ch 3, text accompanying n 37). In n 18, it was also mentioned how this was made possible by bartering practices. For the 'political grammar' of the legal officers responsible for the operation, see Sá e Silva (2020).

[31] Of course, when the bartering rationality is heavily grounded on legislation, it sounds odd to say that it thwarts the popular will. In order to put it in a slightly different way, I would say that the decentralisation of power boosted by the bartering rationality tends to legitimate and promote a longstanding disguise for thwarting the rationality of the public law in comparison with private law. I refer here to a similar preoccupation expressed a long time ago, more specifically 1945, by Carnelutti (1960: 292), but concerned with the difference between the civil and criminal law: 'In civil law, the parties have their hands free; in criminal they must have them tied.'

they actually tend to extend noncompliance and perpetuate the deflation of power. Bartering results in a kind of new compliance standard to be followed by the parties. The new standard acquires the status of legal norm and thus becomes part of the arena's non-intended legal ordering, bringing about a very specific set of consequences amid the dynamics of noncompliance within the arena. Bartered agreements, like any other kind of legal regulation, cannot assure that conflicts will be solved nor that the parties will act accordingly, but only that expectations of behaviour will be created. In this way they introduce a new difference, this time bartered by the parties, between compliant and noncompliant behaviour. By implication this means the creation of more opportunities for noncompliance as well as, for the reasons previously presented (see chapter six, text between nn 9 and 10), for potential conflicts, since they function as support for new demands, claims, and refusals. Bartered agreements add new symbols of legally codified power that, not being followed by sufficient increments in the basis of fulfilment of expectations, tend to be just another token alongside the set of statutes, administrative acts, and court decisions that were violated in the first place. As a mere token, that is, a symbol without the capacity to effectively mobilise commitments or enforce decisions, they are capable of triggering spiralling effects in at least three different ways. First, the new agreed compliance always sets a lower standard of compliance than the non-bartered one (ie, the standard of full compliance). Second, just like any regulation, the terms agreed are likewise prone to noncompliance, which creates a kind of persistent need for new agreements to deal with new and existing noncompliance. Third, those whose behaviour was recognised as noncompliant can then selectively use any of the agreed standards as a justifying symbol as if they were 'in the right'. Obviously, such a spiral results in an intrinsic incongruity in the determination of the content of legal norms within the arena: the proliferation of different standards of compliance varying according not only to the degrees of compliance but also the contingent agreements made by some of the actors. The case of *Feira da Sé* is a good illustration of how this happens in practice.

As detailed in the third chapter (see section 3.3), a comprehensive initiative was taken by the MPCE against the municipality to force the removal of street vendors from public spaces. Among the norms being violated by the vendors and the municipality, one was particularly important. I called it *Norm A*, which prohibits the general use of public squares for itinerant commerce, except with the proper permit and to sell specific goods. I also thoroughly examined many of the norm's fragments in all of the three possible degrees of interpretation, what now can be understood as the full standards of compliance in the sense that they point out the non-bartered conditions provided by legislation under which a behaviour may be deemed as compliant or noncompliant. After many failed attempts to enforce the norm, the actors came to a bartering agreement that resulted in the TAC between the MPCE, the municipality, and a committee representing the vendors.[32] As briefly mentioned earlier, among the terms of the agreement, there was one with the following provision (Third Clause, section 2):

> During the transition phase, the street vendors commit themselves to: (i) carry out the market during the period between 00:00 and 07:00 in the morning, and until this time vacate the square and its surroundings and deliver the square clean; (ii) clear the roads located in the market area and its surroundings.

For the sake of facilitating the reasoning, let us call the permission contained in this clause a *bartered form of Norm A*, which has the following deontic expression:

(A.5*) It permits the use of the Praça Dom Pedro II for itinerant commerce between 00:00 and 07:00 in the morning.

I used the asterisk in A.5* to mark the fragment as a bartered norm, that is, a norm specifically created by the parties involved in the agreement. As a permission the norm makes legal a behaviour that otherwise would be illegal. However, one must be careful in calling it a permission, as while it does have such modal expression, it is paradoxically based on a particular requirement: the parties had to recognise that this use of the public square is actually illegal (see the First Clause and Third Clause, section 1, of the TAC). The norm thus creates a kind of permitted illegality by legally allowing a form of noncompliance with *Norm A*, that is, the *first form of disobedience of Norm A*, as I called it earlier (see chapter five, text following n 3). And this treatment of noncompliance has two noteworthy consequences.

First, it demonstrates how such bartering agreements always lower the standard of compliance with a given norm, at least in what refers to the norm's spheres of validity. This decrease in the standard of compliance furthermore tends to have expansive effects. In arenas of noncompliance, as norms are likely to be used as tokens for strategic purposes by the actors of the arena, the bartered norm tends to expand its spheres of validity to the spheres of the non-bartered norm. A.5*, for instance, has a clear space of validity – Praça Dom Pedro II and its surroundings – and a life span – four months. In practice, however, it was applied for the whole area that instantiated the arena, which included not only the mentioned square and its surroundings, but also all the streets, avenues, other public squares, and sidewalks that together formed the somewhat fluid spatial demarcation of *Feira da Sé*. It set, too, a practical precedent for those who were deemed as noncompliant (the municipality and the vendors): even after its temporal validity expired (ie, 2 November 2008), the market continued to take place after midnight. This overextension in practice of the bartered

[32] See pp 127–122 of the case 0063506-61.2007.8.06.0001.

norm reveals another facet of making the law flexible: what is initially established to serve as a transitional rule in order to increase the compliance with a given norm, may instead contribute to the stabilisation of its noncompliance. This leads to the second consequence.

I briefly mentioned that the practices of implementation may render a norm nonbinding. The issuance of A.5*, to the extent it decreases the standard of compliance of *Norm A*, is also a form of making *Norm A* nonbinding, that is to say, it empties the possibilities of legally insisting on full compliance of *Norm A*. In this specific sense, at least regarding part of its spatial sphere of validity, *Norm A* becomes nonbinding when subjected to bartering. It is true that this does not change the fact that it remains a norm in its structure and that it legally provides for certain commands and prohibitions to be followed by those who fall under its scope, including the actors of the bartering process. But in such terms, one is invariably led to face – at least from the point of view of legal theory – what appears to be an oxymoron: how can there be the existence of legal but nonbinding commands and prohibitions? Here underlies a very subtle phenomenon that, as was advanced earlier (see p 136), stems from the flexibilisation of the law by the use of bartering arrangements: they pragmatically change the structure of norms, providing rules of conduct with characteristics of offers of regulation.[33]

The distinction between 'rules of conduct' and 'offers of regulation' was elaborated on by Blankenburg, though in another context, in his attempt to conceptualise the efficacy of the regulation of social relations from external addressees (ie, those who are not state administrative staff).[34] The former refers to legal norms that regulate behaviour by means of establishing 'commands and prohibitions (such as criminal law)', which can be obeyed or disobeyed. The latter corresponds to those norms, often found in private law, with another structure: 'they provide offers of regulation for social relationships and for relationships to things (eg, contractual regulations, property regulations), which can or cannot be used' (Blankenburg 1977: 36–37). Whilst obedience and disobedience imply a mandatory behaviour (ie, a conduct that ought to be performed by the norm addressee), use and non-use assume an option. That is why Friedman (1975: 80) called attention to the fact that 'formally at least, *use* is a matter for actors to decide for themselves'. Easily seen in the realm of private law (eg, contracts, marriages, and wills), offers of regulation might entail commands and prohibitions, for instance, through procedural rules or formal requirements, but they do not primarily rely on punishments and rewards as techniques for channelling behaviour. Instead, they give actors the competence to decide whether they will make use of the regulation, and frequently the power to determine

[33] See ch 4, n 18.

[34] In order to avoid misunderstandings, the term efficacy employed here corresponds to what he actually called validity (*Geltung*) and not efficacy (*Wirksamkeit*); see Blankenburg (1977: 41).

according to their own will the form, the extension, and the effects of the relation between them.

Issued as an administrative regulation of the public space and providing a series of sanctions for those who breach it, it is clear that *Norm A* is a rule of conduct at syntactic and semantic levels. However, when noncompliance is introduced into the norm through bartered agreements, such as in A.5*, one can observe how the norm in arenas of noncompliance may pragmatically be turned into a matter for the norm addressees and, especially, enforcement agencies to decide for themselves. It is in this sense that high grades of noncompliance might lead to practices of bartering that render a norm nonbinding in its structure. Instead of having their expectations oriented and their behaviour regulated by definitions of what is allowed and what is prohibited, actors are caught in a highly contingent dynamic in which legal norms, once turned into offers of regulation, can hardly serve as a codification for power to circulate, thus hampering the mobilisation of resources for collective action. With power itself being an increasingly scarce resource in this context, we are presented with what seems to be the guiding problem of pervasive noncompliance: can law solve what the law cannot solve?

Concluding Remarks

In his research handbook on development and the informal economy, Charmes (2020: 1–2) lists four reasons why the concept of informality should be revisited despite the fact that so much literature has been produced about it. First, there is still widespread confusion between what is informal and what is illegal. Second, informality, due to its magnitude and historical trends, has been presented as 'the new normal'.[1] Third, the boundaries that define which activities are informal may shift in such a way that what was illegal can become legal or tolerated, not to mention the changes in the notion of work and employment.[2] Finally, vis-à-vis the increase in governmental agendas addressing the transition from the informal to the formal economy, there is a growing need to understand the relation between the state and actors – and among actors themselves – involved with such activities.

These reasons highlight not only the difficulties underlying the concept, but also how informality has been playing a major role in understanding a wide swath of notions, such as development, work, employment, governance, and growth. Its pervasiveness, nonetheless, goes far beyond economic definitions and political agendas. As I argued, at the root of informality lies another comprehensive, yet generally unnoticed – or at best improperly treated – phenomenon: that of noncompliance. Whilst it is true that much attention has been paid to the former over the past five decades, the same cannot be said about the latter, which is one of its constitutive features. If despite all the academic efforts there is still much to be investigated with respect to informality, a domain that – in the words of Charmes (2019: 218) – today remains 'largely unrecognized, misunderstood and unexplored' and whose 'methods of data collection are still open to innovation', then the study of noncompliance, one could easily say, is yet to even be born.

This book has attempted to take the first steps in this direction. I first provided an account of its nature, that is, what can be conceived as noncompliance and by which forms it can be assessed as such, and second, I mapped its most striking impacts. This twofold endeavour also had the intention of filling some important gaps that, as I see them, are hampering a better understanding of informality itself as well as the functioning of the legal system in contexts where noncompliance with the law is widespread. I conclude by restating these

[1] In this vein, see Jütting and Laglesia (2009: esp 11) and, corroborating them, Stuart et al (2018).

[2] Regarding the latter, 'the transformation of wageworkers into self-entrepreneurs' (Charmes 2019: 4) seems to be the most striking example nowadays.

gaps and how they were tackled by the approach offered here, in the hope that further steps might be taken by others.

Charmes was right in asserting that there is still a widespread confusion between what is informal and what is illegal. His concern is by no means insignificant. The distinction between both concepts has been underlying almost every attempt to define informality, be it at scholarly levels or through international agreements.[3] However, much of the confusion seems to derive not from the possible meanings of what may be 'informal', but rather from a shallow comprehension of what is involved in defining what is 'illegal'. Even the scholars who have realised that the whole conceptual enterprise behind the various definitions of informality – or more generally, unobserved economies – could be summarised in choosing the particular set of rules being violated suffer from a similar hindrance:[4] the lack of a proper understanding of what is at stake in the concept of illegality and thus in the definition of noncompliant behaviour. It is here that Charmes's (2020: 1) plea has to be taken seriously: 'far from being confined to economic approaches, informality needs to be addressed, surveyed and understood from the points of view of other social sciences'. This book offered one point of view that so far has been bypassed in the studies of informality, namely the point of view of the law, or – to put it in a less ambiguous manner – jurisprudence, and by doing so it brings some important analytical gains.

A legally oriented perspective is capable of justifying why informality is necessarily a kind of illegality. A legally relevant behaviour is either legal or illegal, and a *tertium non datur*. This, of course, does not make the assessment of legality easier.[5] On the contrary, the complexity involved is precisely what moves the legal profession. It is about not only hermeneutical difficulties embodied in legal texts, but also making sense of an intricate relation of organisations and authorities that play multiple roles in the very determination of what is legal or illegal. The penalty for not taking this complexity into consideration is clear: we are unable to identify the standards according to which a behaviour is legal or illegal in a given context, and by implication formal or informal. This book tackles the problem by showing this complexity through the concept

[3] I already made some incursions in this regard (see section 1.2).

[4] Feige is a remarkable example, since he is the one who emphasises the role of illegality in the definition of informality. What I am calling attention to is the fact that it should not be assumed by default, for instance, that norm addressees 'attempt to conceal their behaviors and authorities try to detect them' (Feige 2016a: 6). Such an assumption takes for granted a legal system in which public authorities are necessarily compliant with the law.

[5] Nor does it set aside the problems of labelling a behaviour as illegal or criminal. There is plenty of literature dealing with this, especially within the so-called sociology of deviance. A summary of all traditions of this field would be pointless here. For a few examples, see the contributions of Lemert (1967), Becker (1963), and Goffman (1963). In the context of street vending, see Duneier (1999: esp 306 fn 8). However, only by recognising the 'question of legality' is it possible to cope with the struggles of those affected; see eg, the case of street vendors in India (Jhabvala 2010: xii–xiii).

of noncompliance. However, it does so with a further warning: the assessment of illegality should not be reduced to the behaviour of norm addressees. The organisations and authorities that matter for the definition of such standards are likewise implicated in the equation. Therefore, just as noncompliance is not restricted to the behaviour of norm addressees, studies of informality should not be restricted to the assessment of disobedience.

There is another gap also worth mentioning. Whereas the study of informality has been captivating different disciplines, ranging from macroeconomic statistics to ground-level qualitative approaches, it remains curiously absent in legal scholarship, even though the phenomenon itself is intrinsically connected to law, abundantly present in society, and in many cases as conspicuous as daylight. When one realises that the large size of informality reflects a state of massive illegality, one is forced to question the very foundations of the legal system. This is not to say that challenges of implementation and problems of law enforcement have not received any attention from lawyers or legal scholars in general.[6] The issue here – at least from the point of view of jurisprudence – is much more problematic. It has to do with the tension between the validity and efficacy of the legal system.

As Kelsen (1967: 211 [1960: 215]) once said, 'the correct determination of this relationship is one of the most important and at the same time most difficult problems of a positivistic legal theory'. And even before making this statement, he had his own way of framing this relationship, that is, the validity of the legal system depends on a specified minimum of efficacy below which it ceases to exist.[7] However, as the numbers of informality seem to pinpoint, the real challenge nowadays is not to ascertain whether the validity of the legal system can survive low grades of efficacy, but rather how it does so.

This book approached this question by examining the impacts of noncompliance using the case of street vending as a sample. Whether the conclusions can be further generalised (and to what extent) or contrasted with other cases is still open to discussion. As it is proper to any scientific work, there might also be criticisms of the approach chosen here. Whichever the pathway chosen, legal scholars cannot simply ignore the fact that noncompliance is much larger and more pervasive than we are inclined to believe. And we are lagging behind in recognising this.

[6] This has been a concern since at least the 1970s; see in this regard Mayntz (1988). *cf* Teubner (1987: 27–29 [1985: 326–29]).

[7] See Kelsen earlier (1992: 59–60 [1934: 68–69]) and later (1949: 41–42 and 118–22, 1967: 211–14 [1960: 215–20]). In the same vein, see Hart (1994: 103–04 and 294–95) and, adding the 'test of exclusion' to that of efficacy, Raz (1980: 206).

Bibliography

Alexy, R (1979) 'Zum Begriff des Rechtsprinzips' in W Krawietz, K Opalek, A Peczenik, and A Schramm (eds), *Argumentation und Hermeneutik in der Jurisprudenz* (Berlin, Duncker & Humblot).

—— (1986) *Theorie der Grundrechte* (Frankfurt am Main, Suhrkamp) [English translation 2002].

—— (2002) *A Theory of Constitutional Rights*, translated by J Rivers (Oxford, Oxford University Press).

Allport, FH (1954) 'The Structuring of Events: Outline of a General Theory with Applications to Psychology' 61 *Psychological Review* 281, https://doi.org/10.1037/h0062678.

Amaral, GL do, JE Olenike, LMF Amaral, CL Yazbek, and F Steinbruch (2019) 'Quantidade de Normas Editadas no Brasil: 31 Anos da Constituição Federal de 1988' (Curitiba, IBPT).

Almeida, FPL de (2020) *Constitution: The Darwinian Evolution of a Societal Structure* (Baden-Baden, Nomos).

Aragão, TAM (2012) *Doce Som Urbano: O Triângulo e as Territorializações dos Vendedores de Chegadinho em Fortaleza*, master's thesis (Universidade Federal do Rio Grande do Sul), lume.ufrgs.br/handle/10183/60601.

Araujo, FCB and E Moita (2018) 'The Problems of Under-Inclusion in Marine Biodiversity Conservation: The Case of Brazilian Traditional Fishing Communities' 10 *Asian Bioethics Review* 261, https://doi.org/10.1007/s41649-018-0068-6.

Araujo, FCB (2021) *Os Direitos das Comunidades Tradicionais Pesqueiras vis-à-vis o Direito Brasileiro das Áreas Marinhas Protegidas*, doctoral dissertation (Universidade de Brasília and Aix-Marseille Université).

Augel, J (ed) (1985) *Leben in Armut: Überlebensstrategien in Brasilianischen Elendsvierteln* (Mettingen, Brasilienkunde-Verlag).

Austin, R (1994) '"An Honest Living": Street Vendors, Municipal Regulation and the Black Public Sphere' 103 *Yale Law Journal* 2119, scholarship.law.upenn.edu/faculty_scholarship/817.

Ávila, H (2007) *Theory of Legal Principles* (Dordrecht, Springer).

—— (2011) *Teoria dos Princípios: Da Definição à Aplicação dos Princípios Jurídicos*, 12th edn (São Paulo, Malheiros).

Bacchetta, M, E Ernst, and JP Bustamante (2009) *Globalization and Informal Jobs in Developing Countries: A Joint Study of the International Labour Office and the Secretariat of the World Trade Organization* (Geneva, International Labour Organization and World Trade Organization).

Bachelard, G (1947) *La Formation de l'Esprit Scientifique : Contribution à une Psychanalyse de la Connaissance Objective* (Paris, Librairie Philosophique J Vrin) [English translation 2002].

—— (2002) *The Formation of the Scientific Mind: A Contribution to a Psychoanalysis of Objective Knowledge*, translated by MMcA Jones (Manchester, Clinamen).

Baer, MH (2009) 'Governing Corporate Compliance' 50 *Boston College Law Review*.

Baldwin, DA (1971) 'Money and Power' 33 *The Journal of Politics* 578.

Barnard, CI (1968) *The Functions of the Executive*, 30th anniversary edn (Cambridge, Massachusetts, Harvard University Press) [first published 1938].

Barnes, JA (1954) 'Class and Committees in a Norwegian Island Parish' 7 *Human Relations* 39, https://doi.org/10.1177/001872675400700102.

Barton, JH (1975) 'Behind the Legal Explosion' 27 *Stanford Law Review* 567, https://doi.org/10.2307/1228327.

Baum, RC (1976) 'Introduction to Part IV: Generalized Media in Action' in JJ Loubser, RC Baum, A Effrat, and VM Lidz (eds), *Explorations in General Theory in Social Science: Essays in Honor of Talcott Parsons, Vol 2* (New York, The Free Press).

Becker, HS (1963) *Outsiders: Studies in the Sociology of Deviance* (New York, The Free Press).
Bhowmik, SK (2010a) 'Introduction' in SK Bhowmik (ed), *Street Vendors in the Global Urban Economy* (New Delhi, Routledge).
—— (2010b) 'Preface and Acknowledgements' in SK Bhowmik (ed), *Street Vendors in the Global Urban Economy*, XXI–XXII (New Delhi, Routledge).
—— (ed) (2010c) *Street Vendors in the Global Urban Economy* (New Delhi, Routledge).
Blankenburg, E (1977) 'Über die Unwirksamkeit von Gesetzen' 63 *ARSP: Archiv für Rechts- und Sozialphilosophie* 31.
Bobbio, N (2007) 'Le Sanzioni Positive' in *Dalla Struttura Alla Funzione: Nuovi Studi Di Teoria Del Diritto*, e-book edn (Bari, Gius Laterza & Figli) [first published 1971].
Bourdieu, P (2018) 'Social Space and the Genesis of Appropriated Physical Space' 42 *International Journal of Urban and Regional Research* 106, https://doi.org/10.1111/1468-2427.12534.
Bourdieu, P and L Wacquant (1992) *An Invitation to Reflexive Sociology* (Cambridge, Polity Press).
Brizio, L, D Bernales, and A Zea (2013) 'La Importancia del Comercio Ambulatorio para el Desarrollo de la Vida en la Ciudad. Estudio de Caso: Ambulante de Comida Árabe' 6 *La Colmena* 69, http://revistas.pucp.edu.pe/index.php/lacolmena/article/view/12504.
Bromley, R (2000) 'Street Vending and Public Policy: A Global Review' 20 *International Journal of Sociology and Social Policy* 1, https://doi.org/10.1108/01443330010789052.
Bronfenbrenner, M (1968) 'Inflation and Deflation' in DL Sills (ed), *International Encyclopedia of the Social Sciences*, Vol 7 (Chicago and New York, The Macmillan Company & The Free Press).
Buarque de Holanda, S (1995) *Raízes do Brasil*, 26th edn (São Paulo, Companhia das Letras) [English translation 2012] [1st edn 1936].
—— (2012) *Roots of Brazil*, translated by G H Summ (Notre Dame, Notre Dame Press).
Bulygin, E (1965) 'Der Begriff der Wirksamkeit' in EG Valdés (ed), *Lateinamerikanische Studien zur Rechtsphilosophie* (Neuwied am Rhein, Luchterhand).
Burton, SJ (ed) (2000) *The Path of the Law and Its Influence: The Legacy of Oliver Wendell Holmes, Jr* (Cambridge, Cambridge University Press), https://doi.org/10.1017/CBO9780511527432.
Calabria, CRA (2018) *The Efficacy of the Inter-American Court of Human Rights: A Socio-Legal Study Based on the Jurisprudence of the Inter-American Court of Human Rights Concerning Amnesty Laws, Indigenous Rights, and Rights of Detainees*, doctoral dissertation (Manchester University).
Caminha, A (1893) *A Normalista* (Rio de Janeiro, Magalhães & C).
Carnelutti, F (1960) 'La Equidad en el Juicio Penal (Para la Reforma de la Corte de Assises)' in *Cuestiones sobre el Processo Penal*, translated by SS Melendo (Buenos Aires, Libreria El Foro).
Charmes, J (2002) 'Is Asking for "Place of Work" a Pertinent and Efficient Way to Better Measure and Understand the Category of Homeworkers, and More Generally, Outworkers in the Labour Force?' in *On Measuring Place of Work* (Geneva, ILO).
—— (2009) 'Concepts, Measurement and Trends' in JP Jütting and JR Laiglesia (eds), *Is Informal Normal? Towards More and Better Jobs in Developing Countries* (Paris, OECD Publishing).
—— (2012) 'The Informal Economy Worldwide: Trends and Characteristics' 6 *Margin: The Journal of Applied Economic Research* 103, https://doi.org/10.1177/097380101200600202.
—— (2019) *Dimensions of Resilience in Developing Countries* (Cham, Springer), https://doi.org/10.1007/978-3-030-04076-5.
—— (2020) 'Why and How Should the Informal Economy Be Revisited after 50 Years?' in J Charmes (ed), *Research Handbook on Development and the Informal Economy* (Cheltenham, Edward Elgar Publishing), https://doi.org/10.4337/9781788972802.00009.
Chazkel, A (2007) 'Beyond Law and Order: The Origins of the Jogo do Bicho in Republican Rio de Janeiro' 39 *Journal of Latin American Studies* 535, https://doi.org/10.1017/S0022216X07002830.
—— (2011) *Laws of Chance: Brazil's Clandestine Lottery and the Making of Urban Public Life* (Durham, Duke University Press).

Chen, M (2005) 'Rethinking Informal Economy: From Enterprise Characteristics to Employment Relations' in N Kudva and L Benería (eds), *Rethinking Informalization: Poverty, Precarious Jobs and Social Protection* (Cornell University Open Access Repository), ecommons.cornell.edu/handle/1813/3716.

Chernilo, D (2002) 'The Theorization of Social Co-Ordinations in Differentiated Societies: The Theory of Generalized Symbolic Media in Parsons, Luhmann and Habermas' 53 *British Journal of Sociology* 431, https://doi.org/10.1080/0007131022000000581.

Contreras, V and J Thomas (1993) *Surviving on the Street: The Ambulatory Street Traders of Santiago* (Santiago, ILO, PREALC), catalog.hathitrust.org/Record/101085147.

Cossio, C (1964) *La Teoria Egologica del Derecho y el Concept Juridico de Libertad*, 2nd edn (Buenos Aires, Abeledo-Perrot).

DaMatta, R and E Soárez (1999) *Águias, Burros e Borboletas: Um Estudo Antropológico do Jogo do Bicho* (Rio de Janeiro, Rocco).

Dantas, EWC (2014) *A Cidade e o Comércio Ambulante: Estado e Disciplinamento da Ocupação do Espaço Público em Fortaleza (1975–1995)* (Fortaleza, Imprensa Universitária).

Dawes, A (2018) 'The Struggle for Via Bologna Street Market: Crisis, Racial Denial and Speaking Back to Power in Naples Italy' 70 *The British Journal of Sociology* 377, https://doi.org/10.1111/1468-4446.12347.

DIEESE (2014) 'Diálogo Social: Para Transformar o Trabalho no Brasil', March, www.dieese.org.br/projetos/informalidade/revista.pdf.

Dillinger, J (2019) 'The Most Dangerous Cities in the World', 30 July, www.worldatlas.com/articles/most-dangerous-cities-in-the-world.html.

DiMento, JF (1986) *Environmental Law and American Business: Dilemmas of Compliance* (New York, Springer Science+Business Media).

Donovan, MG (2002) *Space Wars in Bogotá: The Recovery of Public Space and Its Impact on Street Vendors*, master's thesis (Massachusetts Institute of Technology), dspace.mit.edu/handle/1721.1/16811.

Duneier, M (1999) *Sidewalk* (New York, Farrar, Straus and Giroux).

—— (2002) 'What Kind of Combat Sport Is Sociology?' 107 *American Journal of Sociology* 1551, www.journals.uchicago.edu/t-and-c.

Dworkin, R (1977a) 'Hard Cases' in *Taking Rights Seriously* (Cambridge, Harvard University Press).

—— (1977b) 'The Model of Rules I' in *Taking Rights Seriously* (Cambridge, Harvard University Press).

—— (1985) *A Matter of Principle* (Cambridge, Harvard University Press).

Edelman, LB, S Petterson, E Chambliss, and HS Erlanger (1991) 'Legal Ambiguity and the Politics of Compliance: Affirmative Action Officers' Dilemma' 13 *Law & Policy* 73.

Ehrlich, E (1913) *Grundlegung der Soziologie des Rechts* (Munich and Leipzig, Duncker & Humblot) [English translation 2017].

—— (2017) *Fundamental Principles of the Sociology of Law*, translated by WL Moll (London, Routledge).

Elwert, G, H-D Evers, and W Wilkens (1983) 'Die Suche nach Sicherheit: Kombinierte Produktionsformen im sogenannten Informellen Sektor' 12 *Zeitschrift für Soziologie* 281.

Epstein, AL (1968) *Politics in an Urban African Community* (Manchester, Manchester University Press).

Escobar, A (1995) *Encountering Development: The Making and Unmaking of the Third World* (New Jersey, Princeton University Press).

ETCO (2018) 'Relatório de Atividades 2018' (São Paulo, ETCO), www.etco.org.br/wp-content/uploads/relatorioanual2018.pdf.

Evers, H-D (1987) 'Subsistenzproduktion, Markt und Staat. Der Sogenannte Bielefelder Verflechtungsansatz' 39 *Geographische Rundschau* 136.

Farzin, S (2006) *Inklusion/Exklusion: Entwicklungen und Probleme einer systemtheoretischen Unterscheidung* (Bielefeld, Transcript Verlag).

Feige, EL (ed) (1989) *The Underground Economies: Tax Evasion and Information Distortion* (Cambridge, Cambridge University Press).

—— (1990) 'Defining and Estimating Underground and Informal Economies: The New Institutional Economics Approach' 18 *World Development* 989, https://doi.org/10.1016/0305-750X(90)90081-8.

—— (2016a) 'Reflections on the Meaning and Measurement of Unobserved Economies: What Do We Really Know about the "Shadow Economy"?' 2 *Journal of Tax Administration* 5, http://jota.website/index.php/JoTA/article/view/69/52.

—— (2016b) 'Professor Schneider's Shadow Economy (SSE): What Do We Really Know? A Rejoinder' 2 *Journal of Tax Administration*, http://jota.website/index.php/JoTA/article/view/109/78.

Frankel, A, S Katovich, and H Vedvig (2016) *'Forced into Breaking the Law': The Criminalization of Homelessness in Connecticut* (New Haven, Yale Law School), law.yale.edu/sites/default/files/area/center/schell/criminalization_of_homelessness_report_for_web_full_report.pdf.

Freire, D (2019) 'Beasts of Prey or Rational Animals? Private Governance in Brazil's Jogo Do Bicho' 46 *Latin American Perspectives* 230, https://doi.org/10.1177/0094582X19846519.

Freyre, G (2003) *Casa-Grande & Senzala: Formação da Família Brasileira sob o Regime da Economia Patriarcal*, 48th edn (São Paulo, Global) [English translation 1986] [1st edn 1933].

—— (1986) *The Masters and the Slaves: A Study in the Development of Brazilian Civilization*, translated by S Putnam, 2nd English-language edn, revised, (Berkeley, Los Angeles and London, University of California Press).

Friedman, LM (1975) *The Legal System: A Social Science Perspective* (New York, Russell Sage Foundation).

—— (2016) *Impact: How Law Affects Behavior* (Cambridge and London, Harvard University Press).

Garrn, H (1969) 'Rechtswirksamkeit und faktische Rechtsgeltung: Ein Beitrag zur Rechtssoziologie' 55 *ARSP: Archiv für Rechts- und Sozialphilosophie / Archives for Philosophy of Law and Social Philosophy* 161, www.jstor.org/stable/23678400.

Geiger, T (1964) *Vorstudien zu einer Soziologie des Rechts. Mit einer Einleitung und internationalen Bibliographie zur Rechtssoziologie von Paul Trappe*, edited by H Maus and F Fürstenberg (Neuwid am Rhein, Luchterband).

Gessner, V (1976) *Recht und Konflikt: Eine soziologische Untersuchung privatrechtlicher Konflikte in Mexiko* (Tübingen, JCB Mohr [Paul Siebeck]) [Spanish translation 1986].

—— (1986) *Los Conflictos Sociales y la Administracion de Justicia en Mexico*, translated by R Marsiske (Mexico, Universidad Nacional Autonoma de Mexico), biblio.juridicas.unam.mx/bjv/detalle-libro/261-los-conflictos-sociales-y-la-administracion-de-justicia-en-mexico-1a-reimp.

Giacomolli, NJ and VG de Vasconcellos (2015) 'Justiça Criminal Negocial: Crítica à Fragilização da Jurisdição Penal em um Cenário de Expansão dos Espaços de Consenso no Processo Penal' 20 *Novos Estudos Jurídicos* 1108, https://doi.org/10.14210/nej.v20n3.p1108-1134.

Giddens, A (1968) '"Power" in the Recent Writings of Talcott Parsons' 2 *Sociology* 257, https://doi.org/10.1177/003803856800200301.

Gidi, A (2003) 'Class Actions in Brazil: A Model for Civil Law Countries' 51 *The American Journal of Comparative Law* 311, https://doi.org/10.2307/3649151.

Goffman, E (1963) *Stigma: Notes on the Management of Spoiled Identity* (New Jersey, Prentice-Hall).

Greshoff, R and G Kneer (eds) (1999) *Struktur und Ereignis in theorievergleichender Perspektive: Ein diskursives Buchprojekt* (Wiesbaden, Springer Fachmedien Wiesbaden).

Griffith, SJ (2016) 'Corporate Governance in an Era of Compliance' *William & Mary Law Review* 57 (6), 2075–2140, scholarship.law.wm.edu/wmlr/vol57/iss6/4.

Grimm, D (ed) (1990) *Wachsende Staatsaufgaben – Sinkende Steuerungsfähigkeit des Rechts* (Baden-Baden, Nomos Verlagsgesellschaft), https://doi.org/10.5771/9783845261393.

—— (1991) *Die Zukunft der Verfassung* (Frankfurt am Main, Suhrkamp).

—— (2016) *Constitutionalism: Past, Present, and Future* (New York, Oxford University Press).

Grinover, AP, AM Gomes Filho, AS Fernandes, and LF Gomes (2005) *Juizados Especiais Criminais: Comentários à Lei 9.099 de 26.09.1995*, 5th edn (São Paulo, Editora Revista dos Tribunais).

Günther, G (1979) 'Life as Poly-Contexturality' in G Günther (ed), *Beiträge zur Grundlegung einer operationsfähigen Dialektik II* (Hamburg, Felix Meiner).

Habermas, J (1987a) *The Theory of Communicative Action Volume 2. Lifeworld and System: A Critique of Functionalist Approach*, translated by T McCarthy (Boston, Beacon Press).

—— (1987b) *Theorie des Kommunikativen Handelns Band 2. Zur Kritik der Funktionalistischen Vernunft*, 4th edn (Frankfurt am Main, Suhrkamp) [English translation 1987a].

Hart, HLA (1983) 'Kelsen's Doctrine of the Unity of Law' in *Essays in Jurisprudence and Philosophy* (Oxford, Clarendon Press).

—— (1994) *The Concept of Law*, 2nd edn (Oxford, Clarendon Press).

Hart, K (1973) 'Informal Income Opportunities and Urban Employment in Ghana' 11 *The Journal of Modern African Studies* 61, www.jstor.org/stable/159873.

Hartog, F (2003) *Régime d'Historicité : Présentisme et Expériences du Temps*, e-book edn (Paris, Éditions du Seuil) [English translation 2015].

—— (2015) *Regimes of Historicity: Presentism and Experiences of Time*, translated by S Brown (New York, Columbia University Press).

—— (2016) 'Toward a New Historical Condition' in *Historisierung* (Stuttgart, JB Metzler), https://doi.org/10.1007/978-3-476-05460-9_18.

Hawkins, K, 1984) *Environment and Enforcement: Regulation and the Social Definition of Pollution* (Oxford, Clarendon Press), https://doi.org/10.1093/acprof:oso/9780198275145.001.0001.

Hilgartner, S and CL Bosk (1988) 'The Rise and Fall of Social Problems: A Public Arenas Model' 94 *American Journal of Sociology* 53, www.jstor.org/stable/2781022.

Hilhorst, D and BJ Jansen (2010) 'Humanitarian Space as Arena: A Perspective on the Everyday Politics of Aid' 41 *Development and Change* 1117, https://doi.org/10.1111/j.1467-7660.2010.01673.x.

Hillebrecht, C (2009) 'Rethinking Compliance: The Challenges and Prospects of Measuring Compliance with International Human Rights Tribunals' 1 *Journal of Human Rights Practice* 362, https://doi.org/10.1093/jhuman/hup018.

Hirschl, R (2008) 'The Judicialization of Mega-Politics and the Rise of Political Courts' 11 *Annual Review of Political Science* 93, https://doi.org/10.1146/annurev.polisci.11.053006.183906.

Holmes, OW (1997) 'The Path of the Law' 110 *Harvard Law Review* 991, https://doi.org/10.2307/1342108.

Hoopes, J (2003) *False Prophets: The Gurus Who Created Modern Management and Why Their Ideas Are Bad for Business Today* (Cambridge, Perseus Publishing).

Hume, D (1960) *A Treatise of Human Nature*, edited by LA Selby-Bigge, reprinted edn (London, Oxford University Press) [1st edn 1888].

Hummel, C (2017) 'Disobedient Markets: Street Vendors, Enforcement, and State Intervention in Collective Action' 50 *Comparative Political Studies* 1524, https://doi.org/10.1177/0010414016679177.

—— (2018) 'Bribery Cartels: Collusive Corruption in Bolivian Street Markets' 53 *Latin American Research Review* 217, https://doi.org/10.25222/larr.342.

Hutter, BM (1997) *Compliance: Regulation and Environment* (Oxford, Clarendon Press).

IBGE (2012) *Síntese de Indicadores Socais: Uma Análise das Condições de Vida da População Brasileira* (Rio de Janeiro, IBGE), biblioteca.ibge.gov.br/index.php/biblioteca-catalogo?view=detalhes&id=282173.

—— (2019a) Pesquisa Nacional por Amostra de Domicílios Contínua: Trimestre Móvel Jun.-Ago. 2019 (Rio de Janeiro, IBGE).

—— (2019b) *Pesquisa Nacional por Amostra de Domicílios Contínua: Terceiro Trimestre de 2018 Out.-Dez. 2018* (Rio de Janeiro, IBGE).

ILO (1972) *Employment, Incomes and Equality: A Strategy for Increasing Productive Employment in Kenya* (Geneva, ILO).

—— (1996) *1996 Labour Review: Latin America and the Caribbean* (Geneva, ILO).

—— (2002a) *On Measuring Place of Work* (Geneva, ILO) www.ilo.org/global/statistics-and-databases/WCMS_087887/lang--en/index.htm.

—— (2002b) *Resolution Concerning Decent Work and Informal Economy* (Geneva, ILO), www.ilo.org/asia/info/WCMS_098314/lang--en/index.htm.

—— (2002c) *Women and Men in the Informal Economy: A Statistical Picture* (Geneva, ILO), www.wiego.org/sites/default/files/migrated/publications/files/ILO-Women-Men-Informal-2002.pdf.

—— (2013a) *19th International Conference of Labour Statisticians, Resolution I: Resolution Concerning Statistics of Work, Employment and Labour Underutilization* (Geneva, ILO), www.ilo.org/global/statistics-and-databases/standards-and-guidelines/resolutions-adopted-by-international-conferences-of-labour-statisticians/WCMS_230304/lang--en/index.htm.

—— (2013b) *Measuring Informality: A Statistical Manual on the Informal Sector and Informal Employment* (Geneva, ILO), www.ilo.org/global/publications/ilo-bookstore/order-online/books/WCMS_222979/lang--en/index.htm.

—— (2015) *Recommendation 204 Concerning the Transition from the Informal to the Formal Economy* (Geneva, ILO).

—— (2018) *Women and Men in the Informal Economy: A Statistical Picture* (Geneva, ILO).

Itikawa, LF (2006) *Trabalho Informal nos Espaços Públicos no Centro de São Paulo: Pensando Parâmetros para Políticas Públicas*, doctoral dissertation (Universidade de São Paulo), https://doi.org/10.11606/T.16.2006.tde-03032010-154458.

—— (2010) 'Clandestine Geometries: Mapping Street Vending in Downtown Sao Paulo' in SK Bhowmik (ed), *Street Vendors in the Global Urban Economy* (New Delhi, Routledge).

Jakobsen, KA (2000) 'Apresentação' in K Jakobsen, R Martins, and O Dombrowski (eds), *Mapa do Trabalho Informal: Perfil Socioeconômico dos Trabalhadores Informais na Cidade de São Paulo* (São Paulo, Fundação Perseu Abramo).

Jhabvala, R (2010) 'Foreword' in SK Bhowmik (ed), *Street Vendors in the Global Urban Economy* (London, New York, and New Delhi, Routledge).

Johnson, C (1966) *Revolutionary Change* (Boston, Little, Brown and Company).

Jonas, H (1979) *Das Prinzip Verantwortung: Versuch einer Ethik für die technologische Zivilisation* (Frankfurt am Main, Suhrkamp).

Jowell, J (1977) 'The Limits of Law in Urban Planning' 30 *Current Legal Problems* 63, https://doi.org/10.1093/clp/30.1.63.

Jütting, JP and JR de Laiglesia (eds) (2009) *Is Informal Normal? Towards More and Better Jobs in Developing Countries* (Paris, OECD Publishing).

Kamunyori, SW (2007) *A Growing Space for Dialogue: The Case of Street Vending in Nairobi's Central Business District*, master's thesis (Massachusetts Institute of Technology), dspace.mit.edu/handle/1721.1/40123.

Kant, I (1920) *Prolegomena zu einer jeden künftigen Metaphysik, die als Wissenschaft wird auftreten können*, edited by K Vorländer, 6th edn (Leipzig, Felix Meiner) [English translation 2004] [1st edn 1783].

—— (2004) *Prolegomena to Any Future Metaphysics That Will Be Able to Come Forward as Science: With Selections from the Critique of Pure Reason*, edited and translated by G Hatfield, revised edn (Cambridge, Cambridge University Press).

Kapiszewski, D and MM Taylor (2013) 'Compliance: Conceptualizing, Measuring, and Explaining Adherence to Judicial Rulings' 38 *Law & Social Inquiry* 803, https://doi.org/10.1111/j.1747-4469.2012.01320.x.

Kellow, A (2009) 'Arenas of Power by Theodore J. Lowi' 68 *Australian Journal of Public Administration* 484, https://doi.org/10.1111/j.1467-8500.2009.00652.x.

Kelsen, H (1934) *Reine Rechtslehre. Einleitung in die rechtswissenschaftliche Problematik* (Leipzig and Vienna, Franz Deuticke) [English translation 1992].

—— (1949) *General Theory of Law and State*, translated by A Wedberg (Cambridge, Harvard University Press).

—— (1959) 'Eine "Realistische" und die Reine Rechtslehre, Bemerkungen zu Alf Ross: On Law and Justice' 10 *Österreichische Zeitschrift für öffentliches Recht* 1.

—— (1960) *Reine Rechtslehre*, 2nd edn (Vienna, Österreichische Staatsdruckerei) [English translation 1967] [Portuguese translation 1998].

—— (1967) *Pure Theory of Law*, translated by M Knight (Berkeley and Los Angeles, University of California Press).

—— (1979) *Allgemeine Theorie der Normen* (Vienna, Manz) [English translation 1991].

—— (1991) *General Theory of Norms*, translated by M Hartney (Oxford, Clarendon Press).

—— (1992) *Introduction to the Problems of Legal Theory*, translated by BL Paulson and SL Paulson (Oxford, Clarendon Press).

—— (1998) *Teoria Pura do Direito*, translated by JB Machado, 6th edn (São Paulo, Martins Fontes).

Kindermann, H (1989) 'Alibigesetzgebung als Symbolische Gesetzgebung' in R Voigt (ed), *Symbole der Politik, Politik der Symbole* (Opladen, Leske u Budrich), https://doi.org/10.1007/978-3-322-97194-4.

Kitschelt, F (1984) *Überlebensstrategien von Fischern in Port Morant/Jamaika*, doctoral dissertation (Universität Bielefeld).

—— (1987) *Die Kunst zu Überleben: Reproduktionsstrategien von Fischern in Jamaika* (Saarbrücken and Fort Lauderdale, Breitenbach).

Kitschelt, H (1980) *Kernenergiepolitik: Arena eines gesellschaftlichen Konflikts* (Frankfurt am Main and New York, Campus-Verlag).

Koselleck, R (1979) 'Historia Magistra Vitae: Über die Auflösung des Topos im Horizont neuzeitlich bewegter Geschichte' in *Vergangene Zukunft: Zur Semantik geschichtlicher Zeiten* (Frankfurt am Main, Suhrkamp) [English translation 2004].

—— (2004) 'Historia Magistra Vitae: The Dissolution of the Topos into the Perspective of a Modernized Historical Process' in *Futures Past: On the Semantics of Historical Time*, translated by K Tribe (New York, Columbia University Press).

Krein, JD and MW Proni (2010) 'Economia Informal: Aspectos Conceituais e Teóricos', *Série Trabalho Decente no Brasil*, Documento de trabalho no 4 (Brasília, OIT), www.ilo.org/brasilia/publicacoes/WCMS_227055/lang--pt/index.htm.

La Porta, R and A Shleifer (2014) 'Informality and Development' 28 *Journal of Economic Perspectives* 109, https://doi.org/10.1257/jep.28.3.109.

Lautmann, R (1971) *Wert und Norm: Begriffsanalysen für die Soziologie*, 2nd edn (Opladen, Westdeutscher Verlag).

Lemert, EM (1967) *Human Deviance, Social Problems, and Social Control* (Englewood Cliffs, Prentice-Hall).

Lévi-Strauss, C (1955) *Tristes Tropiques* (Paris, Plon) [Portuguese translation 1957].

—— (1957) *Tristes Trópicos*, translated by W Martins (São Paulo, Anhembi).

—— (1958) *Anthropologie Structurale* (Paris, Plon) [English translation 1963].

—— (1963) *Structural Anthropology*, translated by C Jacobson and BG Schoepf (New York, Basic Books).

Lin, TCW (2006) 'Compliance, Technology, and Modern Finance' 11 *Brooklyn Journal of Corporate, Financial & Commercial Law* 159, brooklynworks.brooklaw.edu/bjcfcl/vol11/iss1/6.

Lindahl, H (2013) *Fault Lines of Globalization: Legal Order and the Politics of A-Legality* (Oxford, Oxford University Press).

Lintelo, DJH te (2010) 'Advocacy Coalitions Influencing Informal Sector Policy: The Case of India's National Urban Street Vendors Policy' in SK Bhowmik (ed), *Street Vendors in the Global Urban Economy* (New Delhi, Routledge).

Llancar, CA (2009) 'Informalidad y Comercio Ambulante. Algunas Notas Preliminares' 3 *Summa Humanitatis* 1, http://revistas.pucp.edu.pe/index.php/summa_humanitatis/article/view/2328.

Long, N (1968) *Social Change and the Individual: A Study of the Social and Religious Responses to Innovation in a Zambian Rural Community* (Manchester, Manchester University Press).

—— (2001) *Development Sociology: Actor Perspectives* (London and New York, Routledge).

Lopes Filho, JM (2014) *Os Precedentes Judiciais no Constitucionalismo Brasileiro Contemporâneo* (Salvador, Juspodivm).

Lopes, FCR (2006) *A Centralidade da Parangaba Como Produto Da Fragmentação de Fortaleza (CE)*, master's thesis (Universidade Federal do Ceará).

Lopes Jr, A (2002) 'Justiça Negociada: Utilitarismo Processual e Eficiência Antigarantista' in S de Carvalho and A Wunderlich (eds), *Diálogos Sobre a Justiça Dialogal: Teses e Antíteses sobre os Processos de Informalização e Privatização da Justiça Penal* (Rio de Janeiro, Lumen Juris).

Loubser, JJ, RC Baumm, A Effrat, and VM Lidz (eds) (1976) *Explorations in General Theory in Social Science: Essays in Honor of Talcott Parsons, Vol 2* (New York, The Free Press).

Lowi, TJ (1964) 'American Business, Public Policy, Case-Studies, and Political Theory' 16 *World Politics* 677, https://doi.org/10.2307/2009452.

—— (1970) 'Decision Making vs. Policy Making: Toward an Antidote for Technocracy' 30 *Public Administration Review* 314, https://doi.org/10.2307/974053.

—— (1972) 'Four Systems of Policy, Politics, and Choice' 32 *Public Administration Review* 298, https://doi.org/10.2307/974990.

—— (1975) 'Party, Policy, and Constitution in America' in *The American Party Systems: Stages of Political Development*, 2nd edn (New York, London, and Toronto, Oxford University Press).

—— (1978) 'Public Policy and Bureaucracy in the United States and France' in DE Ashford (ed), *Comparing Public Policies: New Concepts and Methods* (Beverly Hills and London, SAGE Publications, Inc).

—— (2009) *Arenas of Power*, edited by NK Nicholson (Boulder, Paradigm publishers), https://doi.org/10.4324/9781315635958.

Luhmann, N (1976) 'Generalized Media and the Problem of Contingency' in JJ Loubser, RC Baum, A Effrat, and VM Lidz (eds), *Explorations in General Theory in Social Science: Essays in Honor of Talcott Parsons, Vol 2* (New York, The Free Press).

—— (1981a) *Politische Theorie im Wohlfahrtsstaat* (Munich and Vienna, Günter Olzog Verlag) [English translation 1990].

—— (1981b) 'Symbiotische Mechanismen' in *Soziologische Aufklärung 3* (Opladen, Westdeutscher Verlag).

—— (1987) *Rechtssoziologie*, 3rd edn (Opladen, Westdeutscher Verlag) [English translation 2014].

—— (1989) *Ecological Communication*, translated by J Bednarz Jr (Chicago, The University of Chicago Press).

—— (1990) *Political Theory in the Welfare State*, translated by J Bednarz Jr (Berlin, de Gruyter).

—— (1991) *Soziale Systeme: Grundriß einer allgemeinen Theorie*, 4th edn (Frankfurt am Main, Suhrkamp) [Spanish translation 1998] [English translation 1995d] [1st edn 1984].

—— (1992) 'Zur Einführung' in M Neves *Verfassung und Positivität des Rechts in der peripheren Moderne: Eine theoretische Betrachtung und eine Interpretation des Falls Brasilien* (Berlin, Duncker & Humblot).

—— (1993) *Das Recht der Gesellschaft* (Frankfurt am Main, Suhrkamp) [English translation 2004].

—— (1995a) 'Inklusion und Exklusion' in *Soziologische Aufklärung 6* (Opladen, Westdeutscher Verlag).

—— (1995b) 'Jenseits von Barberei' in *Gesellschaftsstruktur und Semantik* (Frankfurt am Main, Suhrkamp).

—— (1995c) 'Kausalität im Süden' 1 *Soziale Systeme* 7, www.soziale-systeme.ch/leseproben/luhmann.htm.

—— (1995d) *Social Systems*, translated by J Bednarz Jr and D Baecker (Stanford, Stanford University).

—— (1996) *Die Realität der Massenmedien* (Opladen, Westdeutscher Verlag) [English translation 2000b].

—— (1997a) *Die Gesellschaft der Gesellschaft* (Frankfurt am Main, Suhrkamp) [English translation 2012, 2013].

—— (1997b) 'Globalization or World Society: How to Conceive of Modern Society?' 7 *International Review of Sociology* 67, https://doi.org/10.1080/03906701.1997.9971223.

—— (1998) *Sistemas Sociales: Lineamientos para una Teoría General*, translated by S Pappe and B Erker (Rubí, Antropos; México, Universidad Iberoamericana; Santafé de Bogotá, CEJA, Pontificia Universidad Javeriana).
—— (2000a) *Die Politik der Gesellschaft*, edited by A Kieserling (Frankfurt am Main, Suhrkamp).
—— (2000b) *The Reality of Mass Media*, translated by K Cross (Stanford, Stanford University).
—— (2004) *Law as a Social System*, translated by KA Ziegert (Oxford, Oxford University Press).
—— (2005a) 'Die Weltgesellschaft' in *Soziologische Aufklärung 2*, 5th edn (Wiesbaden, Springer Fachmedien Wiesbaden) [first print 1971].
—— (2005b) 'Einfache Sozialsysteme' in *Soziologische Aufklärung* 2, 5th edn (Wiesbaden, Springer Fachmedien Wiesbaden) [first print 1972].
—— (2008a) *Ökologische Kommunikation: Kann die moderne Gesellschaft sich auf ökologische Gefährdungen einstellen?* 5th edn (Wiesbaden, VS Verlag für Sozialwissenschaften) [English translation 1989] [first published 1986].
—— (2008b) 'Beyond Barbarism' 14 *Soziale Systeme* 38, https://doi.org/10.1515/sosys-2008-0104.
—— (2012) *Theory of Society, Vol 1*, translated by R Barret (Stanford, Stanford University).
—— (2013) *Theory of Society, Vol 2*, translated by R Barrett (Stanford, Stanford University).
—— (2014) *A Sociological Theory of Law*, translated by E King-Utz and M Albrow, 2nd edn (Abingdon, Oxon and New York, Routledge).
—— (2015a) 'Die Funktion des Rechts: Erwartungssicherung oder Verhaltenssteuerung?' in *Ausdifferenzierung des Rechts: Beiträge zur Rechtssoziologie und Rechtstheorie*, 2nd edn (Frankfurt am Main, Suhrkamp) [first print 1974].
—— (2015b) 'Gerechtigkeit in den Rechtssystemen der modernen Gesellschaft' in *Ausdifferenzierung des Rechts: Beiträge zur Rechtssoziologie und Rechtstheorie*, 2nd edn (Frankfurt am Main, Suhrkamp) [first print 1973].
—— (2015c) 'Konflikt und Recht' in *Ausdifferenzierung des Rechts: Beiträge zur Rechtssoziologie und Rechtstheorie*, 2nd edn (Frankfurt am Main, Suhrkamp) [1st edn 1981].
—— (2015d) 'Positivität des Rechts als Voraussetzung einer modernen Gesellschaft' in *Ausdifferenzierung des Rechts: Beiträge zur Rechtssoziologie und Rechtstheorie*, 2nd edn (Frankfurt am Main, Suhrkamp) [first print 1970].
Manning, PK (1988) 'Review of "To Punish or Persuade: Enforcement of Coal Mine Safety" by John Braithwaite' 28 *British Journal of Criminology* 559.
Mascareño, AA (2012) *Die moderne Lateinamerikas. Weltgesellschaft, Region und Funktionale Differenzierung* (Bielefeld, Transcript Verlag).
—— (2015) 'Grenzen der Kontrolle: Institutionalisierung und Informalisierung des Raums. Das Beispiel Lateinamerika' in P Goeke, R Lippuner, and J Wirths (eds), *Konstruktion und Kontrolle: Zur Raumordnung sozialer Systeme* (Wiesbaden, Springer VS).
Mascareño, AA, AS da Silva, D Loewe, and D Rodríguez (2016) 'Redes Informales e Instituciones Democráticas en América Latina' 59 *Dados* 683, https://doi.org/10.1590/00115258201689.
Maturana, HR (1980) 'Introduction' in HR Maturana and FJ Varela *Autopoiesis and Cognition: The Realization of the Living* (Dordrecht, D Reidel Publishing Company).
Mayntz, R (1988) 'Berücksichtigung von Implementationsproblemen Bei der Gesetzesentwicklung. Zum Beitrag Der Implementationsforschung Zur Gesetzgebungstheorie' in D Grimm and W Maihofer (eds), *Gesetzgebungstheorie und Rechtspolitik* (Opladen, Springer Fachmedien Wiesbaden).
Meirelles, HL and JE Burle Filho (2016) *Direito Administrativo Brasileiro*, 42nd edn (São Paulo, Malheiros).
Méndez, JE, G O'Donnell, and PS Pinheiro (eds) (1999) *The (Un)Rule of Law and the Underprivileged in Latin America* (Notre Dame, University of Notre Dame Press).
Miller, GP (2017) 'Compliance: Past, Present and Future' 48 *University of Toledo Law Review* 437.
—— (2020) *The Law of Governance, Risk Management, and Compliance*, 3rd edn (New York, Wolters Kluwer).

Moita, E (2018) 'Indicadores, Interesses e Governamentalidade: A Caminho de uma Pós-Democracia na Era da Governança Global?' in M Neves and M Palma (eds), *Sociologia Constitucional e Governança Global: Novas Perspectivas* (Belo Horizonte, Lumen Juris).
Moore, GE (1993) *Principia Ethica*, edited by T Baldwin (Cambridge, Cambridge University Press).
Motala, S (2002) 'Organizing in the Informal Economy: A Case Study of Street Trading in South Africa' *Series on Representation and Organization Building*, SEED Working Paper 36 (Geneva: ILO), www.ilo.org/empent/Publications/WCMS_117700/lang--en/index.htm.
Müller, F (1994) *Strukturiende Rechtslehre*, 2nd edn (Berlin, Duncker & Humblot).
—— (2013a) 'Fragen zu Methode und Methodik' in *Essays zur Theorie von Recht und Verfassung, von Methodik und Sprache*, 2nd edn (Berlin, Duncker & Humblot).
—— (2013b) 'Reine Sprachlehre – Reine Rechtslehre – Aufgaben einer Theorie des Rechts. Notizen zu Kelsen und Wittgenstein' in *Essays Zur Theorie von Recht und Verfassung, von Methodik und Sprache*, 2nd edn (Berlin, Duncker & Humblot).
Münch, R (1982) *Theorie des Handelns: Zur Rekonstruktion der Beiträge von Talcott Parsons, Emile Durkheim und Max Weber* (Frankfurt am Main, Suhrkamp) [partial English translation 1987].
—— (1987) *Theory of Action: Towards a New Synthesis Going Beyond Parsons* (London and New York, Routledge & Kegan Paul).
Neves, M (1988) *Teoria da Inconstitucionalidade das Leis* (São Paulo, Saraiva).
—— (1992) *Verfassung und Positivität des Rechts in der peripheren Moderne: Eine theoretische Betrachtung und eine Interpretation des Falls Brasilien* (Berlin, Duncker & Humblot) [Portuguese translation 2018].
—— (1994) 'Entre Subintegração e Sobreintegração: A Cidadania Inexistente' *Dados – 37 Revista de Ciências Sociais* 253 [English translation 2005].
—— (1995) 'Do Pluralismo Jurídico à Miscelânea Social: O Problema da Falta de Identidade da(s) Esfera(s) de Juridicidade na Modernidade Periférica e Suas Implicações na América Latina' 4 *Direito em Debate* 7 [English translation 2003], www.revistas.unijui.edu.br/index.php/revistadireitoemdebate/article/view/885/600.
—— (2001a) 'Do Consenso ao Dissenso: O Estado Democrático de Direito a Partir e Além de Habermas' in J Souza (ed), *Democracia Hoje: Novos Desafios para a Teoria da Democracia Contemporânea* (Brasília, Editora Universidade de Brasília).
—— (2001b) 'Justiça e Diferença numa Sociedade Global Complexa' in *Democracia Hoje: Novos Desafios para a Teoria da Democracia Contemporânea*, edited by Jessé Souza (Brasília: Editora Universidade de Brasília).
—— (2003) 'From Legal Pluralism to Social Miscellany: The Problem of the Lack of Identity of the Legal Sphere(s) in Peripheral Modernity and its Implications for Latin America' in CA Rodríguez (ed), *Law and Society in Latin America* (9 *Beyond Law: New Work on Law and Social Change from Latin America and Around the World* 125) (Bogotá, ILSA).
—— (2005) 'Between Under-Integration and Over-Integration: Not Taking Citizenship Seriously' in J Souza and V Sinder (eds), *Imagining Brazil* (Lanham, Lexington Books).
—— (2006) *Entre Têmis e Leviatã: Uma Relação Difícil. O Estado Democrático de Direito a Partir e Além de Luhmann e Habermas* (São Paulo, Martins Fontes).
—— (2011) *A Constitucionalização Simbólica*, 3rd edn (São Paulo, WMF Martins Fontes) [English translation 2022].
—— (2013) *Entre Hidra e Hércules: Princípios e Regras Constitucionais Como Diferença Paradoxal do Sistema Jurídico* (São Paulo, WMF Martins Fontes) [English translation 2021].
—— (2018) *Constituição e Direito na Modernidade Periférica: Uma Abordagem Teórica e uma Interpretação do Caso Brasileiro*, translated by ACL Costa and revised by E Moita (São Paulo, WMF Martins Fontes).
—— (2021) *Constitutionalism and the Paradox of Principles and Rules: Between the Hydra and Hercules* (Oxford, Oxford University Press).
—— (2022) *Symbolic Constitutionalization*, translated by Kevin Mundy (Oxford, Oxford University Press).

Nonet, P and P Selznick (2017) *Law and Society in Transition: Toward Responsive Law*, 2nd edn (New York, Routledge) [first published 1978].

O'Donnell, G (1999) 'Polyarchies and the (Un)Rule of Law in Latin America: A Partial Conclusion' in JE Méndez, G O'Donnell, and PS Pinheiro (eds), *The (Un)Rule of Law and the Underprivileged in Latin America* (Notre Dame, University of Notre Dame Press).

OECD (2002) *Measuring the Non-Observed Economy: A Handbook* (Paris, OECD Publications Service), www.oecd.org/sdd/na/measuringthenon-observedeconomy-ahandbook.htm.

Oliveira Neto, ES and GCM Cabral (2020) 'Pena de Prisão e Proporcionalidade: Contribuição a Partir do Paradigma da Justiça Penal Negocial' 173 *Revista Brasileira de Ciências Criminais* 169.

Olivier de Sardan, J-P (1995) *Anthropologie et Développement: Essai En Socio-Anthropologie du Changement Social* (Marseille and Paris, APAD and Karthala) [English translation 2005], www.documentation.ird.fr/hor/fdi:010007659#.

—— (2005) *Anthropology and Development: Understanding Contemporary Social Change* (London and New York, Zed Books).

Palmieri Júnior, V (2017) *A Gourmetização em uma Sociedade Desigual: Um Estudo Sobre a Diferenciação no Consumo de Alimentos Industrializados no Brasil*, doctoral dissertation (Universidade Estadual de Campinas).

Parsons, T (1960) 'Authority, Legitimation, and Political Action' in *Structure and Process in Modern Societies* (New York, The Free Press).

—— (1962) 'The Law and Social Control' in WM Evan (ed), *Law and Sociology: Exploratory Essays* (New York, The Free Press of Glencoe).

—— (1963a) 'On the Concept of Influence' 27 *The Public Opinion* 37.

—— (1963b) 'On the Concept of Political Power' 107 *Proceedings of the American Philosophical Society* 232.

—— (1968) 'On the Concept of Value-Commitments' 38 *Sociological Inquiry* 135.

—— (1970) 'Some Problems o General Theory in Sociology' in JC McKiney and EA Tiryakian (eds), *Theoretical Sociology: Perspectives and Developments* (New York, Appleton-Century-Crofts).

—— (1976) 'Social Structure and the Symbolic Media of Interchange' in PM Blau (ed), *Approaches to the Study of Social Structure* (London, Open Books).

Peña, S (1999) 'Informal Markets: Street Vendors in Mexico City' 23 *Habitat International* 363, https://doi.org/10.1016/S0197-3975(99)00012-0.

Peters, HP (1991) 'Risiko-Kommunikation: Kernenergie' in H Jungermann, B Rohrmann, and PM Wiedemann (eds), *Risikokontroversen: Konzepte, Konflikte, Kommunikation* (Berlin and Heidelberg, Springer-Verlag).

Pinheiro, PS (1999) 'The Rule of Law and the Underprivileged in Latin America: Introduction' in JE Méndez, G O'Donnell, and PS Pinheiro (eds), *The (Un)Rule of Law and the Underprivileged in Latin America* (Notre Dame, University of Notre Dame Press).

Rabanal, CR (1990) *Überleben im Slum: Psychosoziale Probleme Peruanischer Elendsviertel*, translated by H Engelbrecht and C Rodriguez-Drescher (Frankfurt am Main, Fischer).

—— (1991) *Cicatrices de la Pobreza: Un Estudio Psicoanalitico*, 2nd edn (Caracas, Editorial Nueva sociedad) [German translation 1990] [1st edn 1989].

Raz, J (1979a) 'Legal Positivism and the Sources of Law' in *The Authority of Law: Essays on Law and Morality* (Oxford, Oxford University Press), https://doi.org/10.1093/acprof:oso/9780198253457.003.0003.

—— (1979b) 'The Functions of Law' in *The Authority of Law: Essays on Law and Morality* (Oxford, Oxford University Press) https://doi.org/10.1093/acprof:oso/9780198253457.003.0009.

—— (1979c) 'The Rule of Law and Its Virtue' in *The Authority of Law: Essays on Law and Morality* (Oxford, Oxford University Press), https://doi.org/10.1093/acprof:oso/9780198253457.003.0011.

—— (1980) *The Concept of a Legal System: An Introduction to the Theory of Legal System*, 2nd edn (Oxford, Clarendon Press).

Renn, O (1992) 'The Social Arena Concept of Risk Debates' in S Krimsky (ed), *Social Theories of Risk* (Westport, Praeger).

Ribeiro, PH (2013) 'Luhmann "Fora do Lugar"? Como a "Condição Periférica" da América Latina Impulsionou Deslocamentos na Teoria Dos Sistemas' 28 *Revista Brasileira de Ciências Sociais* 105, https://doi.org/10.1590/S0102-69092013000300007.

Rincon, MFG (2010) 'Governance of Street Trade in Caracas, Venezuela' in SK Bhowmik (ed), *Street Vendors in the Global Urban Economy* (New Delhi, Routledge).

Roermund, B van (2013) 'Norm-Claims, Validity and Self-Reference' in LD D'Almeida, J Gardner, and L Green (eds), *Kelsen Revisited: Essays on the Pure Theory of Law* (Oxford and Portland, Hart Publishing).

Roever, S (2010) 'Street Trade in Latin America: Demographic Trends, Legal Issues and Vending Organisations in Six Cities' in SK Bhowmik (ed), *Street Vendors in the Global Urban Economy* (New Delh, Routledge).

Rosa, H (2005) *Beschleunigung: Die Veränderung der Zeitstrukturen in der Moderne* (Frankfurt am Main, Suhrkamp) [English translation 2013].

—— (2013) *Social Acceleration: A New Theory of Modernity*, translated by J Trejo-Mathys (New York, Columbia University Press).

Rosa, H and WE Scheuerman (eds) (2009) *High-Speed Society: Social Acceleration, Power, and Modernity* (Pennsylvania, Pennsylvania State University Press).

Ross, A (1959) *On Law and Justice* (Berkeley and Los Angeles, University of California Press).

—— (2019). *On Law and Justice*, edited by JvH Holtermann, translated by U Bindreiter (Oxford, Oxford University Press), https://doi.org/10.1093/oso/9780198716105.001.0001.

Sá e Silva, F de (2020) 'From Car Wash to Bolsonaro: Law and Lawyers in Brazil's Illiberal Turn (2014–2018)' 47 *Journal of Law and Society* S90, https://doi.org/10.1111/jols.12250.

Sands, P, J Peel, A Fabra, and R MacKenzie (2018) *Principles of International Environmental Law*, 4th edn (Cambridge, Cambridge University Press).

Santos, BS (1977) 'The Law of the Oppressed: The Construction and Reproduction of Legality in Pasargada' 12 *Law & Society Review* 5, https://doi.org/10.2307/3053321.

—— (2014) *O Direito Dos Oprimidos: Sociologia Crítica do Direito, Parte 1* (São Paulo, Cortez).

Santos, T dos (1970) 'The Structure of Dependence' 60 *The American Economic Review* 231.

Saussure, F de (1959) *Course in General Linguistics*, translated by W Baskin (New York, The Philosophical Library).

—— (1995) *Cours de Linguistique Générale*, critical edn by T de Mauro, edited by C Bailly and A Séchehaye (Paris, Payot & Rivages) [English translation 1959] [first published 1916].

Schlegel, P and S Racaud (2016) *Urbanization and Street Vending: How Street Vending, an Individual and a Collective Resource, Can Be Integrated into the Urban Governance?* (Nairobi, IFRA).

Schneider, F (2016) 'Comment on Feige's Paper "Reflections on the Meaning and Measurement of Unobserved Economies: What Do We Really Know About the "Shadow Economy"?"' 2 *Journal of Tax Administration* 82, http://jota.website/index.php/JoTA/article/view/108/76.

Schneider, F, A Buehn, and CE Montenegro (2010) 'New Estimates for the Shadow Economies All over the World' 24 *International Economic Journal* 443, https://doi.org/10.1080/10168737.2010.525974.

Scholz, JT (1984) 'Cooperation, Deterrence, and the Ecology of Regulatory Enforcement' 18 *Law & Society Review* 179, https://doi.org/10.2307/3053402.

Schroer, M (2008) 'Raum' in S Fazin and S Jordan (eds), *Lexikon Soziologie und Sozialtheorie: Hundert Grundbegriffe* (Stuttgart, Reclam).

—— (2012) *Räume, Orte, Grenzen: Auf dem Weg zu einer Soziologie des Raums*, 4th edn (Frankfurt am Main, Suhrkamp).

—— (2019) *Räume der Gesellschaft* (Wiesbaden, Springer VS), https://doi.org/10.1007/978-3-658-21964-2.

Schulhofer, Stephen J (1992) 'Plea Bargaining as Disaster' 101 *The Yale Law Journal* 1979, https://doi.org/10.2307/796954.

Schünemann, B (2013) 'Vom Tempel zum Marktplatz. Wie die Strafjustiz scheinbar die ökonomische Theorie des Rechts in Praxis, Government in Governance und Souveranität in Kooperation verwandelt hat' in *Philosophisch-historische Klasse; Vorgetragen in der Sitzung Vom 30. Januar 2009* (Munich, Bayerische Akademie der Wissenschaften), http://publikationen.badw.de/en/039791544.

Searle, JR (1964) 'How to Derive "Ought" from "Is"' 73 *The Philosophical Review* 43, https://doi.org/10.2307/2183201.

Silva, VA da (2005) 'Interpretação Constitucional e Sincretismo Metodológico' in VA da Silva (ed), *Interpretação Constitucional* (São Paulo, Malheiros).

Sinha, S and S Roever (2011) 'India's National Policy on Urban Street Vendors' 2 *WIEGO Policy Brief* 1 (Manchester, WIEGO), www.wiego.org/sites/default/files/migrated/publications/files/Sinha_WIEGO_PB2.pdf.

Skinner, C (2010) 'Street Trading Trends in Africa: A Critical Review' in SK Bhowmik (ed), *Street Vendors in the Global Urban Economy* (New Delhi, Routledge).

Slaughter, A-M (2004) *A New World Order* (Princeton, Princeton University Press).

Sousa, ETO (2015) 'Produção de Territórios na Feira da Rua José Avelino – Fortaleza – CE', master's thesis (Universidade Estadual do Ceará).

—— (2016) 'Feira da Rua José Avelino: Usos do Espaço Público e Questões Sobre o Patrimônio Histórico – Fortaleza – CE' 25 *Geografia* 125.

Srivastava, A, V Ram, M Kurpad, and S Chatterjee (2012) 'Formalising the Informal Streets: A Legislative Review of the Street Vendors (Protection of Livelihood and Regulation of Street Vending) Bill, 2012' 4 *Journal of Indian Law and Society* 247.

Stanfield, JR and B McClintock (1999) 'Welfare State' in PA O'Hara (ed), *Encyclopedia of Political Economy*, Vol 2: *L-Z* (London and New York, Routledge).

Stichweh, R (1995) 'Zur Theorie der Weltgesellschaft' 1 *Soziale Systeme* 29.

—— (2000) 'Systems Theory as an Alternative to Action Theory? The Rise of "Communciation" as a Theoretical Option' 43 *Acta Sociologica* 5.

—— (2016) 'Inklusion/Exklusion, funktionale Differenzierung und die Theorie der Weltgesellschaft' in *Inklusion und Exklusion: Studien zur Gesellschaftstheorie*, 2nd edn, 47–63 (Bielefeld, Transcript Verlag) [extended version of the published in *Soziale Systeme 3*, 1997].

—— (2017) 'Weltgesellschaft' in *Bonner Enzyklopädie der Globalität* (Wiesbaden, Springer Fachmedien Wiesbaden), https://doi.org/10.1007/978-3-658-13819-6_45.

Stuart, E, E Samman, and A Hunt (2018) 'Informal Is the New Normal: Improving the Lives of Workers at Risk of Being Left Behind' *Shaping Policy for Development*, Working Paper 530 (London, Overseas Development Institute), odi.org/en/publications/informal-is-the-new-normal-improving-the-lives-of-workers-at-risk-of-being-left-behind.

Tarantino, A (2006) *Manager's Guide to Compliance: Sarbanes-Oxley, COSO, ERM, COBIT, IFRS, BASEL II, OMB A-123, ASX 10, OECD Principles, Turnbull Guidance, Best Practices, and Case Studies* (Hoboken, John Wiley & Sons, Inc).

Taylor, C (1991) 'Cross-Purposes: The Liberal-Communitarian Debate' in N Rosenblum (ed), *Liberalism and the Moral Life* (Cambridge, Harvard University Press).

Teubner, G (1982) 'Reflexives Recht: Entwicklungsmodelle des Rechts in vergleichender Perspektive' 68 *Archiv für Rechts- und Sozialphilosophie* 13.

—— (1983) 'Substantive and Reflexive Elements in Modern Law' 17 *Law & Society Review* 239, https://doi.org/10.2307/3053348.

—— (1985) 'Verrechtlichung – Begriffe, Merkmale, Grenzen, Auswege' in F Kübler (ed), *Verrechtlichung von Wirtschaft, Arbeit und Sozialer Solidarität: Vergleichende Analysen* (Frankfurt am Main, Suhrkamp) [English translation 1987].

—— (1987) 'Juridification: Concepts, Aspects, Limits, Solutions' in G Teubner (ed), *Juridification of Social Spheres: A Comparative Analysis in the Areas of Labor, Corporate, Antitrust and Social Welfare Law*, translated by P Knight (Berlin, Walter de Gruyter).

—— (1996) 'Globale Bukowina: Zur Emergenz eines transnationalen Rechtspluralismus' 21 *Basler Schriften zur Europäischen Integration* (Basel, Europa Institut an der Universität Basel) [English translation 1997].
—— (1997) '"Global Bukowina": Legal Pluralism in the World Society' in G Teubner (ed), *Global Law Without a State* (Aldershot, Dartmouth).
—— (2008) 'Selbstsubversive Gerechtigkeit: Kontingenz- oder Transzendenzformel des Rechts?' 29 *Zeitschrift für Rechtssoziologie* 9 [English translation 2009], https://doi.org/10.1515/zfrs-2008-0103.
—— (2009) 'Self-Subversive Justice: Contingency or Transcendence Formula of Law?' 72 *Modern Law Review* 1.
—— (2012a) *Constitutional Fragments: Societal Constitutionalism and Globalization*, translated by G Norbury (Oxford, Oxford University Press).
—— (2012b) *Verfassungsfragmente: Gesellschaftlicher Konstitutionalismus in der Globalisierung* (Berlin, Suhrkamp) [English translation 2012a].
United Nations (2022) *The Sustainable Development Goals Report 2022* (New York, United Nations), https://unstats.un.org/sdgs/report/2022/.
United Nations, European Commission, International Monetary Fund, OECD, and World Bank (1993) *System of National Accounts 1993* (New York, United Nations).
Vilanova, L (1997) *As Estruturas Lógicas e o Sistema do Direito Positivo* (São Paulo, Max Limonad).
Villas Bôas Filho, O (2009) *Teoria dos Sistemas e o Direito Brasileiro* (São Paulo, Saraiva).
Wacquant, L (2002) 'Scrutinizing the Street: Poverty, Morality, and the Pitfalls of Urban Ethnography' 107 *American Journal of Sociology* 1468, https://doi.org/10.1086/340461.
Walter, R (1975) 'Buchbesprechung zu Friedrich Müllers "Juristische Methodik"' 97 *Juristische Blätter* 443.
Weber, M (1946) 'Class, Status, Party' in *From Max Weber: Essays in Sociology*, edited and translated by HH Gerth and CW Mills (New York, Oxford University Press).
—— (1947) *The Theory of Social and Economic Organization*, translated by AM Henderson and T Parsons (Glencoe, The Free Press).
—— (2013) *Max Weber-Gesamtausgabe Band I/23: Wirtschaft und Gesellschaft. Soziologie. Unvollendet. 1919–1920*, edited by K Borchardt, E Hanke, and W Schluchter, 1st edn (Tübingen, Mohr Siebeck) [partial English translation 1947], https://doi.org/10.1628/978-3-16-157749-9.
Winter, G (1975) *Das Vollzugsdefizit im Wasserrecht* (Berlin, Erich Schmidt Verlag).
—— (1985) 'Bartering Rationality in Regulation' 19 *Law & Society Review* 219.
Wright, GH von (1963) *Norm and Action: A Logical Inquiry* (London, Routledge & Kegan Paul).
Zhang, Li (2006) 'Contesting Spatial Modernity in Late-Socialist China' 47 *Current Anthropology* 461, https://doi.org/10.1086/503063.

List of Newspaper and Online Reports

BRAZIL

BBC website

Brazil's ilegal numbers game under pressure. 27 January 2012. www.bbc.com/news/world-latin-america-16634941. Accessed on 17 December 2019.

Consultor Jurídico

Abusos podem levar à extinção da delação premiada, diz Gilmar Mendes. 16 November 2020. www.conjur.com.br/2017-nov-16/abusos-podem-levar-extincao-delacao-premiada-gilmar. Accessed on 1 December 2020.

Delação premiada precisa de uma revisão para evitar abusos. 15 December 2017. www.conjur.com.br/2017-dez-15/limite-penal-delacao-premiada-lei-evitar-atuais-abusos. Accessed on 1 December 2020.

Diário do Nordeste

Ambulantes não obedecem fiscais e ficam no Centro. 6 May 2013. diariodonordeste.verdesmares.com.br/editorias/metro/ambulantes-nao-obedecem-fiscais-e-ficam-no-centro-1.125682. Accessed on 10 April 2019.

Ambulantes voltam a lotar ruas e calçadas. By Gioras Xerez on 19 November 2012. diariodonordeste.verdesmares.com.br/editorias/metro/ambulantes-voltam-a-lotar-ruas-e-calcadas-1.688960. Accessed on 23 January 2020.

Estudo avalia ambulantes da José Avelino. By Karla Camila, Raone Saraiva, and Karoline Viana on 6 September 2011. diariodonordeste.verdesmares.com.br/editorias/metro/estudo-avalia-ambulantes-da-jose-avelino-1.719234. Accessed on 23 January 2020.

Madrugada na José Avelino tem maior comércio ao ar livre. By Redação on 27 August 2011. diariodonordeste.verdesmares.com.br/editorias/negocios/madrugada-na-jose-avelino-tem-maior-comercio-ao-ar-livre-1.696937. Accessed on 23 January 2020.

Ocupação irregular gera confronto em feira no Centro. 30 December 2016. diariodonordeste.verdesmares.com.br/editorias/metro/ocupacao-irregular-gera-confronto-em-feira-no-centro-1.1678521. Accessed on 10 April 2019.

Pássaros raros apreendidos em feira. 30 August 2010. diariodonordeste.verdesmares.com.br/editorias/metro/passaros-raros-apreendidos-em-feira-1.472237. Accessed on January 2020.

Por que a feira da Rua José Avelino resiste ao passar dos anos? 16 November 2019. diariodonordeste.verdesmares.com.br/editorias/metro/por-que-a-feira-da-rua-jose-avelino-resiste-ao-passar-dos-anos-1.2175600. Accessed on 10 January 2020.

Presença de ambulantes na Praia do Futuro gera polêmica. 11 July 2017. diariodonordeste.verdesmares.com.br/editorias/metro/presenca-de-ambulantes-na-praia-do-futuro-gera-polemica-1.1785845. Accessed on 3 January 2020.

Estadão

Justiça ordena que barraca de praia de Fortaleza indenize cliente expulsa por convidar ambulante à mesa. 13 August 2019. politica.estadao.com.br/blogs/fausto-macedo/justica-ordena-que-barraca-de-praia-de-fortaleza-indenize-cliente-expulsa-por-convidar-ambulante-a-mesa. Accessed on 3 January 2020.

Folha de São Paulo

Brasil ganha 1,4 milhão de informais em apenas 2 anos. 2 July 2022. www1.folha.uol.com.br/mercado/2022/07/brasil-ganha-14-milhao-de-informais-em-apenas-2-anos.shtml. Accessed on 11 December 2022.

Entenda ponto a ponto as mudanças previstas pelo pacote anticrime de Moro. 4 February 2020. www1.folha.uol.com.br/poder/2019/02/entenda-os-principais-pontos-do-pacote-anticrime-de-moro.shtml. Accessed on 30 November 2020.

Ilegais, apostas esportivas são oferecidas por bicheiros no Rio. 18 August 2017. www1.folha.uol.com.br/esporte/2017/08/1910912-ilegais-apostas-esportivas-sao-oferecidas-por-bicheiros-no-rio.shtml. Accessed on 27 December 2019.

Loteria esportiva ilegal é o novo jogo do bicho em SP. 13 November 2017. www1.folha.uol.com.br/esporte/2017/11/1934937-loteria-esportiva-clandestina-toma-conta-das-ruas-de-sao-paulo.shtml. Accessed on 27 December 2019.

G1

Ambulante morto durante confronto na Rua José Avelino é velado em Fortaleza. 18 August 2021. g1.globo.com/ce/ceara/noticia/2021/08/18/ambulante-morto-durante-confronto-na-rua-jose-avelino-e-velado-em-fortaleza.ghtml. Accessed on 19 August 2021.

Barraca da Praia do Futuro cobra R$ 60 de clientes que consumirem produtos de ambulantes. 14 January 2020. g1.globo.com/ce/ceara/noticia/2020/01/14/barraca-da-praia-do-futuro-cobra-r-60-de-clientes-que-consumirem-produtos-de-ambulantes.ghtml. Accessed on 23 January 2020.

Barraca de praia é autuada no Ceará por expulsar cliente que comprou de ambulante. 5 September 2015. g1.globo.com/ceara/noticia/2015/11/barraca-de-praia-e-autuada-no-ceara-por-expulsar-cliente-que-comprou-de-ambulante.html. Accessed on 5 January 2020.

Como Fortaleza se tornou a região metropolitana mais violenta do Brasil. By Camilla Veras Mota from BBC. 7 March 2019. g1.globo.com/ce/ceara/noticia/2019/03/07/como-fortaleza-se-tornou-a-regiao-metropolitana-mais-violenta-do-brasil.ghtml. Accessed on 22 January 2020.

Feira da José Avelino ocorre sem transtornos nesta quinta, em Fortaleza. 2015. g1.globo.com/ceara/noticia/2015/02/feira-da-jose-avelino-ocorre-sem-transtornos-nesta-quinta-em-fortaleza.html. Accessed on 10 April 2019.

Fiscalização recolhe produtos de ambulantes e gera tumulto na Praia do Futuro. 3 July 2019. g1.globo.com/ce/ceara/noticia/2019/07/03/fiscalizacao-recolhe-produtos-de-ambulantes-e-gera-tumulto-na-praia-do-futuro.ghtml. Accessed on 3 January 2020.

Homem é flagrado oferecendo arma de fogo na Feira da Parangaba, em Fortaleza; veja vídeo. 20 June 2017. g1.globo.com/ceara/noticia/homem-e-flagrado-oferecendo-arma-de-fogo-na-feira-da-parangaba-em-fortaleza-veja-video.ghtml. Accessed on 8 January 2020.

Prefeitura retira ambulantes da Praça da Estação em Fortaleza. 26 April 2013. g1.globo.com/ceara/noticia/2013/04/prefeitura-retira-ambulantes-da-praca-da-estacao-em-fortaleza.html. Accessed on 16 January 2020.

Procon notifica barraca de praia por cobrar R$ 60 de clientes que consumissem produtos de ambulantes em Fortaleza. 20 January 2020. g1.globo.com/ce/ceara/noticia/2020/01/20/procon-notifica-barraca-de-praia-por-cobrar-r-60-de-clientes-que-consumissem-produtos-de-ambulantes-em-fortaleza.ghtml. Accessed on 23 January 2020.

Secretaria abre inquérito de caso de apreensão de mercadorias no Centro. 12 July 2016. g1.globo.com/ceara/noticia/2016/07/secretaria-abre-inquerito-de-caso-de-apreensao-de-mercadorias-no-centro.html. Accessed on 16 January 2020.

Treze são presos em esquema de sonegação que causou prejuízo de mais de R$ 300 milhões ao Ceará. 1 September 2019. g1.globo.com/ceara/noticia/treze-sao-presos-em-esquema-de-sonegacao-que-causou-prejuizo-de-mais-de-r-300-milhoes-ao-ceara.ghtml. Accessed on 12 December 2019.

Vendedor ambulante madruga no Centro de Fortaleza para aumentar as vendas durante a Black Friday. 29 November 2019. g1.globo.com/ce/ceara/noticia/2019/11/29/vendedor-ambulante-madruga-no-centro-de-fortaleza-vender-roupa-durante-a-black-friday.ghtml. Accessed on 15 January 2020.

Nexo

A estrutura política no Brasil se confunde com genealogias e famílias. By Isabela Cruz. 22 November 2020. www.nexojornal.com.br/entrevista/2020/11/21/%E2%80%98A-estrutura-pol%C3%ADtica-no-Brasil-se-confunde-com-genealogias-e-fam%C3%ADlias%E2%80%99. Accessed on 13 January 2021.

O Povo

Catedral de Fortaleza obrigada a fechar as portas. By Vanderlúcio Souza. 6 November 2011. blogs.opovo.com.br/ancoradouro/2011/11/06/catedral-de-fortaleza-fechara-as-portas. Accessed on 21 January 2020.

Empresários e contadores entre os 19 denunciados por fraudes no setor têxtil. 13 March 2018. www.opovo.com.br/noticias/fortaleza/2018/03/justica-aceita-denuncia-contra-19-acusados-de-fraude-no-setor-textil.html. Accessed on 12 December 2019.

Feirantes da Sé e Guarda Municipal entram em conflito neste domingo. 31 August 2014. www.opovo.com.br/noticias/fortaleza/2014/08/feirantes-da-se-e-guarda-municipal-entram-em-conflito-neste-domingo.html. Accessed on 10 April 2019.

Feirantes e fiscais da Prefeitura de Fortaleza entram em conflito na Rua José Avelino. 25 November 2018. www.opovo.com.br/noticias/fortaleza/2017/05/feirantes-e-guardas-municipais-entram-em-confronto-na-jose-avelino.html. Accessed on 10 April 2019.

Feirantes e guardas municipais entram em confronto na José Avelino. 14 May 2017. www.opovo.com.br/noticias/fortaleza/2017/05/feirantes-e-guardas-municipais-entram-em-confronto-na-jose-avelino.html. Accessed on 10 April 2019.

Pesquisa. Retirada de vendedores ambulantes é controversa. 16 September 2016. www20.opovo.com.br/app/opovo/cotidiano/2016/09/16/noticiasjornalcotidiano,3659131/retirada-de-vendedores-ambulantes-e-controversa.shtml. Accessed on 11 September 2020.

Sabor da conquista: conheça a história de sucesso da Pardal. 11 September 2020. blogs.opovo.com.br/radardocomercio/2020/09/11/sabor-de-conquista-conheca-a-historia-de-sucesso-da-pardal. Accessed on 13 December 2022.

Três em cada quatro Fortalezenses admitem comprar itens piratas. 27 October 2016. www20.opovo.com.br/app/opovo/cotidiano/2016/10/27/noticiasjornalcotidiano,3666148/tres-em-cada-quatro-fortalezenses-admitem-comprar-itens-piratas.shtml. Accessed on 18 May 2021.

The Guardian

Operation Car Wash: Is this the biggest corruption scandal in history? 1 June 2017. www.theguardian.com/world/2017/jun/01/brazil-operation-car-wash-is-this-the-biggest-corruption-scandal-in-history. Accessed on 27 November 2020.

Under cover of darkness: inside São Paulo's vast illegal Feirinha night market. 28 November 2017. www.theguardian.com/cities/2017/nov/28/sao-paulo-night-market-bras-feirinha-da-madrugada. Accessed on 27 November 2019.

The Intercept

Secret Brazil Archive. Multiple dates. theintercept.com/series/secret-brazil-archive. Accessed on 30 November 2020.

The Washington Post

How the release of wiretapped conversations in Brazil threatens its democracy. 26 March 2016. www.washingtonpost.com/news/monkey-cage/wp/2016/03/26/how-the-release-of-wiretapped-conversations-in-brazil-threatens-its-democracy. Accessed on 30 November 2020.

COLOMBIA

El Tiempo

El Madrugón de San Victorino, el 'Black Friday' bogotano. 19 December 2017. www.eltiempo.com/bogota/unas-200-000-personas-van-al-madrugon-de-san-victorino-en-diciembre-163450. Accessed on 5 December 2019.

Dinero

En San Victorino, el paro ya les ha costado $24.000 millones. 28 November 2019. www.dinero.com/pais/articulo/en-san-victorino-estan-preocupados-por-el-paro/279658. Accessed on 5 December 2019.

INDIA

India Together

A futile struggle for the right to trade. 18 May 2015. www.indiatogether.org/futile-struggle-for-the-right-to-trade-laws. Accessed on 9 December 2019.

UNITED STATES

The New York Times

Legal pollution. 8 February 1976. www.indiatogether.org/futile-struggle-for-the-right-to-trade-laws. Accessed on 28 January 2021.

Index

www.ingramcontent.com/pod-product-compliance
Ingram Content Group UK Ltd.
Pitfield, Milton Keynes, MK11 3LW, UK
UKHW020819290926
15470UKWH00003B/1260